I M

Second

# Roll of

*for*

## Wigan Metropolitan District

Second World War

# Roll of Honour
*for*

the towns and townships of
## Wigan Metropolitan District

*Including*

**Abram, Appley Bridge, Ashton-in-Makerfield, Aspull, Atherton, Billinge, Blackrod, Golborne, Hindley, Ince-in-Makerfield, Leigh, Orrell, Shevington, Standish, Tyldesley, Up Holland, Wigan**

Researched and compiled
by

# Dr. Eric McPherson

# ANZIO PUBLISHING

First published in Great Britain 2001
by

ANZIO PUBLISHING
99 Walton Road, Sale, Cheshire, M33 4DW

Printed by
A.A. Sotheran Ltd.
14-16, Queen Street, Redcar
Cleveland, TS10 1AF

ISBN
0-9540325-0-0

# *CONTENTS*

# INTRODUCTION

This book has three aims. First to provide a record of the 1800 or so men and women who gave their lives in the Second World War and who had direct family or residence links with one or other of the towns and townships that comprise the area covered.

Secondly, it attempts to provide identification of these casualties of war. All the entries therefore, whenever possible, include service details and information regarding death, family, local connections and the name of the relevant cemetery or memorial. Most people at some time or other will have looked at the names on a memorial and wondered: who were these people? In which regiment did they serve? Where and when did they die? The reason for the inclusion of a particular name on a local memorial is now sometimes difficult to ascertain or establish. With the passing years memories fade, contemporaries and relatives die or leave the district and the name becomes just that – simply a name carved on a stone tablet. The actual person may thus be honoured only annually as one of the many who made the ultimate sacrifice.

Thirdly, this Roll of Honour is offered as a small tribute to these local men and women who gave their lives that we might live in freedom.

The material contained herein has been gathered from many sources. Commonwealth War Graves Commission (CWGC) registers, local and national newspapers, publications, documents, rolls of honour, regimental and other archives, school records, museums, record offices, parish magazines, war veterans and the friends, colleagues, neighbours and relatives of those commemorated. All possible methods of obtaining information have been used – including advertisements, articles, letters to the press and correspondence with people and institutions in the United Kingdom and overseas.

In spite of this, sadly there are some names for which positive identification has not been possible. There are mistakes on some memorials and in local newspaper reports. Misspellings, duplicated entries and incorrect details of rank or regiment make the problems of accurate determination difficult (especially with the more common names), and CWGC registers do not in every case give details of parents or spouses, nor do they always include geographical information.

In relation to the Second World War, the CWGC only take responsibility for members of the Armed Forces (including the Home Guard) and some Merchant Seamen who lost their lives in the period 3 September 1939 – 31 December 1947. Anyone who died after discharge from the service or after 1947 is not officially classified as 'war dead'. Of course, local communities do not always follow these classifications and therefore some names rightly appear on local memorials but are not to be found on official, national ones. Nor are their graves marked with the distinctive 'war grave' headstone.

Unfortunately, the majority of local memorials do not give first names, and few include details of rank, service and regiment. Some commemorate members of the Fire Service, Civil Defence and civilians in addition to members of the Armed Forces and Merchant Navy, but without any distinguishing detail it is sometimes difficult always to be certain of their identity. **APPENDIX ONE** contains the names on local memorials that do not have national recognition, as well as those for which it has not been possible to discover full, positive (or in some cases *any*) information.

There are bound to be difficulties when the arbitrary selection of a geographical area is used as the prime qualification for inclusion in a publication such as this. Nonetheless, I have striven to be consistent in using only those local memorials which are open to the public and which are sited within the defined boundaries. I have included a few townships that, although not strictly included within the present local authority boundary of the Wigan Metropolitan District, are historically associated with the town. All the names that these memorials contain have been entered and researched. There are however some 200 servicemen who sadly (and somewhat mysteriously) are not commemorated on any local memorial even though they had the immediate family links and connections which should have guaranteed their appearance on at least one memorial. These have been included. It has not been possible to ascertain exactly why these names are missing, but it is probable that in the majority of cases it is due to the rather haphazard way by which the names of local casualties were gathered after the war.

I am, of course, indebted to the many people (too numerous to mention) who have assisted in my researches and the production of this book by giving information, loaning documents and books, providing contacts, answering questions and suggesting possible sources and amendments. I am extremely grateful to them all. I would welcome any additional or missing information that anyone can supply and, as it would be foolish to claim that there are no inaccuracies contained within, I would be pleased to receive details of any errors or omissions.

Dr ERIC McPHERSON

*March 2001*

# ABBREVIATIONS

| | |
|---|---|
| AA | Anti-aircraft |
| AB | Able Seaman |
| Air Bmr. | Air Bomber |
| Air Gnr. | Air Gunner |
| Attd. | Attached |
| Bdr. | Bombardier |
| BSM | Battalion Sergeant Major |
| Cpl. | Corporal |
| CSM | Company Sergeant Major |
| CWGC | Commonwealth War Graves Commission |
| CU | Conversion Unit |
| d | Daughter |
| D.E.M.S. | Defensively Equipped Merchant Ship |
| DFC | Distinguished Flying Cross |
| DFM | Distinguished Flying Medal |
| Dvr. | Driver |
| Flt. Lt. | Flight Lieutenant |
| Flt. Sgt. | Flight Sergeant |
| Flying Offr. | Flying Officer |
| Fus. | Fusilier |
| g | Grandson |
| Gdsmn. | Guardsman |
| Gnr. | Gunner |
| h | Husband |
| H.M.S. | His Majesty's Ship |
| L.Bdr. | Lance Bombardier |
| L.Cpl. | Lance Corporal |
| Ldg. Smn. | Leading Seaman |
| Lt. | Lieutenant |
| MC | Military Cross |
| MID | Mentioned in Dispatches |
| MM | Military Medal |
| MN | Merchant Navy |
| Mne. | Marine |
| Ord. Smn. | Ordinary Seaman |
| Ord. Teleg. | Ordinary Telegrapher |
| OUT | Operation Training Unit |
| Pilot Offr. | Pilot Officer |
| PoW | Prisoner of War |
| Pte. | Private |
| RAAF | Royal Australian Air Force |
| RAC | Royal Armoured Corps |
| RAF | Royal Air Force |
| RAF(VR) | Royal Air Force Volunteer Reserve |
| RCAF | Royal Canadian Air Force |

| | |
|---|---|
| Rfmn. | Rifleman |
| RN | Royal Navy |
| s | Son |
| SBA | Sick Bay Attendant |
| Sgmn. | Signalman |
| Sgt. | Sergeant |
| Sjt. | Serjeant |
| Spr. | Sapper |
| Sqdn. | Squadron |
| Sqdn. Ldr. | Squadron Leader |
| Sto. | Stoker |
| Sub Lieut. | Sub Lieutenant |
| Tpr. | Trooper |
| Vol. | Volunteer |
| w | Wife |
| WO | Warrant Officer |
| W.Op. | Wireless Operator |

# LOCAL MEMORIAL CODES AND LOCATION OF LOCAL MEMORIALS

*At the end of each individual entry, a series of letters will be found (BNC/G/W).*
*These represent coded indicators of the local memorial(s) on which the particular*
*name is to be found. Details are given below.*

A      Leigh Road, Atherton.
AB      Abram Council Chamber. (Housed in the Library, Vicarage Road, Abram)
ABC      St John's Church, Warrington Road, Abram.
ABL      Bag Lane Methodist Church, Atherton.
AC      Holy Trinity Church, North Ashton, Ashton-in-Makerfield
ACC      Congregational Church, Hilton Street, Ashton-in-Makerfield.
AGS      Ashton-in-Makerfield Grammar School. (Now housed in Birchall High School, Lodge Lane)
AIM      St Thomas's Church, Warrington Road, Ashton-in-Makerfield.
AMS      Central School, Ashton-in-Makerfield. (Now housed in Cansfield High School)

~~A~~ ~~Appley Lane North, Appley Bridge~~

## ERRATA
Page ix    The abbreviation for Operation Training Unit should be OTU
Page xi    The codes HIC and HIY should refer to St Matthew's not St John's
Page xii    In some entries the code UPH has been used for the memorial at Up Holland

BC      St Aidan's Church, Newton Road, Billinge.
BCC      St Catharine's Church, Black Horse Street, Blackrod.
BDC      Bedford Methodist Church, Breeston Avenue, Leigh.
BHC      St Anne's Church, Beech Hill, Wigan.
BL      The Cemetery, Manchester Road, Blackrod
BMC      Royal British Legion, Bamfurlong. (Now housed in Bamfurlong Methodist Church, Lily Lane, Bamfurlong)
BNC      St Peter's Church, Bryn Road, Bryn.
CUC      Chowbent Unitarian Chapel, Chapel Street, Atherton.
G      Leigh Street, Golborne.
GGC      St Paul's Church, Warrington Road, Goose Green.
GOC      St Thomas's Church, Golborne.
HAC      St Anne's Church, James Street, Hindsford, Atherton.
HBC      St Michael & All Angels' Church, Leigh Road, Howe Bridge, Atherton
HC      St Peter's Church, Liverpool Road, Hindley.
HDC      St David's Church, Haigh Road, Haigh.
HGC      St John's Church, Atherton Road, Hindley Green.
HGS      Hindley & Abram Grammar School. (Still housed in the original building in Park Road, Hindley which is no longer used as a school.)
HIC      St John's Church, Orrell Road, Highfield, Pemberton.
HIY      Lord & Sharman Works Memorial. (Now sited in St John's Highfield Churchyard.)

| | |
|---|---|
| IN | Christ Church, Ince Green Lane, Lower Ince. |
| ISM | St Mary's Church, Warrington Road, Lower Ince. (The stone memorial was not transferred from the demolished church and the details exist only in documentary form.) |
| JC | St James with St Thomas Church, Poolstock, Wigan. |
| KMC | Kendal Street Methodist Church, Wigan. |
| L | Church Street, Leigh. |
| LAS | All Saints' Church, Manchester Road, Leigh. |
| LGS | Leigh Grammar School. (Now housed in Bedford High School, Manchester Road, Leigh.) |
| LMC | St Mary The Virgin Church, Vicarage Square, Leigh. |
| LPC | Christ Church, Schofield Street, Pennington, Leigh. |
| LTA | Twelve Apostles' R.C. Church, Nel Pan Lane, Leigh. |
| LTC | St Thomas's Church, Chapel Street, Leigh. |
| MZC | Mount Zion Independent Methodist Church, Ormskirk Road, Pemberton. |
| NAV | North Ashton Village Club, Rectory Road, Ashton-in-Makerfield. |
| NC | St Mark's Church, Victoria Street, Newtown, Wigan. |
| NSC | St John The Baptist Church, Kirkless Street, New Springs, Wigan. |
| OC | St Luke's Church, Orrell. |
| ORC | Orrell Rugby Football Club, Edge Hall Road, Orrell. |
| OCY | St Luke's Churchyard, Orrell. |
| OUC | Orrell United Reform Church, Orrell. |
| PBC | St Nathaniel's Church, Ridyard Street, Platt Bridge, Wigan. |
| PC | St John's Church, Pemberton. |
| PHW | Police Headquarters, Harrogate Street, Wigan. |
| S | Church Lane, Shevington. |
| SAC | St Andrew's Church, Mort Street, Wigan. |
| SCC | St Catherine's Church, St Catherine's Terrace, Wigan. |
| SGC | St George's Church, Crompton Street, Wigan. |
| SIM | Stubshaw Cross Independent Methodist Church, Bolton Road, Stubshaw Cross. |
| SMC | St Michael & All Angels' Church, Duke Street, Wigan. |
| SSC | St Stephen's Church, Plantation Gates, Whelley, Wigan. |
| SSM | St Marie's R.C. Church, School Lane, Standish. |
| ST | High Street, Standish. |
| STC | St Wilfrid's Church, Standish. |
| T | Tyldesley Cemetery, Hough lane, Tyldesley. |
| TC | St George's Church, Tyldesley. |
| TMC | Tyldesley Methodist Church, Elliot Street, Tyldesley. |
| UP | Grove Road, Up Holland. |
| UPC | St Thomas's Church, School Lane, Up Holland. |
| W | The Cenotaph, Standishgate, Wigan. |
| WGS | Wigan Grammar School, Wigan. (Still in the original building which is no longer a school.) |
| WMC | Westleigh Methodist Church, Westleigh Lane, Westleigh. |
| WPC | All Saints' Parish Church, Standishgate, Wigan. |
| WSB | Whelley School Old Boys. (Housed in St Stephen's Church, Whelley.) |
| X | Name not to be found on any local memorial sited within the stated geographical boundaries. |

*At the going down of the sun and in the morning*
*We will remember them.*

*Lawrence Binyon*


**ABBOTT Eric,** Sto. 1ˢᵗ Class   C/KX595708   R.N.   H.M.S. *Boadicea* 13 June 1944. Aged 19. The destroyer was sunk by German aircraft off Portland Bill. *s of Thomas & Mary, Up Holland.* CHATHAM NAVAL MEMORIAL [UPC/UPH] (See also Harry Kenyon and John Moores.)

**ABBOTT Wilfred,** Pilot Offr. (Nav) 175843 R.A.F.(V.R.) 431 Sqdn. 18 July 1944. Age 23. A Halifax III from Croft attacked railway yards at Vaires. It crashed near the centre of Creil with the loss of all the crew. *s of William & Mary, Stubshaw Cross; h of Dorothy.* CRAMOISY COMMUNAL CEMETERY , FRANCE. [AGS/AIM/SIM]

**ACKERS Harry,** Fus. 3461117 2/8ᵗʰ Bn. Lancashire Fusiliers. Killed in India 9 May 1942. Age 34. *h of Ellen, Leigh.*   DELHI WAR CEMETERY, INDIA. [L/LTC]

**ACKERS Peter,** Fus. 3453602 1/8ᵗʰ Bn. Lancashire Fusiliers. Drowned whilst on duty in England 8 June 1941. Age 25. HINDLEY CEMETERY [HC]

**ACKERS Walter,** Gdsmn. 2723046 2ⁿᵈ Bn. Irish Guards. Killed on the first day of Operation Market Garden - the Arnhem attack in Holland. 17 September 1944. VALKENSWAARD WAR CEMETERY [HIC/W]

**ADAMSON Jack,** Vol. 76ᵗʰ County of Lancaster (Golborne) Bn. Home Guard. While on guard duty, he and a colleague were killed by the explosion of a bomb. 13 September 1940. Aged 18. *s of Mr & Mrs W.* ASHTON-IN-MAKERFIELD (HOLY TRINITY) CHURCHYARD. [AC/NAV] (See also J.H. Davies.)

**ADAMSON Leonard Cook,** Sgmn. 2318694 3ʳᵈ Div. Sigs., Royal Corps of Signals. 8 June 1941. Age 32. *h of Edith May*   WIGAN CEMETERY. [SCC/W]

**ADAMSON Robert,** Pte. 3460943 2ⁿᵈ Bn. Gordon Highlanders. Killed in Belgium 21 September 1944. Age 32. *s of William & Jane; h of Annie, Wigan.* GEEL WAR CEMETERY. [SCC/W]

**AINSCOUGH Harold,** Sto. D/KX138695 R.N. H.M.S. *Drake* 13 September 1944 Age 46 *h of Rose Hannah.*   WIGAN CEMETERY. [X]

**AINSCOUGH Harry,** Pte. 14697127 2ⁿᵈ Bn. Argyll & Sutherland Highlanders. Killed in France 18 July 1944. Age 29. *s of Thomas & Margaret, Wigan; h of Alice.* LA DELIVERANDE WAR CEMETERY. FRANCE. [W]

1

**AINSCOUGH Jack**, Ldg. Teleg. D/JX134179 R.N. H.M.S.*Prince Of Wales*. This battleship was sunk by Japanese aircraft off Kuantan, Malaya, 10 December 1941. Over 300 of the crew of 1612 perished. PLYMOUTH NAVAL MEMORIAL. [IN]

**AINSCOUGH Rowland**, Pte. 978989 2/6th Bn. Queen's Royal Regiment (West Surrey). Killed in Italy 21 September 1944. Aged 24. *s of Enoch & Lilian, Goose Green*. GRADARA WAR CEMETERY, ITALY. [W/GGC]
(It should be noted that this soldier is also mistakenly shown on the Wigan memorial as having died whilst serving in the Royal Artillery - although he was in the Royal Artillery from 1939 to 1944.)

**AITKEN William P. H.**, A.C.2. 994628 R.A.F.(V.R.) 28 November 1940. Aged 24. *s of William & Agnes Hannah; adopted s of Elizabeth Aitken, Wigan*. WIGAN CEMETERY. [W]

**ALDRED James**, Ord. Smn. C/JX351443 R.N. H.M.S. *Curacoa* 2 October 1942. Aged 19. This cruiser, while on escort duty, was rammed and sunk by the troopship liner *Queen Mary*. 338 men died. *s of William & Clara*. CHATHAM NAVAL MEMORIAL. [A]

**ALDRED John Frederick**, Marine. PO/X115495 26 R.M. Lt. A.A. Bty. Royal Marines. Killed in Holland 4 November 1944. Aged 21. *s of Edward & Emma*. SCHOONSELHOF CEMETERY. [A]

**ALDRED Thomas**, A.B. D/SSX18649 R.N. H.M.S. *Kite* 21 August 1944. Aged 25. The sloop was sunk by German U-boat *U-334* off north Norway. PLYMOUTH NAVAL MEMORIAL. [A]
(See also : Albert Grundy; Edward Nelson;Thomas Payne.)

**ALKER Samuel**, Marine. PLY/X2431 Royal Marines. H.M.S. *Glorious* 9 June 1940. Aged 25. *s of Frederick & Clara, Winstanley, Wigan*. The aircraft carrier was sunk by battlecruisers *Gneisenau* and *Scharnhorst* 300 miles west of Narvik. There were only 43 survivors. PLYMOUTH NAVAL MEMORIAL [HIC/W]
(Seven other local men perished when this aircraft carrier was sunk: Walter L. Duckworth; John F.Gorton; John Jameson; Edward Knight; Peter McNicholas; Benjamin T. Starkie and Frederick Swan).

**ALLDRED Thomas**, L.A.C. 1499187 R.A.F.(V.R.) 23 June 1946. Aged 42. *s of William & Ellen h of Annie, Leigh*. LEIGH CEMETERY. [X]

**ALLEN Harold**, Sgt.(W.Op./Air Gnr.) 1058478 R.A.F. (V.R.) 61 Sqdn. 20 August 1942. Aged 22. *s of Albert & Florence, Ashton-in-Makerfield; h of Phyllis*. BILBAO BRITISH CEMETERY, SPAIN. [AIM/AMS]
The name is spelt *Allan* on the AIM memorial.

**ALMOND John**, Elec. Artificer. D/MX60623 R.N. H.M.S. *Dorsetshire* 5 April 1942. Aged 26. The cruiser was on passage from Columbo to the Maldive Islands when it was sunk by Japanese carrier-based aircraft. *Family connections in Atherton*. PLYMOUTH NAVAL MEMORIAL. [LGS]

**ALLSOP Arthur Burt,** Sto. 1st Class. D/KX87718. Fleet Air Arm. He was killed in a road accident. 19 September 1939. Aged 23. PEMBERTON CEMETERY. [SAC]

**AMBROSE Harold,** Sgt. 1059824 R.A.F(V.R.) Died after an accident in Algiers the day before he was to leave for England and demobilisation, 5 October 1945. Aged 36. *s of Harold & Selina; h of Jessie, Leigh.* DELY IBRAHIM WAR CEMETERY [L/LPC]

**ANDERSON Albert,** Gnr. 1472470. 80 Bty., 22 Lt AA Regt. Royal Artillery. Died as the result of a road accident, 31 October 1939. s *of William & Rebecca, Atherton; h of Eva, Leigh.* ATHERTON CEMETERY [A]

**ANDERTON Frederick,** Cpl. 4467609. 1st Bn. Durham Light Infantry. Killed on Cos Island 3 October 1943. Aged 33. He was laid to rest on the Island, but his grave has subsequently been lost and he is therefore commemorated on the memorial appropriate to that theatre of war. *s of Elijah & Mary, Bryn.* ATHENS MEMORIAL [AC/BNC/NAV]

**ANDERTON Harold,** Pilot Offr. (Nav.) 189448 R.A.F.(V.R.) Died 26 May 1945 as a result of an aircraft accident which happened one week before he was to be married. Aged 26. *s of Frederick & Ada, Leigh.* DELY IBRAHIM WAR CEMETERY, ALGERIA. [L/LPC]

**ANDERTON James,** A.C.2 1085594 R.A.F.(V.R.) 211 Sqdn. Died whilst a PoW of the Japanese in Java 18 October 1944. Aged 23. *s of Joseph & Ethel, Atherton.* SINGAPORE MEMORIAL [A]

**ANDERTON Robert,** Pte. 7606694 Royal Army Ordnance Corps. 9 September 1941. Aged 41. *s of William & Margaret; h of Thelma Olive, Hindsford.* ATHERTON CEMETERY. [A]

**ANDERTON Samuel,** Pte. 10558884 Royal Army Ordnance Corps attd. 28 Lt. Anti-Aircraft Regiment, Royal Artillery. Died 22 May 1942 in India. Aged 20. *s of Joseph & Mabel, Lowton.* BHOWANIPORE CEMETERY, CALCUTTA. [G]

**ANDERTON Thomas Richard,** A.B. P/JX266684 R.N. H.M.S. *Holcombe* 12 December 1943. The destroyer was sunk by German U-boat *U-593* off Bougie. Aged 32. *s of Thomas & Margaret; h of Clarice, Hindley Green.* PORTSMOUTH NAVAL MEMORIAL. [L]

**ANDERTON William Cyril,** Gnr. 1808928 242 Bty., 48 Lt AA Regt., Royal Artillery. 16 May 1945 in the Far East. Aged 23. *s of Daniel & Winifred, Wigan.* SINGAPORE MEMORIAL [X]

**ANGLESEA John,** Engine Room Artificer D/MX102924. H.M. Submarine *Simoon.* 19 November 1943. Aged 21. The submarine was sunk in the Dardanelles Approaches by German U-boat *U-565.* *s of Richard & Margaret, Lower Ince.* PLYMOUTH NAVAL MEMORIAL [IN/ISM]

**ARKWRIGHT Frederick,** Dvr. T/14695668 723 Gen. Transport Coy. Royal Army Service Corps. Died 1 February 1945 in Belgium. Aged 27. *s of Joseph & Alice, Goose Green.* SCHOONSELHOF CEMETERY [W/GGC]

**ARKWRIGHT William Eric,** Gnr. 1156560 112 (The West Somerset Yeomanry) Field Regt., Royal Artillery. Killed 2 July 1944 in Normandy. Aged 21. BAYEAUX MEMORIAL [WGS]

**ARMER William Roy,** Lieut. 293212 10th Bn. Highland Light Infantry (City of Glasgow Regt.) Killed in action in France 29 June 1944. Aged 21. *s of William & Lily, Worthington.* ST. MANVIEU WAR CEMETERY. [AS/HDC/STC/WGS]

**ARMSTRONG George,** Sto. 1st Class. P/K23779 R.N. H.M.Tug *St Abbs* 1 June 1940. Aged 43. The tug was attacked and sunk by German aircraft during the Dunkirk evacuation. He was recalled to the service on the outbreak of war, having served in the R.N. 1914-36. *s of William & Mary, Spring View, Ince.* PORTSMOUTH NAVAL MEMORIAL . [W]

**ARNOLD Thomas,** Sgt. (Nav) 1515414 R.A.F. (V.R.) 10 Sqdn. 27 March 1944 Aged 21. A Halifax III bomber from Melbourne was lost on an attack on Essen. Five of the crew of seven perished. *s of John & Alice; h of Alice, Garswood.* HOTTON WAR CEMETERY [AC/AMS/NAV]

**ARROWSMITH John Critchley,** Sgt. 1514783 R.A.F. (V.R.) 102 Sqdn. 12 November 1943. Aged 21. He was a crew member of a Halifax from Pocklington which was shot down by a flak ship in the target area whilst engaged on mine-laying operations off the Frisians *s of Kenneth & Annie, Leigh.* RUNNYMEDE MEMORIAL [L/LGS]

**ASCROFT Frank,** Pte. 7616968 17 Ordnance Store Coy., Royal Army Ordnance Corps. Died of wounds 21 December 1941 in Egypt.. Aged 23. *s of Sam & Sarah Jane, Newtown.* HELIOPOLIS WAR CEMETERY, EGYPT. [W]

**ASHALL William,** Fus. 3457618 10th Bn. Lancashire Fusiliers. Killed in India 9 May 1943. Aged 29. *s of Thomas & Alice, Billinge; h of Doris.* RANGOON MEMORIAL. [BC]

**ASHCROFT Herbert,** Gnr. 1536484 Royal Artillery Died of wounds in Egypt 10 September 1943. Aged 26. *s of Herbert & Mary, UpHolland.* HELIOPOLIS WAR CEMETERY. [UPH/UPC]

**ASHCROFT John,** Spr. 14376217 103 Army Troops Coy. Royal Engineers. 20 April 1946. Aged 36. *s of William & Mary; h of Betsy, Hindley.* PHALERON WAR CEMETERY, ATHENS. [X]

**ASHCROFT Norman,** Cpl. 3523175 2nd Bn. The Parachute Regiment, Army Air Corps. He was killed in Tunisia 30 November 1942 Aged 33. He has no known grave. *s of James & Alice; h of May.* MEDJEZ-EL-BAB MEMORIAL, TUNISIA. [SCC/W]

**ASHTON Colin**, Fus. 14241646 2nd Bn. The Lancashire Fusiliers. Killed in action 5 October 1943. Aged 27. He has no known grave. *s of Cyril & Mary, Ince; h of Mary.* ATHENS MEMORIAL. [X]

**ASHTON George Andrew**, L. Bdr. 1732403 416 Bty., 81 Heavy AA Regt., Royal Artillery. Died in a military hospital, 20 August 1941. Aged 21. *s of Andrew & Anne, Leigh.* LEIGH CEMETERY [X]

**ASHTON William**, Dvr. 14242599 Royal Engineers. Died 26 March 1943 Aged 31. *h of Florrie.* HINDLEY CEMETERY [X]

**ASHTON William Thomas**, Sgt. 3530049 30 Lt. AA Regt., Royal Artillery. Died of wounds in Italy, 17 February 1944. Aged 35. ANZIO WAR CEMETERY, ITALY. [A/HBC]

**ASHURST George Arthur**, Dvr. T/279892 R.A.S.C. Died 2 December 1941 Aged 31 *h of Hilda, Wigan.* WIGAN CEMETERY [SMC/W]

**ASHURST Jack Hall**, A.C.1. 1082219 R.A.F. (V.R.) Died 26 October 1944 while a PoW of the Japanese. Aged 29 *s of Ernest & Mary, Pemberton.* SINGAPORE MEMORIAL [X]

**ASHURST James Fearnley**, L. Cpl. 2934500 2nd Bn. Queen's Own Cameron Highlanders. Died 3 June 1943. Aged 27. *s of William & Margaret; h of Doris. Family connections in Wigan & St Helens.* SUTTON (ST NICHOLAS & ALL SAINTS) CHURCHYARD, LANCASHIRE. [X]

**ASHURST John**, L.A.C. 1480779 R.A.F. (V.R.) 654 Sqdn. Killed 7 September 1943. Aged 20. *s of Henry & Margaret , Lamberhead Green.* CATANIA WAR CEMETERY, ITALY. [PC]

**ASHURST Kenneth**, Flt. Sgt. 553270 R.A.F. 61 Sqdn. 16 February 1942. Aged 19. A Manchester I bomber from Woolfox Lodge on a mining operation was hit by flak and crashed into the sea off Terschelling. The bodies of three members of the crew were washed ashore and buried in Westerschelling. *s of Agnes; h of Marjory, Orrell.* RUNNYMEDE MEMORIAL. [X]

**ASHURST Thomas**, Pte. 3855465 1/7th Bn. Queen's Royal Regiment (West Surrey). Killed in action in Libya 23/24 October 1942. *s of Mr & Mrs R.* EL ALAMEIN WAR CEMETERY. [HGC]

**ASPEY Ernest**, Fus. 1427071 7th Bn. Royal Welch Fusiliers. Killed in Germany 14 April 1945 Aged 30. *s of Joseph & Margaret; h of Dorothy, Standish.* BECKLINGEN WAR CEMETERY GERMANY. [ST/STC]

**ASPEY William**, W.O. (Air Gnr.) 1437583 *D.F.M.* R.A.F. 7 Sqdn. Age 22. Killed 8 August 1944 as a member of the crew of a Lancaster which bombed the Normandy battle area and which crashed near Bolbec. *s of Thomas & Mary, Wigan.* BOLBEC COMMUNAL CEMETERY [STC/W]

**ASPINALL Harry,** Flt. Sgt.(Air Gnr.) 1101769 *D.F.M.* R.A.F. (V.R.) 61 Sqdn. 23 April 1944. Aged 28. A member of the crew of a Lancaster III bomber which exploded and crashed on a raid on Brunswick. HANOVER WAR CEMETERY. [A/CUC/HBC/LGS]

**ASPINALL Jacob,** L.A.C. 1504396 R.A.F. (V.R.) 180 Sqdn. Killed 9 November 1942. Aged 21. *s of Thomas & Ethel, Platt Bridge.* INCE-IN-MAKERFIELD CEMETERY. [PBC]

**ASPINALL William Francis,** L.Cpl. 7901246 48th Royal Tank Regiment, R.A.C. Killed North Africa 21 April 1943. Aged 24. *s of John & Emily.* MEDJEZ-EL-BAB WAR CEMETERY. [L/LGS]

**ASTLEY John,** Air Mech. 1st Class. FAA/FX84377 R.N. H.M.S. *Avenger.* 15 November 1942. Aged 22. The escort carrier was torpedoed by *U-155* west of Gibraltar with the loss of over 600 crew. *s of Thomas & Annie, Standish.* FLEET AIR ARM MEMORIAL, LEE ON SOLENT. [HDC/ST/STC]

**ATHERTON Henry,** Gnr. 1082719 150 (South Nottinghamshire Hussars) Field Regt. Royal Artillery. 21 March 1942. Aged 26. *h of Mary Elizabeth, Wigan.* PEMBERTON CEMETERY. [X]

**ATHERTON Jack,** Gnr. 1533026 153 Bty., 51 H.A.A. Regt. Royal Artillery. Killed in the Middle East, 27 April 1941 Aged 23. *s of William & Edith; h of Mary, Orrell.* TOBRUK WAR CEMETERY, LIBYA. [OC]

**ATHERTON James,** Ch. Stoker. P/KX 75862 R.N. H.M.S. *Cossack* 23 October 1941. Aged 36. This destroyer on escort duty was torpedoed by *U-563* in the North Atlantic. *s of Henry & Margaret; h of Margaret, Wigan.* PORTSMOUTH NAVAL MEMORIAL. [W]
(See also the entries for two other local men who died in this action: John Hargreaves; Thomas Ralph Rainford.)

**ATHERTON John,** Sjt. 3522744 7th Bn. Manchester Regiment 9 June 1944. Aged 37. *h of Florence.* LEIGH CEMETERY. [L]

**ATHERTON John,** Gdsmn. 2613216 3rd Bn. Grenadier Guards. Killed in action 21 May 1940 during the period leading up to the withdrawal to Dunkirk. Aged 26. *s of John & Margaret Atherton, Wigan.* ESQUELMES WAR CEMETERY, BELGIUM.[W]

**ATHERTON John,** Dvr. 10691019 24th Tank Brigade Signals., Royal Corps of Signals. Died of wounds 9 August 1944 in France. Aged 23. *s of William & Elizabeth, Golborne.* BROUAY CEMETERY, FRANCE [G/GOC]

**ATHERTON Joseph,** Cpl. PLY/X103460 No. 3 Royal Marine Commando. Died of wounds in France 23 August 1944 Aged 23. *s of Joseph & Annie; h of Mary, Lower Ince.* RANVILLE WAR CEMETERY, NORMANDY. [IN/ISM]

**ATHERTON Thomas Hodson**, Pte. 3858464 2nd Bn. The Loyal Regiment (North Lancashire). Killed during the battle for Singapore. 23 January 1942. Aged 23. He has no known grave. SINGAPORE MEMORIAL [L/LTC]

**ATHERTON Wilfred Paul**, Pte. 7519793 2 Light Field Ambulance, Royal Army Medical Corps. 22 November 1941. *s of Arthur & Margaret; h of Rachel Jane, Hindley.* KNIGHTSBRIDGE WAR CEMETERY, ACROMA, LIBYA. [X]

**AUSTIN James**, Fus. 3127333 2nd Bn. Royal Scots Fusiliers. Died in hospital in Italy 13 October 1943. Aged 35. BARI WAR CEMETERY, ITALY. [IN]

**BAGGALLEY Albert**, Spr. 2125725 16 Bomb Disposal Coy., Royal Engineers. Killed during an exercise in Wales 28 April 1942. Aged 31. *s of William & Mary; h of Martha Ellen.* PEMBROKE DOCK MILITARY CEMETERY, PEMBROKE, WALES. [SGC/W]

**BAILEY William**, Gnr. 1492190 154 Bty., 52 Lt. AA Regt.. Royal Artillery. Lost his life at sea 26/27 April 1941. Aged 23. ATHENS MEMORIAL. [W]

**BAINES David**, Gnr. 859714 127 Field Regt., Royal Artillery. Killed 19 July 1943 during the invasion of Sicily. Aged 27. *s of David & Eliza; h of Mary, Hindley.* CATANIA WAR CEMETERY. [X]

**BALDWIN Jack**, Sgt (W. Op./Air Gnr.) 625671 *D.F.M.* R.A.F. 44 Sqdn. 14 October 1940 Aged 19. A Hampden bomber from Waddington was shot down by a night fighter while on an operation to Berlin. *s of William & Elizabeth, Wigan.* BERLIN 1939-45 WAR CEMETERY. [X]

**BALL Albert**, Pte. 3534876 West Yorkshire Regiment (The Prince of Wales's Own) Died in hospital in India, 12 September 1944 Aged 27 *s of Albert & Anne* IMPHAL WAR CEMETERY. [L]

**BALL John Sidney**, Pte. 3541174 13th Bn. King's Regiment (Liverpool). Killed in action 3 May 1943 in India while operating behind enemy lines with General Wingate's Chindits. Aged 21. *s of John S. & Evelyn May.* RANGOON MEMORIAL. [T]
(This soldier's father, John Sidney Ball Snr., also died in the Second World War)

**BALL John Sidney**, Cpl. 13024669 Pioneer Corps. 11 October 1945. Aged 44. *h of Evelyn May.* TYLDESLEY CEMETERY. [T]
(The father of John Sidney Ball, Jr. who also died serving in HMF)

**BANKS Eli**, Gnr. 1784006 280 Bty., 87 H.A.A. Regt., Royal Artillery. Died 20 June 1942 in the Middle East. Aged 21. *Family connections in Orrell.* BEIRUT WAR CEMETERY, LEBANON [OC/UP/UPC]

**BANKS John**, Pte. 3453455 2nd Bn. South Lancashire Regiment (Prince of Wales's Volunteers) Died in a Bombay hospital 24 July 1945 Aged 28. *Family connections in Kitt Green.* KIRKEE WAR CEMETERY, INDIA. [PC]

**BANKS Peter**, Sgt. (Air Gnr.) 2205640 R.A.F.(V.R.) 625 Sqdn. 15 December 1944. Aged 20. A Lancaster I bomber from Kelstern was lost on a raid on Ludwigshafen. All the crew perished. *s of Peter & Maria, Wigan.* RHEINBERG WAR CEMETERY, GERMANY. [SCC/W/WSB]

**BANKS Robert**, Flt. Lt. (Pilot) 147209 R.A.F. (V.R.) 625 Sqdn. 13 September 1944. His Lancaster I bomber from Kelstern was shot down during a raid on Frankfurt. All the members of the crew were killed.. *s of Florence & Robert, Standish; h of Joan.* DURNBACH WAR CEMETERY, GERMANY. [SGC/ST/STC]

**BARBER Joseph**, Dvr. T/14320309 Royal Army Service Corps, Attd. H.Q. 22nd Armd. Bde. Died of injuries in Italy, 29 July 1944. Age 31. *s of Edwin & Alice; h of Ada. Leigh & Hindley Green.* CASERTA WAR CEMETERY, ITALY. [L]

**BARKER Benjamin**, Sgt. 1015142 R.A.F. (V.R.) Killed 14 February 1944 in a flying accident in South Africa whilst completing pilot training. Age 32. *s of Joseph & Margaret, Wigan; h of Mabel.* KIMBERLEY (WEST END) CEMETERY, SOUTH AFRICA [NC/SCC/W]

**BARKER Horace**, Sig. D/J55340 R.N. H.M.S. *Courageous.* 17 September 1939. Aged 39. West of Ireland, this aircraft carrier was torpedoed and sunk by *U-29.* 519 of her crew were lost. PLYMOUTH NAVAL MEMORIAL [W/WPC]
(See also: Harold Hocken and Percival Waldron.)

**BARKER Jack**, Tpr. 3451667 108th (1/5th Bn. Lancashire Fusiliers) Regtiment, R.A.C. Died of typhus in a military hospital in Egypt, 2 May 1943. Aged 24. *s of Samuel James & Annie, Wigan.* HELIOPOLIS WAR CEMETERY, EGYPT. [W]

**BARNES Albert**, Pte. 3655298 2nd Bn. South Lancashire Regiment (Prince of Wales's Volunteers). Killed 1 April 1945 in Burma. Aged 24. *s of John & Esther, Ince-in-Makerfield.* TAUKKYAN WAR CEMETERY, BURMA. [IN]

**BARNES Alfred James**, L. Sgt. 2762343 The Black Watch (The Royal Highland Regiment). Killed in action in Normandy 17 June 1944. Aged 31. *s of John & Esther, Wigan; h of Margaret.* BASLY CHURCHYARD, FRANCE. [W/WPC]

**BARNES Geoffrey**, Sgt.(Air Gnr.) 981748 R.A.F. (V.R.) 144 Sqdn. 8 December 1941. Aged 21. A Hampden I bomber from North Luffenham on a raid to Aachen was lost with all the crew. HEVERLEE WAR CEMETERY, BELGIUM. [B]

**BARNES James**, Cpl. 3656375 1st Bn. South Lancashire Regiment (The Prince of Wales's Volunteers) Killed in action in Normandy 27 June 1944. Aged 24. *s of Mr & Mrs James, Higher Ince; h of Joan Ivy.* HERMANVILLE WAR CEMETERY. [IN]

**BARNES Norman**, Pte. 3861027 10th Bn. The Loyal Regiment (North Lancashire). 15 February 1941. Aged 26. *s of Ann, Standish; h of Winifred, Coppull.* COPPULL PARISH CHURCHYARD EXTENSION [STC]

**BARNES Ronald,** A.C.2. 1125364 R.A.F.(V.R.) Killed in a training flight in South Africa 24 February 1942. Aged 19. *s of John & Geraldine, Wigan.* JOHANNESBURG (BRAAMFONTEIN) CEMETERY. [SMC/W]

**BARNES William,** A.B. D/SSX20221 R.N. H.M.S. *Mahratta* 25 February 1944. Aged 28. This destroyer on escort duty was sunk by the U-boat *U-956* in the Barentz Sea. *s of George & Susan, Leigh; h of Catherine.* PLYMOUTH NAVAL MEMORIAL. [L/LTA]
(See also: James Clare; Owen Dootson; James R. Speakman; Alfred H. Urmston.)

**BARNES William,** Spr. 2117002 144 Field Park Sqdn. Royal Engineers. Killed 27 June 1943 in North Africa. Age 29 *s of Ernest & Helen, Wigan; h of Margaret, Ince.* BONE WAR CEMETERY, ALGERIA. [ISM]

**BARNETT John,** Pte. 3856871 2$^{nd}$ Bn. The Loyal Regiment (North Lancashire). Died of wounds received in the battle to hold Singapore, 14 February 1942. Aged 22. *s of John & Ann, Spring View, Ince.* SINGAPORE CIVIL HOSPITAL GRAVE MEMORIAL. [IN/ISM]
(This particular battalion was very heavily involved in the bitter struggle to defend Singapore. It was practically wiped out and no fewer than 32 local men were killed or died in captivity as a result of this action.)

**BARNETT Joseph,** W.O.II C.S.M. 3521930 2$^{nd}$ Bn. The Border Regiment. Killed 23 March 1944 in the Far East. Aged 36. He has no known grave. *h of Veronica, Wigan.* RANGOON MEMORIAL. [W]

**BARNSLEY William,** Fus. 3453433 2/6$^{th}$ Bn Lancashire Fusiliers. Killed in an accident involving a military vehicle, 20 August 1940. Aged 22. HIGHFIELD (ST MATTHEW) CHURCHYARD. [X]

**BARON Thomas,** Cpl. 3451665 1/5$^{th}$ Bn Lancashire Fusiliers. Died 27 July 1941. Aged 22. *h of Nora, Pemberton.* HIGHFIELD (ST MATTHEW) CHURCHYARD. [MZC/W]

**BARRETT William,** Dvr. T/67590 Royal Army Service Corps. Died in Harefield Hospital 4 April 1940. *h of Victoria.* HINDLEY CEMETERY. [HGC]

**BARROW, Harry Victor,** Sgt. 1006181 R.A.F. 190 Sqdn. 15 April 1945. Aged 25. *s of Edwin & Beatrice, Bickershaw; h of Doris Irene, Wigan.* RUNNYMEDE MEMORIAL. [B]

**BARTON Francis (Frank),** Gnr. 1695561 3 Bty., 6 H.A.A. Regiment, Royal Artillery. Died 11 October 1943 while working on the Burma-Siam railway as a PoW of the Japanese. Aged 29. *s of William & Florence, h of Elizabeth, Ashton-in-Makerfield.* KANCHANABURI WAR CEMETERY.[ACC]

**BARTON Frank,** Dvr. T/157208 Royal Army Service Corps. Died of wounds 22 January 1943 in the Middle East. Aged 23. *s of Richard & Daisy, Leigh.* TRIPOLI WAR CEMETERY. [L]

**BARTON George**, A.B  R/JX181454  R.N.  H.M.S. *Minster*  8 June 1944.  Aged 24.  The netlayer, H.M.S. *Minster* (ex Southern Railway) was sunk by a mine off the Normandy beaches.  *s of Richard & Ellen, Ince*.  His brother Thomas died as a PoW of the Japanese.  PORTSMOUTH NAVAL MEMORIAL. [IN]
(See also: Colin Daniels; Frank Marsh.)

**BARTON John**, Sgt. (Nav.)  1434967  R.A.F. (V.R.)  Died 31 March 1943.  Aged 21.  *s of William & Elizabeth, Orrell*.  ORRELL (ST JAMES) R.C. CHURCHYARD. [OC]

**BARTON Thomas**, Gnr.  1111233   135 (The Hertfordshire Yeomanry) Field Regiment, Royal Artillery.  Died  23 July 1943 while working on the Burma-Siam railway as a P.O.W. of the Japanese.  Aged 35.  *s of Richard & Ellen, Ince; h of Mary Jane, Ince*.  KANCHANABURI WAR CEMETERY, THAILAND. [IN]
(His brother George died in service with the Royal Navy.)

**BARTON Thomas**, Sgt. (Air Bomber)  1621407  R.A.F. (V.R.)  103 Sqdn.  30 August 1944.  Aged 25.  A member of the crew of a Lancaster I bomber from Elsham Woods on a raid on Stettin. Twenty-three other Lancasters were lost on this operation.  *s of John & Rachel; h of Edna, Platt Bridge*.  KIEL WAR CEMETERY, GERMANY. [PBC]

**BARTON Walter**, L.A.C.  1051433  R.A.F. (V.R.)  Died 24 February 1945 in York County Hospital.  Aged 24.  *h of Amy Barton, Aspull*.  WIGAN CEMETERY [AS/BHC/W]

**BATE Charles**, Gnr.  14322422  3 Calibration Troop, Royal Artillery.  Killed on active service in India 10 April 1945.  Aged 20.  *s of William & Emma, Atherton*.  RANCHI WAR CEMETERY. [A/LGS]

**BATE Ernest**, Tpr.  7911621  12th Royal Lancers, R.A.C.  Died of wounds in Italy 29 May 1944.  Aged 24.  *s of William & Nelly, Ashton-in-Makerfeld; h of Anne, Haydock*.  NAPLES WAR CEMETERY, ITALY.  [AIM]
(His name is spelt *Bates* in some local sources.)

**BATES, James**, Sjt.  3527108  1st Bn. East Lancashire Regiment.  Killed in action, 4 September 1944 in France.  Aged 29.  *Stubshaw Cross; Ashton-in-Makerfield*.  PERNES CEMETERY. [BNC]

**BATTERSBY James**, Tpr.  3781371  Royal Armoured Corps.  9 March 1946.  Aged 32.  ATHERTON CEMETERY. [X]

**BATTERSBY Kenneth**, Fus.  14729028  4th Bn. Royal Welch Fusiliers.  Killed in action 7 December 1944.  Aged 18.  *s of Thomas & Ellen, Leigh*.  LEOPOLDSBURG WAR CEMETERY, BELGIUM. [L]

**BATTERSBY Robert Stanley**, Fus.  3781198  8th Bn.  Royal Fusiliers (City of London Regiment).  Killed in action in Italy 8 September 1944. Aged 34  *s of Frank & Annie; h of Ada, Leigh*.  CORIANO RIDGE WAR CEMETERY, ITALY. [L/LTC]

**BAUGH Annie**, Pte. W/85106 Auxiliary Territorial Service. Died 9 January 1942. Aged 25. *d of John & Ann*. ATHERTON CEMETERY. [A/HBC]

**BAUM Alfred James**, Sgt. (Obs.) 581137 R.A.F. 49 Sqdn. Killed in action 12 August 1940 when his Hampden bomber, on a raid on Dortmund, was brought down by flak. *His family lived in Astley*. REICHSWALD FOREST WAR CEMETERY, GERMANY. [X]

**BAXENDALE Thomas**, Gnr. 4467760 6 Maritime Regiment, Royal Artillery. Drowned 26 July 1943. Aged 33. LONG ISLAND NATIONAL CEMETERY, NEW YORK. [W]

**BAXTER John**, Gnr. 884646 1 Medium Regiment, Royal Artillery. Killed in Belgium 22 May 1940 during the withdrawal to Dunkirk. Aged 19. *s of Ellen, Atherton*. BRUYELLE WAR CEMETERY, BELGIUM. [A]

**BAXTER William Parker**, Sgt. (W.Op./Air Gnr) 1381903 R.A.F.(V.R.) 166 Sqdn. A member of the crew of a Wellington on a bombing mission to Dortmund 24 May 1943. It was shot down by a night fighter and crashed near Eindhoven. *s of Walter John & Gwendoline; h of Martha*. EINDHOVEN (WOENSEL) GENERAL CEMETERY, HOLLAND. [L/LTC]

**BAYBUTT Ernest**, Pte. 3529192 1st Bn. The Manchester Regiment. Died 10 October 1943 while working on the Burma-Siam railway as a PoW of the Japanese. Aged 26. THANBYUZAYAT WAR CEMETERY, BURMA. [W/PC]

**BAYBUTT Thomas Henry**, Fus. 3860405 1st Bn. Royal Irish Fusiliers. Killed in action 13 August 1943 in Sicily. Aged 28. *s of Mr. & Mrs. R. Orrell*. CATANIA WAR CEMETERY, ITALY. [OC/OCY]

**BAYNES Charles James**, Sgt. (Flt. Eng.) 1054757 R.A.F.(V.R.) 103 Sqdn. 25 July 1944 in France. Aged 24. This Lancaster I bomber from Elsham Wolds on a raid on Stuttgart crashed near Orleans. *s of Dennis & Margaret Ann, Pemberton*. JOUY-LE-POTIER CEMETERY. [HIY/W] (His name is given as *Baines* in some sources.)

**BEACON James Francis**, Ldg. Air Fitter. FX89494 R.N. H.M.S. *Heron*. Died 4 February 1943. WIGAN CEMETERY. [X]

**BELL Albert**, Bdr. 838430 Royal Artillery. Died 7 July 1944. Aged 25. *s of Capt. W. & Annie*. LEIGH CEMETERY. [LPC]

**BELL Donald**, Sgt. 1002123 R.A.F.(V.R.) Died 11 December 1942 Aged 22. *s of James & May*. PENNINGTON (ST MICHAEL) CHURCHYARD. [X]

**BELL Frederick James**, W.O.(Air Gnr.) 972074 R.A.F.(V.R.) 83 Sqdn.. 22 December 1944. Aged 24. After a raid on Politz, the Lancaster III was returning to base but was diverted to Metheringham. It crashed in fog. Only one member of the crew survived. *s of Mr. & Mrs. William, Atherton; h of Freda, Hampstead Norris*. HAMPSTEAD NORRIS (ST MARY) NEW CHURCHYARD, HAMPSHIRE. [A]

**BELL James Henry**, Dvr. T/122231 Royal Army Service Corps. Died as a PoW in Italy 5 January 1943. Aged 23. *s of Thomas & Ellen, Pemberton.* CASERTA WAR CEMETERY. [HIC/HIY/W]

**BELLIS Harold**, Gdsmn. 3652644 3rd Bn Grenadier Guards. Killed in action 28 May 1940, during the withdrawal to Dunkirk. Aged 23. *s of Jesse & Frances, Golborne.* BAS-WARNETON COMMUNAL CEMETERY BELGIUM. [G/GOC]
(The brother of Jesse who was also killed on active service.)

**BELLIS Jesse**, Pte. 3654514 13th.(2/4th Bn. The South Lancashire Regt.) Bn., The Parachute Regiment. A.A.C. Killed 4 January 1945. Aged 24. *s of Jesse & Frances, Golborne.* HOTTON WAR CEMETERY, BELGIUM. [G/GOC]
(The brother of Harold who was also killed)

**BELSHAW Emanuel**, Cpl. 2650397 2/6th Bn. The East Surrey Regiment. Killed in France, 9 May 1945. Aged 40. *s of Emanuel & Jane, Lower Ince; h of Elsie May, Surrey.* CLICHY NEW COMMUNAL CEMETERY, FRANCE. [X]

**BELSHAW James**, Gdsmn. 2615048 1st Bn. Grenadier Guards. Killed in action in Germany 3 April 1945. Aged 29. *s of James & Rachel, Wigan; h of Elizabeth.* RHEINBERG WAR CEMETERY. [NC/W]

**BELSHAW Robert**, Gdsmn. 2618466 4th Bn. Grenadier Guards. Killed by enemy action in London, 20 October 1940. Aged 24. *s of Joseph & Margaret, Spring View, Ince.* INCE-IN-MAKERFIELD CEMETERY. [IN]

**BENNETT Arthur**, Pilot Offr. (Nav.) 151351 R.A.F.(V.R.) 9 Sqdn. 10 May 1944. Aged 25. This Lancaster III bomber took off from Bardney to attack Lille railway yards but exploded in flight over the target. All seven members of the crew were killed on this - their first – sortie, but one has no known grave and is commemorated on the Runnymede Memorial. *s of George & Lily.* HELLEMMES-LILLE COMMUNAL CEMETERY. [SSC/W/WGS]

**BENNETT George**, Gnr. 861804 88 Field Regt. Royal Artillery. Killed 12 September 1944 in the Far East . He has no known grave. Aged 26. *h of M.E., Golborne.* SINGAPORE MEMORIAL. [G/GOC]

**BENNETT Henry**, Gnr. 959870 Royal Artillery Died 29 November 1943. Aged 25. *s of John & Ann Bennett; h of Martha Bennett.* INCE-IN-MAKERFIELD CEMETERY. [X]

**BENNETT James**, L. Cpl. 3445474 2nd Bn. The Lancashire Fusiliers. Killed 7 August 1943. Aged 32. *s of William & Susan ,Up Holland; h of Alice.* CATANIA WAR CEMETERY, ITALY. [UPH/UPC]

**BENNETT John**, Spr. 14642471 1044 Docks Operating Coy. Royal Engineers. Died of wounds 16 December 1944 whilst serving in Belgium. Aged 21. *s of Alma & Elizabeth Bennett, Beech Hill, Wigan.* SCHOONSELHOF CEMETERY, ANTWERP. [BHC/W]

**BENNETT Stephen**, Gnr. 1713861 77 H.A.A. Regt. Royal Artillery. Killed 1 July 1942 in the Far East. Aged 31. *s of Thomas & Rebecca.* DJAKARTA WAR CEMETERY. [ABC]
(In some sources his name is given as *Steven.*)

**BENNETT Sydney**, L.A.C. 999380 R.A.F.(V.R.) Killed in action in the Middle East 7 March 1943. Aged 22. *s of David & Elizabeth; h of Agnes.* TRIPOLI WAR CEMETERY. [IN/ISM/W]

**BENSON Peter Henry**, Sgt. (W.Op./Air Gnr.) 997100 R.A.F.(V.R.) Killed in the Middle East 28 June 1942. Aged 24. *s of Thomas & Martha.* FAYID WAR CEMETERY, EGYPT. [ABC]

**BENT Joseph Laurence**, Pte. 3463074 6th Bn. The Green Howards Killed in France 27 June 1944. Aged 26. *s of James & Catherine, Pemberton.* HOTTOT-LES-BAGNES CEMETERY. [MZC/W/WGS]

**BENTHAM Henry**, Sgt. (W.Op./Air Gnr.) 552444 R.A.F. 107 Sqdn. 30 August 1940. Aged 18. A Blenheim bomber targeted to attack aerodromes was shot down by flak in Holland. *s of Joseph & Ellen, Hindsford.* BERGEN-OP-ZOOM WAR CEMETERY, HOLLAND. [A/HAC/LGS]

**BERRY Henry**, Dvr. 3386185 Royal Army Service Corps. Died 22 June 1942. Aged 21. *s of James & Mary, Up Holland.* WIGAN CEMETERY. [UPH/UPC]

**BERRY John**, Cpl. 3523570 7th Bn. The Cheshire Regiment. Killed 14 March 1944 in Italy. Aged 37. *s of Samuel & Ann; h of Florence.* BEACH HEAD WAR CEMETERY, ANZIO. [SCC/W]

**BERRY Joseph**, A.B. D/JX249537 R.N. H.M.S. *President* but lost in s.s. *Barberrys* 26 November 1942. The cargo ship s.s. *Barberrys,* on passage from the USA to the Clyde, was sunk by *U-663* west of Newfoundland. *Parents lived in Wigan; h of Alice, Lower Ince.* PLYMOUTH NAVAL MEMORIAL [ISM/BHC/SAC/W]

**BERRY William Ernest**, Pte. 3528955 1st Bn The Manchester Regiment. Killed 1 October 1943 in the Far East. *s of James & Mary Ann, Up Holland .* THANBYUZAYAT WAR CEMETERY, BURMA. (UPH/UPC]

**BERTRAND Lorenzo (Lawrence)**, Sgt. (Air Gnr.) 1050195 R.A.F.(V.R.) 428(R.C.A.F.) Sqdn. Killed 8 April 1943. Aged 22. REICHSWALD FOREST WAR CEMETERY. [IN/ISM]

**BIBBY Edward**, P.O. P/JX145572 R.N. H.M.S. *Byrsa.* Died in 92nd General Hospital, Naples, December 1944. Aged 35. *s of James & Elizabeth, Platt Bridge; h of Phyllis Minnie.* NAPLES WAR CEMETERY, ITALY. [PBC]

**BIBBY Stanley**, Pte. 3778656 5th Bn. The King's Regiment (Liverpool). Died of wounds D-Day, 6 June 1944. Aged 31. BAYEAUX MEMORIAL. [PBC/HGC]

**BIMSON John,** 970880 Sgt. R.A.F. (V.R.) 105 Sqdn. A Blenheim bomber on a Wilhelmshaven raid was shot down by a night-fighter and crashed near Groningen, Holland. 1 March 1941. *Mr. & Mrs. E.* GRONINGEN GENERAL CEMETERY, HOLLAND. [AS/HGS/ISM/NSC]

**BIRCH Robert Horace,** L.A.C. 1010493 R.A.F.(V.R.) Died in the Middle East 6 July 1943. Aged 29. *s of William & Catherine, Wigan.* RAMLEH CEMETERY, ISRAEL. [SSC/W/WSB]

**BIRCHALL Edwards,** L.Cpl. 3856261 18th (5th Bn. The Loyal Regiment [North Lancashire]) Regt., Reconnaissance Corps. Died while working on the Burma-Siam railway as a PoW of the Japanese, 8 June 1943. Aged 24. *s of James & Jane, Hindley.* [X]

**BIRCHALL Eric,** Sgt.(W.Op./Air Gnr.) 1076673 R.A.F.(V.R.) 44 Sqdn. 24 December 1943. Aged 21. He was a member of the crew of a Lancaster I bomber which took off from Dunholme Lodge tasked to bomb Berlin. It was shot down and all eight members of the crew were killed. *s of Thomas & Edith, Orrell; h of Betty.* HANOVER WAR CEMETERY. [PC]

**BIRCHALL James,** Pte. 5682350 7th Bn. Oxfordshire & Buckinghamshire Light Infantry. Killed 9 September 1943 in Italy. Aged 20. *s of James & Beatrice, Abram.* SALERNO WAR CEMETERY, ITALY. [ABC]

**BIRCHALL Peter,** Gnr. 1823583 117 Bty., 30 Lt.A.A. Regt. Royal Artillery. Killed 20 April 1945 in Italy. Aged 42. *s of Peter & Ellen; h of Margaret.* BARI WAR CEMETERY, ITALY. [L]

**BIRCHALL Stanley,** Cpl. 4204665 1st Bn. Royal Welch Fusiliers. Died of wounds in India 1 June 1944. Aged 27. *s of Walter & Alice, Leigh.* IMPHAL WAR CEMETERY, INDIA. [BDC/L/LGS]

**BIRD Thomas,** Pte. 3854665 2nd Bn. The Loyal Regiment (North Lancashire). Killed in the defence of Singapore, 21 January 1942. Aged 30. He has no known grave. *s of William & Eliza, Spring View, Ince.* SINGAPORE MEMORIAL [IN/ISM]

**BIRKETT Colin,** Pte. 3523144 70th Bn. The King's Regiment (Liverpool). Died of wounds in a military hospital 24 December 1940. Aged 30. *s of Thomas & Ellen, Lower Ince; h of Nellie, Spring View, Ince.* INCE-IN-MAKERFIELD CEMETERY. [ISM]

**BISHOP Horace M.** Cpl. 980692 R.A.F. (V.R.) Died in hospital in the Middle East 28 June 1942. Aged 28. *s of Bernard & Mary Ann.* BASRA WAR CEMETERY, IRAQ. [L/LAS/LTC]

**BLADES Robert Whitaker,** Flt. Sgt. 1056405 R.A.F.(V.R.) 92 Sqdn. Killed 9 November 1942 in a Spitfire operation in the Western Desert. Aged 21. *s of Robert Alfred & Sarah May, Orrell.* ALAMEIN MEMORIAL. [OC]

**BLAKEMORE Samuel,** L.Sjt. 3453513 2/5<sup>th</sup> Bn. The Lancashire Fusiliers. Killed in Normandy 30 July 1944. Aged 26. *Mr.& Mrs. S., Lowton.* FONTENAY-LE-PENSEL WAR CEMETERY [X]

**BLEAKLEY Charles,** Fus. 4208516 Royal Welch Fusiliers and No.1 Commando. Killed on manouvres 18 September 1942. Aged 20. *s of Thomas & Emily B., Higher Ince.* INCE-IN-MAKERFIELD CEMETERY. [IN]

**BLYTON James,** Gdsmn. 2703132 Scots Guards. Died of wounds 6 March 1945. Aged 22. *s of Walter & Margaret, Spring View.* REICHSWALD FOREST WAR CEMETERY,GERMANY. [IN]

**BOARDMAN Clifford,** L.A.C. 980284 R.A.F. Died as a PoW of the Japanese 26 December 1942. *s of William & Margaret, Digmoor.* YOKOHAMA WAR CEMETERY, JAPAN. [UPC/UPH]

**BOARDMAN Gerald Mortimer,** Sgt. 1495951 R.A.F.(V.R.) 75 Sqdn. 9 April 1943. Aged 20. His Stirling I bomber took off from Oakington to raid Duisburg. It was lost without trace. *s of Frederick & Sabina Jane.* RUNNYMEDE MEMORIAL [HGS/WGS]
(It is unusual to find someone commemorated on two school memorials but Sgt. Boardman was a pupil for some years at both Hindley & Abram and Wigan Grammar Schools.)

**BOARDMAN Harry,** Sgt.(Flt. Engr.) 549441 R.A.F. 467(R.A.A.F.) Sqdn. 11 November 1944. Aged 22. A Lancaster I bomber took-off from Waddington to raid Hamburg but crashed near Stelle with the loss of all but one of the crew. Sgt. Boardman was the only non-Australian in a crew of seven. KEIL WAR CEMETERY [L/LTC]

**BOARDMAN James,** Fus. 3447943 6<sup>th</sup> Bn. Royal Scots Fusiliers. Killed 5 September 1944. Aged 30. *s of John & Mary Ann, Leigh.* KESTERLEE WAR CEMETERY, BELGIUM. [X]

**BOARDMAN Robert Cecil,** Sgt.(W.Op/Air Gnr.) 1028039 R.A.F.(V.R.) 44(Rhodesia)Sqdn. A member of the crew of a Lancaster I which was lost without trace on an operation to Plzen 14 May 1943. Aged 20. *s of Joseph & Elizabeth Ellen, Tyldesley.* RUNNYMEDE MEMORIAL. [T/TC/TMC]

**BOARDMAN William,** Wireman. D/MX674004 R.N. H.M.L.C.T. 462. Died 1 October 1945 in India after an operation. Aged 19. *s of Moses & Jane Elizabeth, Ashton-in-Makerfield.* MADRAS WAR CEMETERY. [AGS/AIM]

**BOARDMAN William Arnold,** Cpl. 3457524 11<sup>th</sup> Bn. The Lancashire Fusiliers. Died 16 October 1944 in Italy. Aged 29. *h of Constance, Pemberton.* FAENZA WAR CEMETERY. [MZC/PC/W]
(This soldier was shown originally on the Mount Zion memorial as named *Taylor.* He is now commemorated additionally by the name under which he served and by which he is shown on other memorials.)

**BODELL Edward Thomas,** Gnr. 1082834. 191(The Hertfordshire & Essex Yeomanry) Field Regt. Royal Artillery. Died of pneumonia 19 April 1944. Aged 26. *h of Anne Marie, Leigh.* LEIGH CEMETERY. [L]

**BOLAND Thomas,** A.C.1. 1526384 R.A.F.(V.R.) Died in the Royal Infimary, Lancaster. 26 March 1945. WIGAN CEMETERY. [W]

**BOLD Alec,** Dvr. 7906387 79 Assault Squadron, Royal Engineers. Killed in Holland 8 November 1944. Aged 25. *s of John & Adeline Dorothy, Billinge.* BERGEN-OP-ZOOM WAR CEMETERY. [BC]

**BOLTON George,** Fus. 3531240 4th Bn. Royal Northumberland Fusiliers. Killed in action Normandy 17 August 1944. Aged 24. *s of George & Elizabeth, Wigan.* BAYEAUX WAR CEMETERY. [W]

**BOLTON Harold,** Dvr. T/99421 Royal Army Service Corps. He died of gunshot wounds as a result of a tragic accident in the United Kingdom. 8 June 1940. Aged 21. WIGAN CEMETERY. [SCC/W]

**BOLTON John Bernard,** Pte. 3529726 1st Bn. The Manchester Regiment. Killed 16 June 1943 in the Far East. Aged 25. *s of George & Edith, Billinge.* KANCHANABURI WAR CEMETERY. [BC]

**BOND Harry,** L.Cpl. 14674764 1st Bn. Royal Norfolk Regiment. Killed Normandy, 7 August 1944. Aged 23. *s of Henry & Catherine; h of Ellen, Parbold.* TILLY-SUR-SEULLES WAR CEMETERY, FRANCE [AP/APC]

**BOND Levi,** L.Cpl. 7606505 2/4th Bn. King's Own Yorkshire Light Infantry. 29 December 1943 in Italy. Aged 33. *s of Wilfred & Margaret Ashton-in-Makerfield; h of Catherine, Ashton-in-Makerfield* MINTURNO WAR CEMETERY, ITALY. [AIM]

**BOON Frank,** Pte. 3858823 2nd Bn. The Loyal Regiment (North Lancashire). Died in November 1944 in the Far East. Aged 26. He has no known grave. *Mr.& Mrs. H., Golborne.* SINGAPORE MEMORIAL [G/GOC]
(This battalion was practically wiped out in the vain attempt to defend Singapore. No fewer than thirty-two local men died while serving in the battalion.

**BOOTH David,** Fus. 3451896 2/5th Bn. Lancashire Fusiliers. Killed in action in France 8 July 1944. Aged 26. *s of David & Alice, Standish.* CAMBES-EN-PLAINE CEMETERY. [SSM/STC]

**BOWERMAN Basil Eric,** Dvr. T/14609445 R.A.S.C. Died 31 July 1943. Aged 30. *s of William Herbert & Mary Jane, Upton; h of Ella, Golborne.* FARNWORTH (ST LUKE) CHURCHYARD, WIDNES. [X]

**BOWKER William Arthur,** A.C.2. 1133886 R.A.F. (V.R.) Killed in an aircraft accident 15 June 1941. Aged 34. *s of William Arthur & Jane, Tyldesley; h of Ann, Tyldesley.* TYLDESLEY CEMETERY. [T/TMC]

BOYDELL Alfred, Sgt.(Flt. Engr.) 1486601 R.A.F.(V.R.) 100 Sqdn. A member of the crew of a Lancaster III bomber which was shot down by a night-fighter over Holland 15 June 1943. Aged 20. *s of James & Margaret Ellen, Leigh.* JONKERBOS WAR CEMETERY, HOLLAND. [L/LAS/LTC]

BOYDELL John, Rflmn. 44127844 2nd Bn. The King's Royal Rifle Corps. Died of wounds in Holland 25 December 1944. Aged 26. WEERT (SWARTBROEK) CHURCHYARD. [L/LMC]

BOYDELL Ronald, Sgt. 989148 R.A.F. (V.R.) 78 Sqdn. 4 May 1943. Aged 23. The Halifax II bomber was lost without trace during a raid on Dortmund. *s of Frederick & Sobia, Tyldesley.* RUNNYMEDE MEMORIAL. [T/TC/TMC]

BOYERS Cyril, Dvr. T/189549 Royal Army Service Corps Attd. 2 H.A.A. Regt. Royal Artillery. Died 26 April 1941 during the withdrawal from Greece. Aged 25. He has no known grave. *s of Robert & Martha; h of Phyllis, Bryn.* ATHENS MEMORIAL. [AIM/AMS]

BOYES James, Spr. 2134782 50 Field Coy. Royal Engineers. Died of wounds in Holland, 30 October 1944. Aged 36. He landed in France on D-Day JONKERBOS WAR CEMETERY, HOLLAND. [L]

BOYLAN Frederick, Rflmn. 11062273 The Cameronians (Scottish Rifles) Killed 16 February 1945 in Holland. Aged 29. *h of M.E. Boylan, Wigan.* GROESBEEK MEMORIAL CEMETERY. [SSC/W]

BRABBS William, Gnr. 394171 135 (Hertfordshire Yeomanry) Field Regt., Royal Artillery. 23 August 1941. Aged 43. *h of Emily, Leigh.* LEIGH CEMETERY. [L]

BRADBURN Joseph, Flying Offr. 157696 *D.F.C.* R.A.F. (V.R.) 44 Sqdn. Killed 10 May 1944. Aged 24. His Lancaster III bomber had taken off from Dunholme Lodge to bomb factories at Gennevilliers but was shot down. EVREUX COMMUNAL CEMETERY, FRANCE. [AGS]

BRADBURY John, Pte. 4127843 2nd Bn. The Cheshire Regiment. Killed 9 February 1943 in Italy. Aged 24. *s of James & Bertha; h of Emily, Bryn.* CASERTA WAR CEMETERY, ITALY. [X]

BRADLEY Joseph Charles, L.Cpl. 14512593 8th Bn. The Royal Scots (The Royal Regiment.) 14 September 1944. Aged 20. *s of Mabel, Orrell.* KASTERLEE WAR CEMETERY, BELGIUM. [X]

BRADLEY William, Bdr. 1078297 3 Airlanding Anti-Tank Bty., Royal Artillery. Killed 9 June 1944 during the invasion of Normandy. Aged 30. *s of William & Rachel, Rainford.* RANVILLE WAR CEMETERY. [ORC]

BRADSHAW Victor Charles, Fus. 4195902 Royal Welch Fusiliers. 20 November 1939. Aged 20. *s of Lancelot Charles & Elizabeth, Standish.* WARRINGTON CEMETERY. [ST/STC]

**BRAGG William P.** Gnr. 3530603 Royal Artillery Killed 8 August 1944 in the Middle East. Aged 24. *s of Thomas & Martha, Wigan.* MOASCAR WAR CEMETERY, EGYPT. [JC/W]

**BRAMWELL William,** Sjt. 13062153 Pioneer Corps. Died 26 May 1942. Aged 25. WIGAN CEMETERY. [W]

**BRANNON John,** Spr. 2136668 91 Field Coy. Royal Engineers. Killed on D-Day 6 June 1944. Aged 36. HERMANVILLE WAR CEMETERY, NORMANDY. [SSM/ST]

**BRAZENDALE Ernest Godfrey,** L.A.C. 1357175 R.A.F. (V.R.) Died 7 July 1943 while working on the Burma-Siam railway as a PoW of the Japanese. KANCHANABURI WAR CEMETERY, THAILAND. [L]

**BRETHERTON John,** Spr. 2196447 1 Parachute Squadron, Royal Engineers. Killed at Arnhem, 20 September 1944. Aged 27. *s of James & Ellen, Wigan.* ARNHEM OOSTERBEEK WAR CEMETERY, HOLLAND. [HIC/W]

**BRICKLEY Thomas,** Gnr. 1071908 Royal Artillery. Drowned at Tollesbury, East Sussex, 9 October 1939. Aged 32. COLCHESTER CEMETERY. [L]

**BRIMELOW Ronald,** Sgt. (W.Op./Air Gnr.) 1521038 R.A.F. (V.R.) 625 Sqdn. 11 April 1944. Aged 21. A Lancaster III from Kelstern was to bomb railway yards at Aulnoye but crashed near Amiens. Only one member of the crew survived. *s of Ralph & Mary, Wigan.* ST PIERRE CEMETERY, AMIENS, FRANCE. [BHC/W/WPC]

**BRINDLE Frank,** W.O.(Pilot) 1477971 R.A.F. (V.R.) 4 January 1946. Aged 23. The pilot of a Liberator of Coastal Command which was forced down by fog. All eight members of the crew were killed. *s of Richard & ary Elizabeth.* STAVANGER CHURCHYARD, NORWAY. [BDC/L/LGS]

**BRINDLE Nathaniel,** Cpl. 968898 R.A.F. (V.R.) Killed in a motor accident in England 10 August 1944. Aged 35. *h of Marian, Wigan.* ORRELL (ST LUKE'S) CHURCHYARD. [OC/OCY]

**BRISCOE Benjamin,** Sgt. 1300474 R.A.F. (V.R.) Killed 30 November 1942. Aged 32. He has no known grave. *s of Richard & Annie; h of Mary Beatrice, Wigan.* RUNNYMEDE MEMORIAL. [W]

**BROADBENT Ned** Sto. 1ˢᵗ Class. D/KX107693 R.N. H.M.S. *Matabele.* 17 January 1942. Aged 25. The destroyer was escorting a Russia-bound convoy when it was sunk by U-boat *U-454* off Kola with the loss of 198 crew. *s of Alfred & Annie; h of Dorothy, Leigh.* PLYMOUTH NAVAL MEMORIAL. [L]
(See also Thomas Mort who died in this action.)

**BROADHURST Henry,** Cpl. 53807 R.A.F. Lost in s.s. *Anselm* 5 July 1941. Aged 25. The passenger liner en route to West Africa was sunk by *U-96* north of the Azores. *s of Henry & Katherine, Atherton.* RUNNYMEDE MEMORIAL. [HBC]

**BROADHURST James,** Sgt. 522691 R.A.F. Died in the Far East, 29 November 1943. Aged 29. *s of Henry & May, Atherton; h of Gladys.* SINGAPORE MEMORIAL. [HBC]

**BROGAN Colin Thomas,** Sto. 1ˢᵗ Class. P/KX150226 R.N. H.M.S. *Puckeridge.* 6 September 1943. Aged 20. The destroyer was sunk by U-boat *U-617* east of Gibraltar *s of Joseph & Isabella; foster s of Mary Barlow, Wigan.* PORTSMOUTH NAVAL MEMORIAL [W]

**BROGAN Edward,** Dvr. T/259728 35 General Transport Coy. Royal Army Service Corps. Killed in Italy 22 May 1944. Aged 33. He has no known grave. *s of Edward & Jane Brogan; h of Minnie Brogan, Wigan.* CASSINO MEMORIAL, ITALY. [NC/W]

**BROGAN John,** Pte. 5125299 8ᵗʰ Bn. The Parachute Regiment, A.A.C. Killed in Normandy 21 August 1944. Aged 21. RANVILLE WAR CEMETERY, FRANCE. [W]

**BROMLEY Jack,** L.A.C. 550718 R.A.F. 53 Sqdn. Killed in action 15 May 1940 in France. Aged 20. *s of Frederick & Ada, Golborne.* RUNNYMEDE MEMORIAL. [AGS/G/GOC]

**BROOKS John Clifford,** Pte. 14827011 Army Catering Corps. Died 25 April 1946 while serving with the Occupational Forces in Germany. Aged 34. *s of John & Ann; h of Eliza.* MUNSTER HEATH WAR CEMETERY GERMANY. [X]

**BROOKS John William,** Dvr. 14822973 719 Artisan Works Coy., Royal Engineers. Killed in a motor accident in Toulon, France, 15 June 1946. Age 20. MAZARGUE (MARSEILLES) CEMETERY. [BDC/L]

**BROOME John,** Dvr. 2115832 232 Field Coy. Royal Engineers. Died 12 March 1945. Aged 34. *s of George & Mary; h of Edith A., Lowton.* ALAMEIN MEMORIAL [X]

**BROOMHEAD James Edward Heaton,** Pte. 3856930 1ˢᵗ Bn. The Loyal Regiment (North Lancashire). Killed 1 April 1943 in North Africa. Aged 21. *s of Pearse & Mary, New Springs.* MASSICAULT WAR CEMETERY, TUNISIA. [AS/NSC] (His brother, John W. Broomhead also died on service)

**BROOMHEAD John W.S.H.,** Pte. 3710434 2/6ᵗʰ Bn. The South Staffordshire Regiment. Died as a result of a road accident in Kent 29 May 1944. Aged 29. *s of Pearse & Mary, New Springs.* HAIGH (ST DAVID) CHURCHYARD. [AS/NSC] (His brother James E.H. Broomhead died on active service.)

**BROUGHTON Stanley Davis,** Sigmn. 2359490. 48 Lt. A.A. Regt., Royal Artillery Signals Section; Royal Corps of Signals. Captured in Singapore February 1942 and died 8 August 1944 in Borneo as a PoW of the Japanese. Aged 40. *s of John Jarvis & Sarah Broughton (Sports Outfitters, Wigan); h of Edith.* LABUAN WAR CEMETERY, NORTH BORNEO. [W/WGS]

**BROWN Edwin**, Marine PO/X111439 Royal Marines H.M.S. *Condor* Died 11 November 1942 in a Scottish hospital. Aged 20. *s of E.A. & J.* GOLBORNE (ST THOMAS) CHURCHYARD. [G/GOC]

**BROWN John**, Gdsmn. 2620221 6th Bn. Grenadier Guards. Killed in action Italy 10 December 1943. Aged 34. He has no known grave. *Parents: Spring View, Ince; h of Hilda Amelia, London.* CASSINO WAR CEMETERY, ITALY. [ISM]

**BROWN Norman**, Fus. 14602507 2nd Bn. Royal Fusiliers (City of London Regiment) He died of wounds 19 September 1944 in Italy. Aged 35. *s of George & Mary Brown, Wigan; h of Minnie Brown, Wigan.* NAPLES WAR CEMETERY, ITALY. [W]

**BROWN Percy**, Sjt. 1803188 40 Lt. A.A. Regt. Royal Artillery. Killed 24 February 1945. Aged 33. *s of George & Mary Elizabeth.* OTTERSUM R.C. CEMETERY, HOLLAND. [W]

**BROWN Stanley (Stanilaus)**, Gnr. 1570749 Royal Artillery. He died in a military hospital on 2 March 1944. Aged 29. *h of Annie Brown, Leigh.* LEIGH CEMETERY. [L]

**BROWN Walter**, Pte. 3389452 1st Bn. Highland Light Infantry (City of Glasgow Regiment). Killed in action 4 March 1945. Age 28. *s of Thomas & Susan.* REICHSWALD FOREST WAR CEMETERY, GERMANY. [BDC/L]

**BROWN William**, Fus. 3451662 1/8th Bn. The Lancashire Fusiliers. Killed in the Dunkirk evacuation. 31 May 1940. Aged 21. *s of Peter & Alice, Boothstown.* LA PARADIS WAR CEMETERY, FRANCE. [X]

**BROWN William Henry**, A.C.1. 1019374 R.A.F. (V.R.) Killed in action in the Sudan 4 July 1942. Aged 29. *s of Walter & Martha, Up Holland; h of Edna.* KHARTOUM WAR CEMETERY, SUDAN. [UPC/UPH]

**BROXON Wilfred John**, Gnr. 1149100 17 Field Regt. Royal Artillery. Died 11 April 1946 in Austria. Aged 23. *s of John & Sarah, Wigan.* KLAGENFURT WAR CEMETERY, AUSTRIA. [X]

**BRYAN Thomas**, Pte. 2818267 4th Bn. The Seaforth Highlanders.(Ross-Shire Buffs, The Duke of Albany's). Killed 10 June 1940 in Belgium. Aged 27. *s of Thomas (killed in the First World War) & Eve, Astley.* DUNKIRK TOWN CEMETERY. [X]

**BRYANT William**, Tpr. 4131875 4th County of London Yeomanry, R.A.C. Killed 3 October 1943 in Italy. *s of Robert Jardine & Sarah Fanny, Astley.* CASSINO MEMORIAL. [T]

**BUCKLEY Arthur Henry**, Dvr. T/68317 Royal Army Service Corps. Died of typhoid in Italy, 3 August 1944. Aged 23. *s of Arthur & Winifred; h of Edna.* NAPLES WAR CEMETERY. [W/WSB]

**BUCKLEY Ernest,** Gnr. 1123238 4 Field Regt. Royal Artillery. Killed in Burma 23 July 1944. Aged 40. *s of John & Martha, Standish; h of Mary Elizabeth, Standish.* IMPHAL WAR CEMETERY. [STC/W]

**BUCKLEY Henry James,** Spr. 1886761 7 Field Regt. Royal Artillery. Died of wounds in the Middle East 30 October 1942. Aged 28. *s of Henry James & Frances, Wigan.* EL ALAMEIN WAR CEMETERY. [W]

**BULLOUGH Norman.** L.Cpl. 6093536 The Queen's Royal Regiment (West Surrey). Died 23 February 1943. Aged 25. *s of Mr. & Mrs. James.* WIGAN CEMETERY. [SGC/W]

**BULPITT John,** Pte. 3865881 !st Bn. The Loyal Regiment [North Lancashire]. Killed 18 February 1944 in Italy. Aged 21. *s of James & Eliza, Pemberton, Wigan.* BEACH HEAD WAR CEMETERY, ANZIO. [W/PC]

**BURKE George Thomas,** Marine 14359 2$^{nd}$ Bn. Royal Marine Engineers. Died 7 February 1946. Aged 24. *s of Peter & Elizabeth, Leigh.* SYDNEY WAR CEMETERY, AUSTRALIA. [X]

**BURKE John,** L.Cpl. 3857108 *M.M.* 1$^{st}$ Bn. The Loyal Regiment (North Lancashire). Killed 25 October 1944 in Italy. *His Mother lived in Ashton-in-Makerfield.* AREZZO WAR CEMETERY, ITALY. [X]

**BURKE William,** Ldg. Sto. D/KX89676 R.N. H.M.S.*Charybdis* 23 October 1943. Aged 27. The cruiser was sunk by German torpedo boats off Northern France. *s of William & Margaret, Tyldesley.* PLYMOUTH NAVAL MEMORIAL. [A]
(See also: William Clayton; Robert Finney; Kenneth Gibson; Richmond Smalley.)

**BURNETT George Michael,** Lieut. 134505 74 Medium Regt. Royal Artillery. Killed 28 April 1943 in North Africa. Aged 28. *s of Frank Ridley; h of Joan Hilda, Pennington, Leigh.* MASSICAULT WAR CEMETERY, TUNISIA. [X]

**BURNS Arthur,** Spr. 14223478 505 Field Coy. Royal Engineers. Killed 19 March 1943 in North Africa. Aged 32. *s of Thomas & Eunice Louisa, h of Dorothy, Poolstock, Wigan.* ENFIDAVILLE WAR CEMETERY. [JC]

**BURNS Thomas,** Gnr. 902561 137 Field Regt. Royal Artillery. Killed 3 January 1942 in the Far East. Aged 23. *s of Thomas & Annie.* SINGAPORE MEMORIAL [G/GOC]

**BURROWS Harry,** Sgt.(Air Gnr.) 2203724 R.A.F.(V.R.) 576 Sqdn. 22 February 1945. Aged 19. His Lancaster I bomber left Fiskerton for a raid on Duisburg but crashed and exploded near Kevelaer. All members of the crew were killed. REICHSWALD FOREST WAR CEMETERY. GERMANY. [ABC]

**BURTON William,** Cpl. 4202463 *M.M.* 1$^{st}$ Bn. Royal Welch Fusiliers. Died of wounds in India 9 May 1944. Aged 30. *He had family connections with Abram and Platt Bridge.* DELHI WAR CEMETERY, INDIA. [ABC/PBC]

**BUTLER Francis (Frank)**, Ord. Smn. Merchant Navy. m.v. *British Vigilance.* 3 January 1943. Aged 20. This tanker was en route from Curacao to Gibraltar but was sunk by U-boat *U-514* east of the Leeward Islands. *s of John & Mary A.* TOWER HILL MEMORIAL. [W]

**BUTLER Francis (Frank)**, Sjt. 838500 58 Anti-Tank Regt. Royal Artillery. Died of wounds 20 November 1944 in Italy. Aged 32. *h of May.* CESENA WAR CEMETERY, ITALY. [W]

**BUTLER John**, Pte. 3860419 11$^{th}$ (H.D.) Bn. The Manchester Regiment. Accidentally killed while on sentry duty 16 October 1940. Aged 25. WIGAN CEMETERY. [W]

**BUTLER John**, Ldg. Smn. C/JX159801 R.N. H.M.S. *Cricket.* Died of wounds in a Royal Naval hospital 27 September 1944. Aged 22. *s of William & Elsie, Leigh.* HASLAR ROYAL NAVAL CEMETERY, GOSPORT. [L]

**BUTTERWORTH James**, Dvr. T/197776 Royal Army Service Corps. Captured at the fall of Singapore and died of malaria 8 March 1944 at a Thailand camp whilst a PoW of the Japanese. Aged 30. *s of Frederick & Helen; h of Eliza Ann, Atherton.* CHUNGKAI WAR CEMETERY, THAILAND. [A]

**BUTTERWORTH John Thomas**, Gnr. 1619602 290 Bty; 93 H.A.A. Regt., Royal Artillery. Died 26 November 1940. Aged 26. STANDISH (ST WILFRED) CHURCHYARD. [ST/STC]

**BUTTERWORTH Robert**, Gnr. 1568747 512 Coast Regt. Royal Artillery. Died 20 September 1941. Aged 27. *s of A. & A., Hindley.* HINDLEY CEMETERY. [X}

**BYROM John**, Sigmn. D/SSX33022 R.N. H.M.S. *Broadwater.* 19 October 1941. Aged 19. This destroyer on convoy escort duty was sunk by U-boat *U-101* in the North-West Approaches. *s of William & Lily, Golborne.* LONDONDERRY CITY CEMETERY. [G/GOC]

**BYRON Robert**, Pte. 3856206 2$^{nd}$ Bn. The Loyal Regiment (North Lancashire). Killed 12 February 1942 during the battle for Singapore. Aged 24. *Mr. & Mrs. T., Ince.* SINGAPORE MEMORIAL. [IN]

**CAFFERY Patrick**, Sto. 1$^{st}$ Class D/SKX910 R.N. H.M.Submarine *Thorn.* 11 August 1942. Aged 21. Sunk by Italian torpedo boat *Pegaso* off Tobruk. *s of William & Margaret; h of Eveline, Whelley.* PLYMOUTH NAVAL MEMORIAL. [W]

**CAHILL Frederick**, Gnr. 1106403 Royal Artillery. Died while serving in the Occupation Forces in Germany, 23 May 1946. Aged 31. *s of Fred & Mary; h of Phyllis, Leigh.* MUNSTER HEATH WAR CEMETERY. [X]

**CAIN William**, Bdr. 833246 25 Field Regiment, Royal Artillery. Killed in Italy 1 October 1944. He has no known grave. CASSINO MEMORIAL [AS]
(Local sources give the spelling of his name as *Caine.*)

**CALLISTER Alfred**, A.B. D/SSX35799 R.N. H.M.S. *Exeter.* 1 March 1942. Aged 21. The cruiser was attacked by a force of Japanese destroyers and cruisers, set on fire and abandoned. *s of Martha Alice, Tyldesley.* PLYMOUTH NAVAL MEMORIAL. [T]

**CAMPBELL Colin**, L.Cpl. 3780768 1<sup>st</sup> Bn. The Royal Leicestershire Regiment. Killed in action in France, 23 August 1944. Aged 32. *s of Charles & Mary; h of Beatrice.* ST DESIR WAR CEMETERY, FRANCE. [X]

**CAMPBELL Colin Alexander**, Pte. 14445234 Royal Army Medical Corps. Died Woolwich Hospital, July 1945. Aged 19. *s of Duncan & Jane, Wigan.* WALLASEY (RAKE LANE) CEMETERY. [X]

**CARNEY William**, Pte. 3964343 1<sup>st</sup> Bn. The Welch Regiment. Killed in action in Italy 5 October 1944. Aged 25. *s of William & Minnie, Atherton; h of Mabel.* CESENA WAR CEMETERY, ITALY. [A]

**CARNEY William**, Pte. 3856942 1<sup>st</sup> Bn. The West Yorkshire Regiment (The Prince of Wales's Own). Killed 12 March 1944 in the Far East. Aged 24. *s of Mr. & Mrs. Michael.* RANGOON MEMORIAL. [X]

**CARR Edward**, Sgt. (Air Gnr.) 998856 R.A.F.(V.R.) 61 Sqdn. 8 March 1943. Aged 28. In the course of a raid on Nuremburg, this Lancaster III bomber is believed to have crashed in the target area. *s of Robert & Anne, Ashton-in-Makerfield.* DURNBACH WAR CEMETERY, GERMANY. [X]

**CARR Edward**, Tpr. 3857355 18<sup>th</sup> (5<sup>th</sup> Bn. The Loyal Regt. [North Lancashire] ) Regiment, Reconnaissance Corps. Killed 15 February 1942 in the Far East. Aged 22. *s of Thomas & Catherine, Hindley.* SINGAPORE MEMORIAL. [X]

**CARR Matthew**, Gnr. 1125394 146 (The Pembroke Yeomanry) Field Regiment, Royal Artillery. Killed 28 March 1943 in Tunisia. Aged 38. *s of William George Henry & Jane; h of Alice, Abram.* MEDJEZ-EL-BAB MEMORIAL CEMETERY, TUNISIA. [IN/PBC]

**CARR Norman**, L.Cpl. 14092277 The Argyll & Sutherland Highlanders (Princess Louise's). Killed in an accident in Palestine 3 May 1947. Aged 20. *s of William H & Catherine, Wigan.* RAMLEH CEMETERY, ISRAEL. [W/WSB]
(Note that this soldier is shown on the Wigan memorial as serving in the South Lancashire Regiment at the time of his death. The details here are as given by CWGC).

**CARRICK George**, Cpl. 14241652 The Lancashire Fusiliers & No. 2 Commando. Killed Salerno 13 September 1943. Aged 28. *s of George & Ethel, Astley.* SALERNO WAR CEMETERY, ITALY. [T]

**CARROLL Joseph**, Pte. 4806766 1<sup>st</sup> Bn. The West Yorkshire Regiment (The Prince of Wales's Own). Died in a military hospital of wounds received in the Burma campaign, 9 June 1944. Aged 24. *s of Michael & Bridget, Leigh.* MAYNAMATI WAR CEMETERY, PAKISTAN. [L]

**CARRUTHERS William Alan,** Sgt. (W.Op./Air Gnr.) 1063043 R.A.F.(V.R.) Killed 26 February 1942. *Mother: Mrs. A.M. Parbold.* TERSCHELLING GENERAL CEMETERY, HOLLAND. [SMC/W]

**CARTER John,** Pte. 3858839 $2^{nd}$ Bn. The Loyal Regiment (North Lancashire). Killed 23 January 1942 in Singapore. Aged 22. *s of Frederick & Lily.* SINGAPORE MEMORIAL. [HIC/W]

**CARTER Stanley,** Sto. $2^{nd}$ Class. D/KX121023 R.N. H.M.S. *Prince of Wales.* 10 December 1941. Aged 24. Sunk by a Japanese aircraft attack using bombs and torpedoes off Malaya. *s of Frederick & Lily; h of Lily, Pemberton.* PLYMOUTH NAVAL MEMORIAL. [HIC/W]
(See also: Jack Ainscough; Harold Jenkins.)

**CARTY Joseph Francis (Frank)** A.C.2 1102865 R.A.F. Died as a PoW of the Japanese 11 June 1943. h of *Harriet, Pemberton.* AMBON WAR CEMETERY, INDONESIA. [W]

**CASEY John,** A.C.1. 966720 R.A.F.(V.R.) Died 14 March 1942. GOLBORNE (ALL SAINTS) R.C. CHURCHYARD. [G/GOC]

**CASHIN Ernest,** Marine PLY/X3732 Royal Marines H.M.S. *Galatea.* 15 December 1941. Aged 21. This cruiser was sunk off Alexandria by the German U-boat *U-557* while returning from North Africa. *s of James Arthur & Anne, Wigan.* PLYMOUTH NAVAL MEMORIAL. [SCC/W/WSB]
(See also: Fred Mann and Herbert Worrall)

**CASSIDY Thomas,** Pte. 3858895 $2^{nd}$ Bn. The Loyal Regiment (North Lancashire). Killed 23 January 1942. Aged 24. *s of Mr. & Mrs. John, Top Lock, Wigan.* SINGAPORE MEMORIAL. [W/AS/NSC]
(This battalion suffered very heavy casualties in the defence of Singapore. Thirty-two local men died.)

**CASWELL Thomas,** Tpr. 3865410 $18^{th}(5^{th}$ Bn. The Loyal Regt. [North Lancashire]) Regt.; Reconnaissance Corps. Died while working on the Burma-Siam railway as a PoW of the Japanese, 7 October 1943. Aged 30. *s of Thomas & Nancy, Ince.* THANBYUZAYAT WAR CEMETERY. [X]

**CATTERALL Herbert,** Fus. 14209555 $2^{nd}$ Bn. The Royal Fusiliers (City of London Regiment). Killed 19 May 1944 in Italy. Aged 22. *s of George & Ellen.* CASSINO WAR CEMETERY. [SCC/W/WSB]

**CATTERALL Robert,** Gdsmn. 2624041 $1^{st}$ Bn. Grenadier Guards. Died of wounds 4 September 1944 in France. Aged 19. *s of John & Ellen, Orrell.* HIGHWOOD LONGUEVNE CEMETERY, FRANCE. [X]

**CAUSEY David,** Sto. $2^{nd}$. Class. C/KX149758 R.N. H.M.S. *Cassandra* 11 December 1944. Aged 20. *s of David & May, Ince.* CHATHAM NAVAL MEMORIAL. [IN]

**CAVANAGH Edward**, Fus. 3452390 2<sup>nd</sup> Bn. The Lancashire Fusiliers. Killed 21 June 1944 in Italy. ORVIETO WAR CEMETERY, ITALY. [W]

**CHADWICK Charles Edward**, Sjt. 404922 7<sup>th</sup> Queen's Own Hussars, R.A.C. Killed 28 April 1942 in the Far East. Aged 27. *s of Roland & Betsy, Bamfurlong.* RANGOON MEMORIAL. [ABC/BMC]

**CHADWICK Cyril**, Sgt.(Flt. Engr.) 1622527 R.A.F.(V.R.) 156 Sqdn. 24 August 1943. Aged 20. The Lancaster III on an operation to Berlin is believed to have crashed and exploded. His body was originally buried in Doberitz. *s of Ernest & Evelyn, Pemberton.* BERLIN 1939-45 WAR CEMETERY. [HIC]

**CHADWICK Ronald**, A.B. P/JX266346 R.N. H.M.S. *President III* (but lost in m.v. *President Doumer)* 30 October 1942. Aged 32. Sunk off Madeira by U-boat *U-604.* It was being used as a troop transport and 260 lives were lost. *h of Annie, Hindley Green.* PORTSMOUTH NAVAL MEMORIAL. [HGC]

**CHARLESON George Slater**, L.A.C. 1069857 R.A.F.(V.R.) Accidently drowned in Egypt 19 October 1942. Aged 36. *s of Richard & Mary Ann; h of Lily.* ALEXANDRIA (HADRA) WAR MEMORIAL CEMETERY. [L]

**CHARLTON George**, Rfn. 3663497 9<sup>th</sup> Bn. The Cameronians (Scottish Rifles). Killed in action in Holland 31 October 1944. Aged 24. *s of James & Ellen; h of Hilda, Tyldesley.* MIERLO WAR CEMETERY, HOLLAND. [T/TC]

**CHARLTON James**, Pte. 2198166 19 Depot Labour Coy., Royal Engineers. Drowned in the port of Le Harve 28 December 1939. Aged 34. *His wife lived in School Lane, Wigan.* STE. MARIE CEMETERY, LE HARVE. [W]

**CHATTERLEY Joseph Simpson**, L.Cpl. 3523473 1<sup>st</sup> Bn The Manchester Regiment. Killed 21 September 1944. Aged 34. He has no known grave. *s of Joseph & Alice, Wigan; h of Hilda Victoria.* SINGAPORE MEMORIAL [W]

**CHEETHAM Ernest**, Sgt.(Nav./Air Bomber) 1138227 R.A.F. (V.R.) Killed in France 29 October 1942. Aged 21. *s of Joseph & Florence, Kitt Green.* TAULE COMMUNAL CEMETERY. [OUC/PC]

**CHEETHAM Gerald**, Fus. 6482292 The Royal Fusiliers and No. 2 Commando. Died of typhoid fever in Sicily 27 October 1943. Aged 24. *s of Thomas James & Charlotte, Orrell.* CATANIA WAR CEMETERY, ITALY. [AGS/OC]

**CHEETHAM Herbert Thomas**, Sgt, (Flt.Engr.) 615248 R.A.F. 102 Sqdn. 22 November 1942. Aged 21. This Halifax II bomber from Pocklington on a raid on Stuttgart crashed near Amiens. All members of the crew were killed. *s of Thomas & Christina. Wigan.* ABBEVILLE COMMUNAL CEMETERY. [SSC/W/WSB]

**CHEETHAM John Lewis**, Gnr. 965723 51 Medium Regt. Royal Artillery. Drowned in Tripolitania 5 June 1943. Aged 25. *s of Joseph & Alice, Leigh.* TRIPOLI WAR CEMETERY,. LIBYA. [L]

**CHEETHAM Robert,** Sgmn. 2597217 Royal Corps of Signals. Died in Chester Hospital 15 June 1942. Aged 37. *s of Thomas & Margaret, Standish Lower Ground.* SHEVINGTON CEMETERY.[X]

**CHILTON Horace,** Pte. 3858491 14th Bn. The Sherwood Foresters (Nottinghamshire & Derbyshire Regiment). Killed 18 September 1944 in Italy. Aged 25. *s of Josiah & Sarah Jane, Abram.* CORIANO RIDGE WAR CEMETERY, ITALY. [ABC]

**CHIVERS Joseph,** L.Cpl. 3461305 2nd Bn. The Lancashire Fusiliers. Died of wounds in Italy 16 May 1944. Aged 21. *s of Joseph & Rose, Atherton.* CASSINO WAR CEMETERY, ITALY. [A]

**CHIVERS William,** Rfn. 3250745 9th Bn. The Cameronians (Scottish Rifles) Killed in action in Holland, 20 February 1945. Aged 23. MILSBEEK WAR CEMETERY, HOLLAND. [L/LTC]

**CHRISTOPHER Richard,** Gnr. 1643779 195 Bty., 65 Lt. A.A. Regt. Royal Artillery. Killed 19 January 1942 in the Middle East. Aged 30. He has no known grave. *s of Richard & Mary.* ALAMEIN MEMORIAL. [SCC/W]

**CLAPPERTON Harold Kenneth,** Lieut. 219886 1st Bn. The Loyal Regiment (North Lancashire). Died of wounds in Tunisia, 25 April 1943. Aged 23. *s of George & Jane Hannah.* THIBAR SEMINARY WAR CEMETERY, TUNISIA. [X]

**CLARE James,** A.B. D/JX340441 R.N. H.M.S. *Mahratta.* 25 February 1944. Aged 19. The destroyer, while on convoy escort duty in the Barentz Sea, was sunk by the German U-boat *U-956.* PLMOUTH NAVAL MEMORIAL. [T]
(See: William Barnes; Owen Dootson; James Speakman; Alfred Henry Urmston.)

**CLARKE Charles Sydney,** Pte. 3713405 1st Bn. The Gordon Highlanders. Killed 27 October 1942. Aged 24. *s of William & Ellen; h of Muriel.* EL ALAMEIN WAR CEMETERY. [W]

**CLARKE Eric,** Sgt. 1025294 R.A.F. (V.R.) Killed 11 December 1942. Aged 22. *s of Peter & Jane, Wigan.* RUNNYMEDE MEMORIAL . [WSB]

**CLARKE John,** Flt. Sgt. 1230372 R.A.F. (V.R.) 547 Sqdn. Killed 18 August 1943 on an anti-submarine patrol in the Bay of Biscay. Aged 21. *s of Frederick & Esther; h of Margaret, Leigh.* RUNNYMEDE MEMORIAL. [L/LGS/LMC/LTC]

**CLARKE Stanley James,** Ldg. Sgmn. D/JX151544 R.N. H.M.S. *Scorpion.* 13 February 1942. Aged 20. In the Banka Straight, this river gunboat was sunk by a Japanese warship. *s of William & Mary, Wigan.* PLYMOUTH NAVAL MEMORIAL. [SSC/W/WSB]

**CLARKSON Ernest,** Bdr. 838594 38 Bty., 14 Anti-Tank Regiment, Royal Artillery. Killed in action in Belgium, 18 May 1940. Aged 24. *h of Isabella.* ASSE-LEZ-BRUXELLES (MALLEMSEBAAN) COMMUNAL CEMETERY. [KMC/W]

**CLAYTON William,** Ord. Teleg. D/JX341388 R.N. H.M.S. *Charybdis.* 23 October 1943. Aged 21. The cruiser was sunk by German torpedo boats off Northern France. *s of James & Emily.* ST. PETER PORT (FOULON) CEMETERY, GUERNSEY. [IN/SCC/W/WSB]
(See also: William Burke; Robert Finney; Kenneth Gibson; Richmond Smalley.)

**CLEATOR James Edmund,** A.B. D/SSX24741 R.N. H.M.S. *Illustrious* He died on shore 9 February 1941 but has no known grave. Aged 21. *s of James & Florence.* PLYMOUTH NAVAL MEMORIAL. [PBC/SCC]

**CLEGG Brian Chadwick,** Flying Offr. 167286 R.A.F. Killed in a flying accident in Ceylon 30 November 1945. Aged 21. *s of Bertram Edwin & Mildred May, Golborne.* TRINCOMALEE WAR CEMETERY, CEYLON.[G/GOC]

**CLEGG John,** Tpr. 3859598 5th Regiment, Recconnaissance Corps. Killed in action in North Africa 19 February 1943. Aged 26. *s of John William & Jane Alice, Leigh. h of Dorothy Clegg.* MEDJEZ-EL-BAB WAR CEMETERY, TUNISIA. [L/LMC]

**CLEGG William Edward,** Sgt (Pilot) 741062 R.A.F. (V.R.) 38 Sqdn. Killed 6 January 1941 while flying a Wellington bomber. Aged 32. *s of William & Charlotte Horridge, Atherton; h of Marjorie Clegg.* EL ALAMEIN WAR CEMETERY. [A/LGS]

**CLEMENTS Edwin,** Pte. 3526566 2nd Bn. The North Staffordshire Regiment (The Prince of Wales's) Killed in Italy 20 February 1944. Aged 30. *s of John & Sarah; h of Eunice Ellen.* ANZIO WAR CEMETERY, ITALY. [W]

**CLEWORTH Edwin,** Gdsmn. 2694813 2nd Bn. The Scots Guards Died of wounds in Libya, 22 June 1941. Aged 25. *s of Peter & Helen.* EL ALAMEIN WAR CEMETERY. [X]

**CLIFT James,** Sto. 1st. Class. D/KX138498 R.N. H.M.S. *Kite.* 21 August 1944. Aged 21. The sloop was sunk by *U-334* off north Norway. *s of William Henry & Emma, Atherton.* PLYMOUTH NAVAL MEMORIAL. [A]
(See also: Thomas Aldred; Albert Grundy; Edward Nelson; Thomas Payne.)

**CLOSE George Henry,** Pte. 3603358 4th Bn. The Border Regiment. Died in Burma 29 May 1944. Aged 28. He has no known grave. *s of John Thomas & Elizabeth Jane.* RANGOON MEMORIAL. [GGC]

**CLOUGH John,** Pte. 4131151 6th Bn. The Cheshire Regiment Killed in action 14 September 1942. Aged 26. *s of John & Elizabeth Alice.* EL ALAMEIN WAR CEMETERY. [X]

**COATES Ernest,** Sigmn. 2330292 Royal Corps of Signals. Died while being held as a PoW of the Japanese. 26 November 1942. Aged 24. *s of Alfred Oscar & Martha.* YOKOHAMA BRITISH COMMONWEALTH WAR CEMETERY, JAPAN. [L/LPC]

**COBB Cyril,** Sjt. 3532454 78 Anti-Tank Regiment, Royal Artillery. Fatally injured while directing a convoy of vehicles. 18 June 1943. Aged 24. *s of Thomas (the Vicar of St. Paul's, Westleigh) & Martha Jane; h of Florence.* MANCHESTER SOUTHERN CEMETERY. [L]

**COE Joseph Harry (Henry),** Cpl. 3607392 5th Bn. The East Lancashire Regiment. Killed in Normandy 16 July 1944. Aged 21. *s of William Henry & Sarah, Tyldesley.* FONTENAY-LE-PESNEL CEMETERY, FRANCE. [LGS/T/TC]

**COLBERT Edward,** Sgt. (Air Bomber) 1134101 R.A.F. (V.R.) 9 Sqdn. 31 August 1943. Aged 27. The Lancaster III bomber was lost without trace on an operation to Munchengladbach. *s of Elizabeth & stepson of Fred Arrowsmith, Atherton.* RUNNYMEDE MEMORIAL. [A]

**COLCLOUGH Clarence,** Stoker 1st Class C/KX107133 R.N. H.M.S. *Welshman.* 1 February 1943. Aged 23. While on passage from Malta to Alexandria, this minelayer was sunk by the German U-boat *U-617.* *s of Betsy, Atherton.* CHATHAM NAVAL MEMORIAL. [A]

**COLEMAN Patrick,** Pte. 3530212 14th Bn. Sherwood Foresters (Nottinghamshire & Derbyshire Regiment.) Killed in a road accident in North Africa, 27 August 1943. Aged 22. *s of Edward & Mary.* MEDJEZ-EL-BAB WAR CEMETERY. [T]

**COLLIER George,** Pte. 3858835 1st Bn. The West Yorkshire Regiment (Prince of Wales's Own). Killed 12 March 1944 in India. Aged 27. He has no known grave. *s of Jeremiah & Elizabeth, Aspull.* RANGOON MEMORIAL. [AS/ASC/HDC]

**COLLIER William Richard,** L.A.C. 646821 R.A.F. Died while a PoW of the Japanese, 8 March 1942. Aged 27. *s of Samuel & Amelia, Leigh; h of A.* SINGAPORE MEMORIAL. [L]

**CONNELLY Laurence,** Pte. 3855217 2nd Bn. The Loyal Regiment (North Lancashire). Killed in action, 15 February 1942 in Singapore. Aged 29. *s of Michael & Alice.* KRANJI WAR CEMETERY, SINGAPORE. [W]

**CONNOLLY John,** Pte. 3526536 2nd Bn. The King's Own Royal Regiment (Lancaster) 22 July 1941. Aged 25. DAMASCUS BRITISH WAR CEMETERY. [W]

**CONNOLLY John Stanilaus,** Spr. 2009593 551 Army Troops Coy., Royal Engineers. Killed 13 May 1942. Aged 22. *s of John & Julia, Higher Ince.* FAYID WAR CEMETERY, EGYPT. [X]

**CONNOR Albert,** Sjt. 6093545 6th Regiment, Reconnaissance Corps. Died 15 January 1943 in West Africa. Aged 25. *s of Daniel & Mary Emily, Bryn.* FREETOWN (KING TOM) CEMETERY SIERRA LEONE. [X]

**CONNOR George,** Pte. 5119053 Pioneer Corps. Died in a Liverpool hospital 24 June 1942. Aged 27. *s of Patrick & Mary Jane.* WIGAN CEMETERY. [X]

**CONNOR Harold**, Sgt. 1004480 R.A.F. (V.R.) 114 Sqdn. Killed 25 February 1942 while attacking enemy communications in a Boston aircraft. Aged 24. He has no known grave. *s of Herbert & Agnes, Beech Hill.* MALTA MEMORIAL. [W]

**CONNOR Horace Arrol**, Sgmn. D/JX149298 R.N. H.M.S. *Bonaventure* 31 March 1941. Aged 21. The cruiser was sunk by the Italian submarine *Ambra* north of Sollum. *s of James & Ellen, Golborne.* PLYMOUTH NAVAL MEMORIAL. [G/GOC]

**CONNOR Stanley**, Pte. 14302680 2/5th Bn. Royal Leicestershire Regiment. Killed 17 October 1944 in Italy. Aged 19. ASSISI WAR CEMETERY, ITALY. [SAC/W]

**CONNORS Joseph**, Lieut. 277030 4th Regiment, Royal Horse Artillery. Killed 6 August 1944 in France. Aged 30. *s of Joseph & Elizabeth Ellen, North Ashton.* SIR CHARLES DE PERCY WAR CEMETERY, FRANCE. [X]

**COOK James Edward**, Pte. 3857566 2nd Bn. The Loyal Regiment (North Lancashire) Killed on 23 January 1942 in Singapore. Aged 20. SINGAPORE MEMORIAL. [ACC]
(This battalion suffered very heavy casualties during the defence of Singapore.)

**COOK George William**, Lieut. 224496 231 Bty., 58 Anti-Tank Regiment, Royal Artillery. Killed in the Middle East, 24 April 1943. Aged 33. *s of William & Amy, Leigh; h of Mary Ann.* MEDJEZ-EL-BAB WAR CEMETERY. [L/LGS]

**COOK Norman**, Tpr. 3531895 Royal Armoured Corps, 8th Armoured Brigade. Died of wounds in the Middle East 7 February 1943. Aged 23. *s of James & Emily; Atherton; h of Alice.* HELIOPOLIS WAR CEMETERY, EGYPT. [A/HAC]

**COOKE Thomas**, L.Cpl. 4975427 2nd Bn. The King's Own Royal Regiment (Lancaster). Died of wounds 22 November 1941. *s of Mr. R., Tyldesley.* TOBRUK WAR CEMETERY. [X]

**COOLEY Jack**, Gnr. C/1031 Royal Canadian Infantry. 10 November 1945 in Canada. Aged 31. *s of Mr. & Mrs. Robert, Atherton; h of Elizabeth, Kingston, Canada.* KINGSTON (CATARAQUI) CEMETERY, CANADA. [X]

**COOPER Robert**, Rfn. 30th Bn. King's Royal Rifle Corps. 14 September 1942. Aged 52. *s of Joseph & Elizabeth; h of Frances, Leigh.* BROOKWOOD MILITARY CEMETERY, WOKING [L]

**COPPOCK Colin Fazackerley**, Marine PLY/X100461 Royal Marines H.M.S. *Neptune.* 19 December 1941. Aged 31. While hunting an Italian convoy, the cruiser ran on to a minefield and sank with the loss of all but one of her entire crew. *s of Jack & Mary Ellen; h of Edna, Shevington.* PLYMOUTH NAVAL MEMORIAL. [S/W]

**CORCORAN John Thomas**, Fus. 3451385 2nd Bn. The Royal Fusiliers (City of London Regiment.) 30 April 1945. Aged 26. *s of Robert & Mary Jane; h of Margaret, Newtown.* VENRAY WAR CEMETERY, HOLLAND. [W]
(The Wigan memorial shows him as serving in The Lancashire Fusiliers.)

**CORCORAN John**, Spr. 3390659 22 Bomb Disposal Coy., Royal Engineers. Killed in an explosion in Essex 19 September 1944. Aged 29. TYLDESLEY CEMETERY. [T]

**CORLESS Daniel**, A.B. D/JX311882 R.N. *H.M.S. President* but lost in *m.v. Corbis*. This tanker, en route from the Persian Gulf to the U.K., was sunk east of East London, South Africa by the German U-boat *U-180* on 18 April 1943. A.B. Corless died in East London (probably in hospital) 1 May 1943. Aged 35. *s of William & Elizabeth Corless, Pemberton.* EAST LONDON (EAST BANK) CEMETERY, SOUTH AFRICA. [PC]

**CORLESS John**, Sgt. 613736 R.A.F. 103 Sqdn. 8 August 1944. Aged 24. A Lancaster I bomber returning from a raid on Fontenay was partially abandoned after an engine caught fire and it crashed near Grantham, Lincolnshire. Only Sgt Corless and the Canadian pilot died. *s of Nora; h of Ann Winifred, Pemberton.* RUNNYMEDE MEMORIAL. [X]

**CORNISH Herbert**, Sgt.(Pilot) 580050 R.A.F. 58 Sqdn. On 24 September 1940, the Whitley V bomber crashed and exploded just after taking off from Linton-on-Ouse on an operation to Berlin. STANDISH (ST WILFRED) CHURCHYARD. [SAC/STC/W]

**CORRY Elias**, L.Cpl. 14296524 1ˢᵗ Bn. Royal Northumberland Fusiliers. Killed 16 February 1945 in Holland. Aged 21. *s of Thomas & Alice, Wigan.* MILSBEEK WAR CEMETERY, HOLLAND [W]

**COTTAM Robert**, W.O.I. 1527137 Royal Artillery (Attd. Indian Army Ordnance Corps.) Drowned in India, 23 May 1943. Aged 24. *s of Thomas & Barbara, Atherton.* GAUHATI WAR CEMETERY, INDIA. [A]

**COTTON Frank**, A.B. D/JX150686 R.N. H.M.S. *Jupiter* Died 24 February 1945 whilst being held as a PoW of the Japanese. Aged 25. *s of Henry & Sarah.* AMBON WAR CEMETERY, INDONESIA. [W/WPC]

**COWBURN Leslie**, Sto. 2ⁿᵈ Class D/KX178779 R.N. H.M.S. *Gould.* 1 March 1944. Aged 19. H.M.S. *Gould* was part of a successful frigate attack on *U-358* but was sunk by the U-boat north of the Azores. *s of James Wilfred & Beatrice, Leigh.* PLYMOUTH NAVAL MEMORIAL. [L/LMC]

**COWLEY John**, Dvr. T/14419241 753 Ambulance Car Coy., Royal Army Service Corps. Killed in action in France 26 December 1944. Aged 19. *s of Sydney & Margaret, Atherton.* LONGUENESS (ST OMER) CEMETERY. [A]

**COX Sydney**, L.Cpl. 7948861 'A' Sqdn. North Irish Hussars, R.A.C. Killed 23 May 1944 in Italy. Aged 32. *s of Ernest & Annie; h of Annie.* CASSINO WAR CEMETERY. [SMC/W]

**CRAGG Harry**, Pte. 13009078 Pioneer Corps. Died 12 November 1945. HAIGH (ST DAVID) CHURCHYARD. [X]

CRAGG Vincent Arthur, Pte. 3461637 2/5<sup>th</sup> Bn.The Royal Leicestershire Regiment. Killed in action 14 September 1943 at Salerno, Italy. Aged 22. SALERNO WAR CEMETERY. [L]

CRAIG Hugh Cuthbert, Sgt. 1169555 R.A.F. (V.R.) 101 Sqdn. 9 July 1942. Aged 22. A member of the crew of a Wellington III bomber which took off from Bourn for a raid on Wilhelmshaven but was lost without trace. None of the five members of the crew has a known grave. *s of John & Catherine; h of Kathleen Daisy.* RUNNYMEDE MEMORIAL. [AIM]

CRAIG Lawrence H. Pte. 3247635 6<sup>th</sup> Bn. The Seaforth Highlanders (Ross-shire Buffs, The Duke of Albany's). Killed in Belgium during the withdrawal to Dunkirk. The actual date of his death is unknown, but it was during the period 10 to 31 May 1940. Aged 19. *He was born in Wigan, but his mother (Blanche) lived in Barnsley.* BEDFORD HOUSE CEMETERY, BELGIUM. [X]

CRITCHLEY Frank, L.Cpl. 3461638 2/5<sup>th</sup> Bn. Royal Leicestershire Regiment. Died of wounds 1 September 1944 in Italy. Aged 35. *s of John & Mary Ann , Leigh; h of Margaret.* MONTECCHIO WAR CEMETERY, ITALY. [L/LMC]

CRITCHLEY John, Gnr. 967047 54 (1/5<sup>th</sup> Bn. Durham Light Infactry) Searchlight Regiment, Royal Artillery. Died of wounds Hamburg 1 September 1945. Aged 28. *s of William & Mary; h of May.* HAMBURG WAR CEMETERY. [W]

CRITCHLEY Walter, A.C.1. 619014 R.A.F. Died as a result of an air crash in Scotland. 31 January 1940. Aged 22. *s of Harry & Jane, Leigh.* LEIGH CEMETERY. [L/LMC]

CROFT Thomas, L.A.C. 950664 R.A.F. (V.R.) Killed 12 April 1942 in South Africa. Aged 22. *s of Thomas & Annie, North Ashton.* JOHANNESBURG (WEST PARK) CEMETERY, SOUTH AFRICA. [AC/AMS/NAV]

CROFT William Alexander, Sgt. 1001839 R.A.F. (V.R.) 144 Sqdn. 24 February 1942. Aged 21. A member of the crew of a Hampden I bomber which was lost without trace. *s of John Edward & Nellie, Orrell.* RUNNYMEDE MEMORIAL. [WGS]

CROMPTON Alfred, Gnr. 1146140 61 Field Regiment, Royal Artillery. Killed in Normandy 8 August 1944. Aged 40. *h of Ethel, Blackrod.* BAYEAUX WAR CEMETERY. [BCC/BL/HDC]

CROMPTON George Arthur, Sgt. 1057218 R.A.F. (V.R.) Died 7 July 1941 following a flying accident whilst undergoing pilot training. Aged 19. *s of Peter & Ann Jane, Prescot; g of Peter, Ashton-in-Makerfield.* ASHTON-IN-MAKERFIELD (HOLY TRINITY) CHURCHYARD. [AC/NAV]

CROMPTON Joseph Henry, Pte. 3533019 1<sup>st</sup> Bn. Manchester Regiment. Died in the Far East while being held as a PoW of the Japanese, 20 October 1943. Aged 24. THANBYUZAYAT WAR CEMETERY, BURMA. [IN]

**CROMPTON William**, Pte. 13083383 Pioneer Corps. Died in Birkenhead Hospital, 25 April 1944. Aged 35. *s of William & Elizabeth*. HAIGH CEMETERY. [NSC]

**CROOK Arthur**, Fus. 3451680 1$^{st}$ Bn. The Lancashire Fusiliers. Killed in Burma 9 April 1944. Aged 25. *Foster s of George & Mary Ann Davies, Wigan*. TAUKKYAN WAR CEMETERY, BURMA. [W]

**CROOK William**, Pte. 1082727 1$^{st}$ Bn. The Cheshire Regiment. Killed in action in Germany 17 April 1945. Aged 29. *h of Annie, Pemberton*. HAMBURG WAR CEMETERY. [W]

**CROOK William**, Cpl. (W. Op.[Air] ) 532528 R.A.F. 44 Sqdn. 24 May 1940. Aged 23. His Hampden bomber was hit by flak and crashed near Aachen, Germany. *s of John Nally & Alice, Wigan*. RHEINBERG WAR CEMETERY. [W/WPC]

**CROSS Harold**, Fus. 3457905 10$^{th}$ Bn. The Lancashire Fusiliers. Killed 30 December 1942 in the Far East. Aged 28. *s of Thomas & Mary, Blackrod; h of Doris*. RANGOON MEMORIAL. [BCC/BL]

**CROSSLAND Wilfred**, A.C.2. 643734 R.A.F. 502 Sqdn. Killed in an airfield accident 18 January 1940. Aged 20. *s of Albert & Florence, Leigh*. WARRINGTON CEMETERY. [L/LAS/LPC/LTC]

**CROSTON James**, Tpr. 3865450 18$^{th}$(5$^{th}$ Bn. The Loyal Regiment [North Lancashire]) Regiment; Reconnaissance Corps. Killed sometime between 5$^{th}$ and 15$^{th}$ February 1942 during the battle for Singapore. Aged 21. *s of Samuel & Ellen, Ince*. SINGAPORE MEMORIAL [IN]

**CROSTON Thomas**, L.A.C. 530013 R.A.F. 211 Sqdn. Died while a PoW of the Japanese. 29 November 1943. Aged 27. *s of Edward Peter & Nellie*. SINGAPORE MEMORIAL. [HBC]

**CULSHAW Cecil Clarke**, Lieut. 273116 380 Bty., 116 Lt. A.A. Regiment. Royal Artillery. Killed in Normandy 18 July 1944. Aged 26. *s of Mr. & Mrs E., Tyldesley; h of Anne*. BROUAY WAR CEMETERY. [T]

**CULSHAW Gerald**, Cpl. 3531046 5$^{th}$ Bn. The Manchester Regiment. Killed during the evacuation of troops to Dunkirk. 2 June 1940. Aged 20. DUNKIRK MEMORIAL. [JC/W/WSB]

**CULSHAW Henry (Harry)**, Sjt. 3856572 1$^{st}$ Bn. The Loyal Regiment (North Lancashire). Killed 30 April 1943 in North Africa. Aged 25. *s of Henry & Mary Elizabeth, Wigan; h of Mary (Molly), Spring View, Ince*. MASSICAULT WAR CEMETERY, TUNISIA. [SGC/W]

**CULSHAW James Stephen**, L.A.C. 981942 R.A.F. (V.R.) Died in hospital 20 August 1944. Aged 23. *s of Thomas & Florence, Standish; h of Dorothy Joan*. FAREHAM (ST JOHN'S SARISBURG) CEMETERY, HAMPSHIRE. [ST/STC]

**CULSHAW Thomas**, Pte. 3653650 1st Bn. South Lancashire Regiment (The Prince of Wales's Volunteers). Taken prisoner by the Germans in France 14 June 1940 and died as a PoW 11 October 1943. Aged 27. *s of John & Annie, Pemberton.* PRAGUE WAR CEMETERY. [W]

**CUNDLIFFE William**, L. Sgt. 840798 25 Field Regiment, Royal Artillery. Killed in action at Tobruk in the Middle East, 20 June 1942. Aged 28. He has no known grave. *s of William & Helen, Leigh; h of Lily, Platt Bridge.* ALAMEIN MEMORIAL [L/LMC]

**CUNLIFFE Henry**, Fus. 3461428 2nd Bn. The Lancashire Fusiliers. Died of wounds in Palermo Hospital Italy, 26 December 1942. Aged 27. *s of John & Sarah, Ashton-in-Makerfield; h of Dorothy.* CATANIA WAR CEMETERY, ITALY. [AIM/AC/NAV]

**CUNLIFFE Herbert**, Spr. 1891840. 159 Railway Construction Coy. Royal Engineers. Lost in the sinking of s.s. *Lancastria* 17 June 1940. Aged 20. During the evacuation of troops and civilians from St. Nazaire following Dunkirk, the passenger ship was bombed and sunk with the loss of over 5000 from the 9000 on board. *s of Mr.& Mrs. J.S., Ashton-in-Makerfield.* DUNKIRK MEMORIAL. (AIM/AMS)
(Twelve other local men perished when this ship was sunk: Frederick Charles Denison; John Fairhurst; Joseph Gaskell; Charles Gibson; William S. Honderwood; William McCormick; Stephen J. Marron; Roger Morgan; Peter Thomason; Frederick Unsworth; Walter Unsworth and Henry Wilson.)

**CUNLIFFE John**, A.B. Merchant Navy. s.s.*Manchester Brigade.* 27 September 1940. Aged 23. The cargo steamer was on passage from Manchester to Montreal and was sunk by U-boat *U-137* west of Malin Head. *s of Frank Edward and Louisa, Astley.* TOWER HILL MEMORIAL. [T]

**CUNLIFFE Thomas**, Sjt. 3451906 *Mentioned in Despatches* 2/5th Bn. The Lancashire Fusiliers. Killed in action in France 29 July 1944. Aged 25. *s of John & Margaret Kate, Garswood; h of Eileen Josephine.* FONTENAY-LE-PESNEL WAR CEMETERY. [AC/AMS/NAV]

**CUNNINGHAM John**, L.Cpl. 4460381 4th Bn. The Parachute Regiment; A.A.C. Killed 12 October 1944 in Greece. Aged 27. *s of Michael & Margaret, Ashton-in-Makerfield.* PHALERON WAR CEMETERY, ATHENS. [X]

**CUNNINGHAM Sydney**, L.Cpl. T/10708685 Royal Army Service Corps & N.A.A.F.I. Died in Holland 24 May 1945. Aged 42. He had served in the First World War. *s of Noah & Margaret; h of Doris Cunningham.* TILBURG GENERAL CEMETERY. [L]

**CURLESS George** Pilot Offr. (Pilot) 177256 R.A.F. (V.R.) 625 Sqdn. 27 August 1944. Aged 21. His Lancaster I from Kelstern was lost without trace on an operation to bomb Kiel. It was lost without trace and none of the seven members of the crew has a known grave. *s of Joseph & Jane, Orrell.* RUNNYMEDE MEMORIAL. [HIY/OC/OCY/UPC/UP]

**CURLESS Joseph**, Cpl. 3780735 5th Bn. The King's Regiment (Liverpool). Died following injuries 13 July 1942. Aged 30. WIGAN CEMETERY. [JC/SCC/W]

**CUSICK Richard**, Gnr. 1830285 84 Bty., 49 Lt. A.A. Regiment, Royal Artillery. Killed 27 November 1942 in the Middle East. Aged 32. MASSICAULT WAR CEMETERY, TUNISIA. [W]

**CUTMORE Edward**, Pte. 14413974 2nd Bn. The Glasgow Highlanders, The Highland Light Infantry (City of Glasgow Regiment). Killed in action in France, 10 July 1944. Aged 20. *s of Mr. & Mrs. T., Leigh.* BAYEAUX MEMORIAL. [L/WMC]

**DALE Alfred**, Pte. T/182779 Royal Army Service Corps; Attd. 35 Lt. A.A. Regiment; Royal Artillery. Captured at Singapore in 1942 and died as a PoW of the Japanese when the ship in which he was being transported from Thailand to Japan was sunk 12 September 1944. Aged 27. *s of Thomas & Sarah, Hindley Green.* SINGAPORE MEMORIAL. [X]

**DANIELS Colin**, A.B. P/JX436463 R.N. H.M.S. *Minster.* 8 June 1944. Aged 19. This netlayer (ex Southern Railway) was sunk by a mine off the Normandy beaches. *s of William & Ada, Newtown.* PORTSMOUTH NAVAL MEMORIAL. [W]
(See also: George Barton; Frank Marsh.)

**DANIELS John**, Pte. 3446749 The Green Howards (Alexandra, Princess of Wales's Own Yorkshire Regiment.) He died in a hospital at Peona, India. 28 December 1945. Aged 33. *h of Clara Daniels, Platt Bridge.* KIRKEE WAR CEMETERY. [PBC]

**DARBYSHIRE George**, Sgt.(Pilot) 1078711 R.A.F. (V.R.) Died 1 October 1942. Aged 21. *s of A & E, Pemberton.* WIGAN CEMETERY. [NC/W]

**DARBYSHIRE Harold**, A.C.1. 1024007 R.A.F. (V.R.) Died 5 November 1941 Aged 28. *h of Gladys Mary.* WIGAN CEMETERY. [W]

**DARBYSHIRE William**, Sub Lieut. R.N.V.R. H.M.S. *Heron.* Died 19 March 1941. Aged 21 *s of Mr & Mrs Henry.* STIVICHALL (ST JAMES) CHURCHYARD, COVENTRY. [WGS]

**DARWELL Percival (Percy)** Bdr. 1024801 599 Coast Regiment, Royal Artillery. Drowned in the South of England, 17 December 1941. Aged 40. LEIGH CEMETERY. [L]

**DAVENPORT Frank**, Flt. Sgt.(Pilot) J/88086 Royal Canadian Air Force (attached to 10 Sqdn. R.A.F.) Killed 20 February 1944. Aged 21. He was the pilot of a Halifax bomber which took off from Melbourne tasked to bomb Leipzig but which was lost with six of the seven members of the crew. He has no known grave. *s of Ernest & Martha of Sovereign Road, Wigan and later Ontario, Canada. They had close connections with Ince (St Mary's) Church (on whose memorial Frank's name was to be found) but the whole family emigrated to Canada in 1926.* RUNNYMEDE MEMORIAL [ISM]

**DAVENPORT Harold,** A.C.1. 980614 R.A.F. Killed 24 February 1941. Aged 20. *s of John & Margaret, Spring View, Ince.* MAIDSTONE CEMETERY, KENT. [IN/ISM]

**DAVENPORT Harry Gordon,** S.B.A. D/MX786238 R.N. H.M.S. *Glendower.* Died 4 March 1946. Aged 18. *s of H & E, Wigan.* WIGAN CEMETERY. [X]

**DAVENPORT Richard James,** Gnr. 1719728 21 Lt. A.A. Regiment, Royal Artillery. Died 29 November 1943 as a PoW of the Japanese when the vessel in which he was being transported sank. Aged 34. SINGAPORE MEMORIAL. [GGC/NC/W]

**DAVIDSON Richard Frederick,** Pte. 2754982 2nd Bn. The Black Watch (Royal Highland Regiment) Killed 21 November 1941. Aged 27. *s of Benjamin & Sarah, Haydock.* KNIGHTSBRIDGE WAR CEMETERY, LIBYA [AIM]

**DAVIES Arthur,** Pte. 5956265 5th Bn. The Bedfordshire & Hertfordshire Regiment. Died while working on the Burma-Siam railway as a PoW of the Japanese. 10 November 1943. Aged 31. *s of Charles George & Mary Hannah, Wigan; h of Nellie.* THANBYUZAYAT WAR CEMETERY. [JC]

**DAVIES Charles,** Gdsmn. 2617718 Grenadier Guards. Died of wounds in Whichmore Hill Hospital, 3 May 1947. Aged 29. *s of William & Sarah Ann, Leigh; h of Eileen* Doris. TOTTENHAM & WOOD GREEN CEMETERY, TOTTENHAM. [L/LTC]

**DAVIES Charles Albert Calvert,** Gnr. 1618576 15 Bty., 6 H.A.A. Regiment, Royal Artillery. Captured at the fall of Singapore and died as a PoW of the Japanese. 16 June 1945. Aged 35. *h of P, Beech Hill, Wigan.* SINGAPORE MEMORIAL. [W]

**DAVIES Gerald,** L.Bdr. 1062660 190 Bty., 10 (6th Bn. Royal Warwickshire Regiment) H.A.A. Regiment, Royal Artillery. Died in Imtarfa General Hospital, Malta. 6 April 1941. Aged 34. IMTARFA CEMETERY, MALTA. [W]

**DAVIES James,** Gnr. 3779002 83 Field Regiment, Royal Artillery. Killed 8 February 1945. Aged 29. *s of Albert & Catherine; h of Elsie, Ince.* JONKERBOS WAR CEMETERY, HOLLAND. [IN]

**DAVIES James Owen,** Sgt.(W.Op./Air Gnr.) 998630 R.A.F. (V.R.) 6 September 1943. Aged 22. A Lancaster III bomber on a raid on Mannheim was hit by a night fighter over the target area. Two members of the crew were captured; the other five were killed. *s of George & Esther Alice, Standish; h of Vera.* DURNBACH WAR CEMETERY. [W/ST/STC]

**DAVIES John Henry,** Volunteer 76th County of Lancaster (Golborne) Bn. Home Guard. While on guard duty, he and a colleague were killed by the explosion of a bomb. 13 September 1940. Aged 33. *s of John & Mary Ann, Ashton-in-Makerfield; h of Anne, Garswood.* ASHTON-IN-MAKERFIELD (HOLY TRINITY) CHURCHYARD. [AC/NAV]     (See also Jack Adamson.)

**DAVIES John Thomas**, Dvr. T/190063 Royal Army Service Corps Died from illness 20 April 1944 while returning from Italy. Buried at sea. Aged 27. BROOKWOOD MEMORIAL. [HIC]

**DAVIES Roy Ellis**, Sgt. (Air Gnr.) 2205997 R.A.F. (V.R.) 17 April 1945. Aged 21. While a Lancaster III was being prepared for operations, a fire broke out and a series of explosions killed four airmen (including Sgt. Davies), wrecked a total of five Lancasters and damaged fourteen other bombers. LEIGH CEMETERY. [T]

**DAVIES Thomas Stanley**, Sgt. 1232668 R.A.F. (V.R.) 10 Sqdn. 7 September 1943. Aged 21. The Halifax II bomber was lost without trace on a raid on Munich. *s of Thomas & Emily, Atherton.* RUNNYMEDE MEMORIAL. [A]

**DAVIES William**, Sick Berth P.O. D/SBR/X6293 R.N. Auxiliary Sick Berth Reserve. H.M.S. *Lanka.* Died of enteric fever while returning from Ceylon 17 May 1945. Aged 44. *s of William & Ellen; h of Mary Elizabeth.* PLYMOUTH NAVAL MEMORIAL. [HBC]

**DAVIES William George**, Fus. 14409772 6th. Bn. Royal Scots Fusiliers. Killed in Normandy 29 June 1944. Aged 19. *s of William & Ellen, London; lived with his grandmother in Leigh.* ST MANVIEU WAR CEMETERY. [L/LPC]

**DAVIS Charles Victor**, Sto. P.O. P/KX88300 R.N. H.M. Submarine *Traveller.* 12 December 1942. Aged 29. Lost with all hands in the Gulf of Taranto. *s of Mr. & Mrs. Albert; h of Lily, Atherton.* PORTSMOUTH NAVAL MEMORIAL. [A/HBC]

**DAVIS Frederick Albert**, L.A.C. 1254025 R.A.F. (V.R.) Died 20 June 1945 in Holland. Aged 26. *s of Frederick & Beatrice, Wigan.* TILBURG GENERAL CEMETERY, HOLLAND. [X]

**DAWBER Edward**, Pte. 3776399 2nd Bn. The Royal Lincolnshire Regiment. Died of wounds in France 20 April 1944. Aged 24. *s of Edward & Mary, Beech Hill, Wigan.* HERMANVILLE WAR CEMETERY. [W]

**DAWSON Sydney**, Gdsmn. 2724353 3rd Bn. Irish Guards. Killed 21 April 1945 in Germany. Aged 21. *s of Samuel & Margaret, Wigan.* BECKLINGEN WAR CEMETERY, GERMANY. [SMC/W]

**DEAKIN Samuel**, Sto. P.O. C/K65208 R.N. H.M.S. *Seamew.* Died 27 April 1942. Aged 37. *h of Fanny, Lower Ince.* INCE-IN-MAKERFIELD CEMETERY. [X]

**DEAN Eric Harold**, Pte. 3855252 Royal Army Ordnance Corps. Died 8 May 1945. Aged 33. *s of John & Mary, Wigan.* OXFORD (BOTLEY) CEMETERY. [X]

**DEAN Frederick**, Tpr. 3964311 Royal Armoured Corps and No. 6 Commando. Killed in Normandy on D-Day, 6 June 1944. Aged 25. *s of John & Annie, Wigan.* HERMANVILLE WAR CEMETERY, FRANCE. [W]
(According to CWGC records, this soldier is incorrectly shown on the Wigan memorial as serving in the Reconnaissance Corps at the time of his death.)

**DEAN George,** Pte. 3864922 18th (5th Bn. The Loyal Regiment [North Lancashire] ) Reconnaissance Corps, R.A.C. Captured at the fall of Singapore and died 14 May 1945 as a PoW of the Japanese. Aged 38. DJAKARTA WAR CEMETERY, INDONESIA. [HIC/W]

**DEAN Herbert,** Dvr. T/182884 Royal Army Service Corps Killed 22 February 1943 in North Africa. Aged 26. ENFIDAVILLE WAR CEMETERY. [SCC/W/WSB]

**DEMPSEY John,** Gnr. 3531896 182 Bty., 65 H.A.A. Regiment, Royal Artillery. Killed 16 May 1941. Aged 23. TYLDESLEY CEMETERY. [LTA]

**DENISON Frederick Charles,** Pte. T/158277 Royal Army Service Corps. Lost in s.s.*Lancastria* 17 June 1940. Aged 31. His body was washed up on a beach near St. Nazaire. PREFAILLES CEMETERY, FRANCE. [L/LMC]
(Twelve other local men perished when this ship was sunk. See the **Herbert Cunliffe** entry for names and details.)

**DENNETT Harold,** Pte. 3195298 6th Bn. The Royal Lincolnshire Regiment. Killed in action in North Africa 22 April 1943. Aged 27. *s of Jesse Herbert & Jane, Billinge.* MASSICAULT WAR CEMETERY, TUNISIA. [BC]

**DENTITH Jack,** Cpl. 14397275 8th Bn. The Royal Scots (The Royal Regiment) Killed in action, 14 September 1944 in Belgium. *h of Alice, Leigh.* KASTERLEE WAR CEMETERY, BELGIUM. [X]

**DENTON Albert,** Rfmn. 3859514 2nd Bn. King's Royal Rifle Corps. Died of wounds in Tunisia, 28 March 1943. Aged 26. *s of John & Jane Ann.* SFAX WAR CEMETERY, TUNISIA. [A]

**DERBYSHIRE Harold,** Sgt. 1451160 R.A.F. (V.R.) Died 17 April 1943. Aged 21. *s of John & Emily, Lowton.* LOWTON ST MARY'S (ST MARY'S) CHURCHYARD. [X]

**DERBYSHIRE Peter,** Asst. Steward. Merchant Navy s.s. *Ceramic* 7 December 1942. Aged 27. This passenger cargo liner en route Liverpool to Australia was sunk by the German U-boat *U-515* west of the Azores. Of the 656 passengers and crew there was only one survivor.. *h of Helen, Wigan.* TOWER HILL MEMORIAL. [WPC]

(The following two entries concern two soldiers named **William Derbyshire** who both had clear connections with Golborne, but only one such name appears on each of the two Golborne memorials. It has not been possible to determine which serviceman is commemorated - or whether the names refer to both men.)

**DERBYSHIRE William,** L.Cpl. 13068476 Pioneer Corps. Killed in Belgium 12 February 1945. Aged 32. *h of Elizabeth, Golborne. Family connections also in Wigan.* SCHOONSELHOF CEMETERY, ANTWERP. [SCC] (See Gnr. Willam Derbyshire, Royal Artillery.)

**DERBYSHIRE William**, Gnr. 1774186 166 Bty., 56 Lt. A.A. Regiment. Royal Artillery. Killed 25 October 1942 in the Middle East. Aged 22. *s of Peter & Hannah, Golborne*. EL ALAMEIN WAR CEMETERY. [G/GOC] (See also L.Cpl. William Derbyshire, Pioneer Corps.)

**DERMOTT Cyril**, Cpl. 3528806 1st Bn. The Manchester Regiment. Killed 21 September 1944 in the Far East. Aged 28. He has no known grave. SINGAPORE MEMORIAL. [SGC/W]

**DEWHURST John**, Pte. 7629866 Royal Army Ordnance Corps Died 1 August 1943. Aged 32. *h of Mary Dewhurst.* WRIGHTINGTON (ST JAMES) CHURCHYARD. [X]

**DEWHURST Thomas**, L.Cpl. 3451908 2nd Bn. The Gordon Highlanders. Killed in Germany 21 February 1945. Aged 26. RHEINBERG WAR CEMETERY, GERMANY. [SCC/W]

**DICKINSON Clifford**, Sgt. 1511926 R.A.F. (V.R.) 44 Sqdn. 28 June 1944. Aged 21. The Lancaster I bomber from Dunholme Lodge crashed into the sea while on an attack on a flying-bomb site at Marqise. Sgt. Dickinson, along with five of his six colleagues, has no known grave. *h of Doris*. RUNNYMEDE MEMORIAL [W/NSC]

**DICKINSON Frederick**, A.B. C/SSX33903 R.N. H.M.S. *Isis*. 20 July 1944 Aged 23. The destroyer was sunk by a mine off Normandy. *s of Thomas & Mary, Bickershaw*. CHATHAM NAVAL MEMORIAL [B]

**DICKINSON Thomas**, Tpr. 3528732 The Nottinghamshire Yeomanry, R.A.C. 26 March 1943 in the Middle East. Aged 26. He has no known grave. *s of Thomas & Ethel, Astley*. MEDJEZ-EL-BAB MEMORIAL, TUNISIA. [T]

**DICKINSON Thomas**, A.C.1. 1105162 R.A.F. (V.R.) 113 Sqdn. Died in a military hospital, India 5 November 1942. Aged 22. *s of James & Ellen, Leigh*. DELHI WAR CEMETERY. [L/LGS/LPC/LTC]

**DISLEY Francis William**, Pte. 14657825 1st Bn. Argyll & Sutherland Highlanders. Killed 12 May 1944 in Italy. Aged 36. *s of William & Catherine; h of Mary, Lower Ince*. CASSINO WAR CEMETERY. [W]

**DIXON Richard John**, Spr. 2141628 220 Field Coy. Royal Engineers. Died of wounds in North Africa 5 May 1943. Aged 37. *h of Elizabeth, Leigh*. ENFIDAVILLE WAR CEMETERY, TUNISIA. [L]

**DOHERTY Frank**, Cpl. 3858759 1st Bn The Manchester Regiment. Died of wounds in France 17 July 1944. RYES WAR CEMETERY, FRANCE. [W]

**DOOLEY John**, Pte. 3964338 2nd Bn. The Devonshire Regiment. Killed 20 April 1945 in Germany. Aged 26. *s of Thomas & May, Higher Ince*. BECKLINGEN WAR CEMETERY. [IN/SCC]

**DOONEY Martin,** Pte. 2819450 1st Bn.The Seaforth Highlanders (Ross-shire Buffs, The Duke of Albany's) Died 8 June 1942 in India. Aged 28. *s of Thomas & Elizabeth, Ashton-in-Makerfield.* MAYNAMATI CEMETERY, PAKISTAN. [X]

**DOOTSON Frederick,** L.A.C. 1032921 R.A.F. (V.R.) Died 7 September 1942. Aged 20. *s of Thomas & Hannah, Ince.* INCE-IN-MAKERFIELD CEMETERY. [X]

**DOOTSON Harry,** Pte. 4038893 7th Bn. King's Shropshire Light Infantry. Died 27 June 1942. Aged 22. *s of Richard & Isobel; h of Elizabeth, Golborne.* GOLBORNE (ST THOMAS) CHURCHYARD. [G/GOC]

**DOOTSON John,** Sjt. 3857390 18th (5th Bn. The Loyal Regiment [North Lancashire]) Regiment, Reconnaissance Corps. Died as a PoW of the Japanese while working on the Burma-Siam railway. 24 June 1945. Aged 25. *s of Joseph & Ellen, Hindley.* KANCHANABURI WAR CEMETERY, THAILAND. [HC]

**DOOTSON Owen,** A.B. D/JX250156 R.N. H.M.S. *Mahratta* 25 February 1944. Aged 20. The destroyer on convoy escort duty was sunk by U-boat *U-956* in the Barentz Sea. *s of Jonah & Margaret, Astley.* PLYMOUTH NAVAL MEMORIAL. [LGS] (See : William Barnes; James Clare; James R. Speakman; Alfred H. Urmston.)

**DOUGLAS Victor,** Gnr. 11417165 *M.M.* 17 Field Regiment, Royal Artillery. Killed in Italy 21 April 1945. Aged 22. *s of Elizabeth (Mrs Holloway) Leigh.* ARGENTA GAP WAR CEMETERY. [L/LMC]
(Some sources give his name as *Victor Douglas Holloway*)

**DOVEY John,** Pte. 3780211 2/7th Bn. The Queen's Royal Regiment (West Surrey). Died of wounds, 14 September 1944 in Italy. Aged 24. *s of Thomas & Mary Ellen, Astley.* MONTECCHIO WAR CEMETERY. [T]

**DRAKE Albert,** Sgt.(W.Op./Air Gnr.) 1049379 R.A.F. (V.R.) 76 Sqdn. Killed 2 March 1944. Aged 21. A Halifax III bomber from Holme-on-Spalding Moor on a raid on Stuttgart crashed near St Die, France. *s of Levy & Sarah Helen, h of Annie, Lowton St Marys.* CHOLOY WAR CEMETERY, FRANCE. [X]

**DRAKE Felix Arthur,** L.A.C. 984612 R.A.F. (V.R.) 217 Sqdn. Died 28 March 1943. Aged 23. *s of Felix & Isabella, Wigan.* KANDY WAR CEMETERY, CEYLON. [AP/APC]

**DRAYCOTT Sydney,** Flt. Sgt. 1094824 R.A.F. (V.R.) Died 11 January 1944. Aged 21. *He had family connections in Astley.* TYLDESLEY CEMETERY. [X]

**DUCKWORTH Walter Leslie,** Air Mech. FAA/FX75993 R.N. H.M.S. *Glorious.* 9 June 1940. Aged 21. The aircraft carrier was sunk by the German battlecruisers *Gneisenau* and *Scharnhorst* 300 miles west of Narvik. Only 43 of the crew survived. *s of Walter, Wigan.* FLEET AIR ARM MEMORIAL, LEE-ON-SOLENT. [JC/SAC/W/WGS]
(See also: Samuel Alker; J.F. Gorton; John Jameson; Edward Knight; Peter McNicholas; B.T. Starkie; F. Swan.)

**DUNCAN Joseph Worthington,** L.Cpl. 14206687 4th Bn. Somerset Light Infantry. Killed 10 July 1944. Aged 21. *s of Harry Don & Margaret, Orrell.* BANNEVILLE-LA-CAMPAGNE WAR CEMETERY, FRANCE. [HIC]

**DUNLOP Benjamin,** Pte. 3859515 2nd Bn. The Essex Regiment. Killed 27 August 1944 in France. Aged 27. *s of William & Mary Alice; h of Hilda, Spring View, Ince.* ST DESIR WAR CEMETERY [IN/ISM]

**DUNN Albert,** A.B. D/JX213672 R.N. H.M.S. *Galatea.* but lost in H.M.S. *Palomares* 9 November 1942. Aged 21. PLYMOUTH NAVAL MEMORIAL. [L/LGS/LTC]

**DUNN Dennis,** L.Cpl. 3461639 2nd Bn. The Lancashire Fusiliers. Killed 23 October 1944 in Italy. Aged 29. *s of Thomas & Mary, Wigan.* FAENZA WAR CEMETERY. [W]

**DUNN William Joseph,** Sgt. 1520456 R.A.F.(V.R.) 75 (R.N.Z.A.F.) Sqdn. 21 July 1944. Aged 23. A Lancaster III bomber from Mepal was lost without trace on an operation over Hamburg. *s of Lawrence & Hilda, Golborne.* RUNNYMEDE MEMORIAL. [G/GOC]

**DUNSTAN Leslie Sneyd,** Third Radio Officer. Merchant Navy, s.s. *Designer.* 9 July 1941. Aged 16. The cargo liner en route to South Africa was sunk by the German U-boat *U-98* with the loss of 68 lives. *s of Bernard & Nellie, Lowton.* TOWER HILL MEMORIAL. [L/LMC]

**DUNSTER Thomas,** Pte. 14234518 Royal Army Ordnance Corps. Killed in Germany while clearing minefields and ammunition dumps. 11 May 1945. Aged 33. *s of Harry & Ann; h of Lottie, Tyldesley. His father was killed in World War I.* REICHSWALD FOREST WAR CEMETERY. [LGS/T/TMC]

**DURKIN Thomas,** Dvr. T/192220 Royal Army Service Corps. Killed in Italy 21 June 1944. Aged 28. *s of Laurence & Winifred; h of Alice.* ASSISI WAR CEMETERY. [L]

**DURKIN Walter,** Pte. 3964336 2nd Bn. The Wiltshire Regiment (Duke of Edinburgh's). Died of wounds in Italy 31 May 1944. Aged 25. *s of Thomas & Mary Ann, Abram.* BEACH HEAD WAR CEMETERY, ANZIO. [ABC]

**DUXBURY Norman Thomas,** Pilot Offr. 157252 R.A.F. (V.R.) Died 5 September 1943. Aged 22. *s of Thomas & B.A.* STANDISH (ST WILFRED) CHURCHYARD. [STC/W/WGS/WPC]

**DWYER William,** Tpr. 14290174 40th (7th Bn. The King's Regiment [Liverpool] ) Royal Tank Regiment, R.A.C. Killed 1 December 1943 in Italy. Aged 21. *s of Edward & Margaret, Bryn.* MINTURNO WAR CEMETERY. [X]

**EAGER J.T.** Cpl. 13116087 R.A.C. Died 13 May 1946. Aged 24. *s of Berthold & Betti Erlich, Wigan.* HAMBURG WAR CEMETERY, GERMANY. [X]

**EASTHAM Samuel,** A.B. C/JX255253 R.N. *H.M.L.S.T.(c) 19.* Died in hospital in Tunis 23 December 1943. Aged 28. *s of Richard Henry & Ellen, Spring View, Ince.* MASSICAULT WAR CEMETERY, TUNISIA. [IN]

**EATOCK Alfred,** Tpr. 3456702 3rd Royal Tank Regiment, R.A.C. Died in a U.K. hospital of burns received during the invasion of France. 23 July 1944. Aged 30. LEIGH CEMETERY. [L/LPC]

**EATON Percy Kenneth,** Pte. 7652976 Royal Army Ordnance Corps. Died 6 February 1946. Aged 28. *h of Alice.* BLACKROD CEMETERY. [X]

**EAVES John Robert,** Fus. 14228748 2nd Bn. The Lancashire Fusiliers. Killed 23 November 1943 in Italy. Aged 34. *s of John & Margaret; h of Edith Ellen.* CASSINO MEMORIAL. [X]

**ECCLES Lucien A.W.J.** W.O. (Pilot) 1931095 R.A.F. (V.R.) 290 Sqdn. Killed in a flying accident in Northern Ireland 15 July 1944. Aged 21. *h of Nellie, Hindley Green.* LEIGH CEMETERY. [X]

**ECCLESTON Harry,** L.Cpl. 3451386 2nd Bn. The Lancashire Fusiliers. Killed in Italy 28 June 1944. Aged 25. *s of James & Margaret, Leigh.* ASSISI WAR CEMETERY. [L]

**ECCLESTON John Henry,** Ldg. Seaman D/SSX25335 R.N. H.M.S. *Gloucester* 22 May 1941. Aged 21. The destroyer was sunk by enemy aircraft off Crete while attempting to pick-up survivors from other ships. *s of Thomas James & Jane, Leigh.* PLYMOUTH NAVAL MEMORIAL. [L]

**ECKERSLEY Harry,** Pte. 3858514 2nd Bn. The Loyal Regiment (North Lancashire). Killed in action in Singapore 23 January 1942, where his battalion suffered very heavy casualties in the vain attempt to defend the colony. Aged 23. He has no known grave. SINGAPORE MEMORIAL. [LGS/T/TC]

**ECKERSLEY Joseph Alban,** Sgt.(Obs.) 998677 R.A.F. (V.R.) 82 Sqdn. 26 January 1942. Aged 21. A Blenheim training flight from Bodney ended when the aircraft crashed into trees bordering the airfield. Two of the crew of three died. *s of James & Maria, Orrell Post.* WATTON (ST MARY) CHURCHYARD, NORFOLK. [OC]

**ECKERSLEY Peter Thorpe,** Lieut. R.N.V.R. H.M.S. *Raven.* 13 August 1940. Aged 36. *s of William & Eva Mary, Tyldesley; h of Audrey. Lieut. Eckersley was Member of Parliament for the Exchange Division of Manchester, 1935-40. He was captain of Lancashire C.C.C. 1929-35.* TYLDESLEY CEMETERY [CUC] (The church also has a memorial window dedicated to him)

**EDGE William Parker,** Sgt. 552818 9th (The Queen's Own Yorkshire Dragoons) Bn., King's Own Yorkshire Light Infantry. Died after an accident in North Africa 4 January 1944. Aged 33. *s of David & Sarah, Atherton.* EL ALIA CEMETERY, ALGERIA. [A]

**EDWARD William Alexander,** Capt. 113752 2$^{nd}$ Bn. Royal Fusiliers (City of London Regiment) Killed 2 August 1944 in Italy. Aged 29. *s of Henry Alex & Hilda Sarah. He was Assistant Registrar at Wigan Technical College.* FLORENCE WAR CEMETERY. [X]

**EDWARDS David John,** Pte. 3527426 2$^{nd}$ Bn The East Lancashire Regiment. Drowned in India 6 October 1943. Aged 28. *s of William John & Florence Louise.; h of Kathleen Minnie, Spring View, Ince.* KIRKEE WAR CEMETERY, INDIA. [IN]

**EDWARDS Eli,** Pte. 3858515 2$^{nd}$ Bn. The Loyal Regiment (North Lancashire). He died as a PoW of the Japanese while working on the Burma-Siam railway, 13 November 1943. Aged 24. THANBYUZAYAT WAR CEMETERY. [IN/ISM]

**EDWARDS Ernest,** Pte. 3530512 2$^{nd}$ Bn. The Border Regiment. Died in India 30 December 1943. Aged 27. *s of William & Mary Ann, Atherton; h of Mary, Tyldesley.* IMPHAL WAR CEMETERY. [A]
(Pte. Edwards is listed on the Atherton memorial as serving in The King's Regiment at the time of his death. CWGC records show the Border Regiment.)

**EDWARDS George Eric,** Spr. 1952944 204 Field Coy., Royal Engineers. Killed at Arnhem 24 September 1944. *s of George & Ethel, Leigh; h of Joyce.* JONKERBOS WAR CEMETERY, HOLLAND. [L/LGS/LMC]

**EDWARDS Thomas,** L.Cpl. 3857037 Corps of Military Police Died 5 November 1944 in India. Aged 33. *s of Mr. & Mrs. T., Platt Bridge; h of J. M.* MADRAS WAR CEMETERY, INDIA.[PBC]

**EDWARDS William,** Tpr. 3528630 18$^{th}$(5$^{th}$ Bn. The Loyal Regiment [North Lancashire]) Regiment., Reconnaissance Corps. Captured at the fall of Singapore and died as a PoW of the Japanese in Palembang Camp 28 June 1945. Aged 33. *s of William & Mary Anne; h of Agnes, Tyldesley.* DJAKARTA WAR CEMETERY, INDONESIA. [X]

**EGAN William Andrew Carneavon,** Tpr. 2992758 The Lovat Scouts. Killed 14 September 1945 in Greece. Aged 22. *s of William & Barbara; h of Marion, Hindley.* PHALERON WAR CEMETERY, ATHENS. [X]

**ELLISON James,** Gdsmn. 2619656 6$^{th}$ Bn. Grenadier Guards Died of wounds 18 March 1943 in North Africa. Aged 30. *s of John & Margaret; h of Patricia.* SFAX WAR CEMETERY, TUNISIA. [A]

**EVANS Aubrey,** Gdsmn. 2737985 1$^{st}$ Bn. Welsh Guards. Died of wounds in Normandy 11 August 1944. Aged 27. *s of Ellis & Annie, Atherton.* SIR CHARLES DE PERCY WAR CEMETERY. [X]

**EVANS Charles Eric,** A.B. P/JX297088 R.N. H.M.S. *Limbourne.* 23 October 1943. Aged 33. This destroyer was damaged so badly by German torpedo boats off Northern France that it had to be sunk. *s of Charles & Mary; h of Annie.* PORTSMOUTH NAVAL MEMORIAL. [W]

**EVANS Clifford**, Sjt. 4616999 7th Bn. The Duke of Wellington's Regiment (West Riding) Killed 24 September 1944. Aged 26. *s of Enoch & Florence. h of Iris.* LEOPOLDSBURG WAR CEMETERY, BELGIUM [T]

**EVANS Gwilym Ivor**, Ord. Seaman D/JX347384 R.N. H.M.S. *Itchen.* 23 September 1943. Aged 20. South-east of Cape Farewell this frigate was sunk by the German U-boat *U-260. s of Thomas & Margaret Elizabeth, Astley.* PLYMOUTH NAVAL MEMORIAL. [T]
(See also: Albert Fairhurst; Ralph Pickering.)

**EVANS Harry**, Sigmn. 2332792 Royal Corps of Signals, Eigth Army Troops Coy. Killed 8 September 1943 in Italy. Aged 25. *s of Thomas & Esther, Atherton.* SALERNO WAR CEMETERY, ITALY. [A]

**EVANS John Mather**, Sgt.(Air Bomber) 535854 R.A.F. 178 Sqdn. 22 August 1944. Aged 27. *s of Cadwallader & Elsie, Lower Ince.* BELGRADE WAR CEMETERY, YUGOSLAVIA. [IN/ISM]

**EVANS Kenneth**, Pte. 7365905 8 Field Ambulance, Royal Army Medical Corps. Killed in action 11 June 1944. Aged 24. He is buried in Hermanville War Cemetery along with 1004 other men – most of whom lost their lives in the first few days after the D-Day invasion of France on 6 June 1944. HERMANVILLE WAR CEMETERY, FRANCE. [L]

**EVERIN Edgar**, Pte. 3860146 7/10th Bn. Argyll & Sutherland Highlanders. Killed 6 April 1943 in Tunisia. Aged 28. *s of Frederick & Emily Gertrude; h of Gladys.* SFAX WAR CEMETERY, TUNISIA. [BCC/BL]

**FAIRCLOUGH Harry**, Gnr. 3441910 3 Bty., 1 Searchlight Regiment, Royal Artillery. Died of wounds in Flanders 8 June 1940 after the Dunkirk Evacuation. Aged 33. *s of Harry & Rachel, Up Holland; h of Ellen.* DUNKIRK TOWN CEMETERY. [UPH/UPC]

**FAIRCLOUGH Henry**, Gdsmn. 2621664 6th Bn. Grenadier Guards. Died 17 March 1943 in North Africa. Aged 23. *s of Henry & Sabina; h of Ann, Platt Bridge.* SFAX WAR CEMETERY, TUNISIA. [PBC]

**FAIRCLOUGH James Henry**, Sub. Lieut.(A) R.N.V.R. H.M.S. *Wagtail* Died 26 October 1944. Aged 31. *s of James & Ada, Leigh; h of Lilian.* RINGLEY (ST SAVIOUR) CHURCHYARD, KEARSLEY, BOLTON. [L/LTC]

**FAIRCLOUGH Norman Douglas**, Flt. Sgt. (Obs.) 997991 R.A.F. (V.R.) 162 Sqdn. Killed in the Middle East 13 August 1942. Aged 25. *s of Herbert & Margaret Alice, Leigh.* HABBANIYA WAR CEMETERY, IRAQ. [L/LGS]

**FAIRHURST Albert**, Ord. Teleg. D/JX401148 R.N. H.M.S. *Itchen.* 23 September 1943. Aged 20. South-East of Cape Farewell this frigate was sunk by U-boat *U-260. s of Henry & Louise, Wigan.* [IN]
(See also: Gwilym Ivor Evans; Ralph Pickering.)

**FAIRHURST Alfred Houghton**, E.R.A. P/MX88713 R.N. H.M.S. *Bentinck.* Died 31 December 1943. *s of Lucy.* WIGAN CEMETERY. [W]

**FAIRHURST Francis Cyril**, Pte. 3523186 1st Bn. King's Regiment (Liverpool). Died 19 May 1943 as a PoW of the Japanese. RANGOON MEMORIAL. [W]

**FAIRHURST Harry**, Dvr. T/10662485 203 Field Ambulance, Royal Army Service Corps. Killed in action in Normandy 8 August 1944. Aged 22. *s of Peter & Martha, Leigh.* BAYEUX WAR CEMETERY. [L/WMC]

**FAIRHURST Henry**, A.C.2. 1047602 R.A.F.(V.R.) Died 13 September 1941. STANDISH (OUR LADY) R.C. CHURCHYARD. [SSM/ST]

**FAIRHURST John**, L.Cpl. 3602334 9th Bn. The Border Regiment. Killed 14 May 1944 in Burma. Aged 26. *s of John & Edith Annie.* IMPHAL WAR CEMETERY. [JC/WGS]

**FAIRHURST John**, Pte. 13002427 50 Coy. Auxiliary Military Pioneer Corps. Lost in the sinking of s.s. *Lancastria* 17 June 1940. Aged 39. DUNKIRK MEMORIAL [HC]
(Twelve other local men perished when this ship was sunk. See the **Herbert Cunliffe** entry for names and details of the loss.)

**FAIRHURST John Ball**, Capt. 85397 The Warwickshire Yeomanry, R.A.C. Killed El Alamein, 2 November 1942. Aged 26. *s of Peter & Minnie. He had family connections with Wigan.* EL ALAMEIN WAR CEMETERY. [WGS]

**FAIRHURST Sydney**, Pte. 3858894 1st Bn. The Loyal Regiment (North Lancashire) Killed in action 21 April 1943 in North Africa. Aged 25. *s of John & Ellen, Worthington.* MEDJEZ-EL-BAB WAR CEMETERY, TUNISIA. [AS/HDC]

**FAIRHURST Thomas**, Tpr. 7899400 2nd Royal Tank Regiment, R.A.C. Killed 5 November 1942 in India. Aged 24. *s of George & Annie, Whelley, Wigan.* BAGHDAD (NORTH GATE) WAR CEMETERY. [SCC/W/WSB]

**FAIRHURST William**, Fus. 3456947 1/8th Bn. The Lancashire Fusiliers. Killed on 9 June 1942 in Bombay, India. Aged 28. KIRKEE WAR CEMETERY, INDIA. [W/PC]

**FARRALL Arthur**, Spr. 1892800 Royal Engineers. Killed by dive bombers during the retreat to Dunkirk 22 May 1940. Aged 20. *s of William & Hannah, Platt Bridge.* DUNKIRK TOWN CEMETERY. [IN]
(Some local sources give the spelling as *Farrell)*

**FARRIMOND Clifford Alexander**, Sgt. 917131 R.A.F. (V.R.) 97 Sqdn. 18 December 1942. Aged 33. His Lancaster I bomber took-off from Woodhall Spa for a raid on Neustadt. It was lost without trace and consequently all seven members of the crew are commemorated on the Runnymede Memorial. *s of James & Amelia.* RUNNYMEDE MEMORIAL. [STC]

**FARRIMOND Eric**, Pte. 14376143 5th Bn. East Lancashire Regiment. Killed in France 8 July 1944. Aged 19. *s of Robert & Ethel, Blackrod.* LA DELIVERANDE WAR CEMETERY. [BCC/BL/STC]
(This soldier's first name is shown on the Blackrod memorial as *Eris.* CWGC records give it as *Eric.*)

**FARRIMOND Ernest**, Cpl. 14206688 Royal Corps of Signals. 24 November 1943. Aged 20. *s of J. & E., Newtown.* WIGAN CEMETERY. [X]

**FARRIMOND John**, Flt. Sgt (W.Op./Air Gnr.) 1114842 R.A.F. (V.R.) 218 Sqdn. 21 August 1942. Aged 21. His Stirling I bomber left Downham Market on a minelaying operation in the Fehmarn Channel in the Baltic but crashed near Schleswig, Germany where the crew were first laid to rest. Since 1945 they have been reburied in Keil War Cemetery *s of John H. & Annie, Lamberhead Green.* KIEL WAR CEMETERY. [X]

**FARRINGTON John**, Tpr. 14353729 The Staffordshire Yeomanry, R.A.C. Died of wounds, Normandy 6 July 1944. Aged 32. LA DELIVERANDE WAR CEMETERY. [L/LAS/LTC]

**FARRINGTON Joseph William**, L.A.C. 1305966 R.A.F.(V.R.) Killed in Italy 3 April 1945. Aged 25. NAPLES WAR CEMETERY. [L]

**FAWCETT John (Jacky)**, Gnr. 1559901 222 Bty., 10 H.A.A. Regiment, Royal Artillery. Killed 19 April 1942. Aged 22. *s of John & Ellen, Newtown.* PIETA MILITARY CEMETERY, MALTA. [W]

**FAZACKERLEY Edward**, Greaser. Merchant Navy s.s.*Ocean Courage.* 15 January 1943. Aged 28. South of the Cape Verde Islands, this cargo ship en route to the U.K. was sunk by German U-boat *U-182.* *s of H. & Rachel.* TOWER HILL MEMORIAL. [L/LMC]
(See also: Joseph Tickle.)

**FAZACKERLEY Harry**, Pte. 14657836 2nd Bn. Queen's Own Cameron Highlanders. Killed in Italy 15 March 1944. Aged 20. *s of Thomas & Bessie, Leigh.* CASSINO WAR CEMETERY. [L/LMC]

**FEARNLEY Roy**, L.Bdr. 3655037 6 Maritime Regiment, Royal Artillery. Accidently drowned in the River Medway at Rochester. 24 December 1944. Aged 22. *s of James & Agnes, Golborne.* FORT PITT MILITARY CEMETERY, KENT. [G/GOC]

**FEARNLEY Stanley**, A.B. D/SSX28545 R.N. H.M.S. *Hermes* 9 April 1942. Aged 21. H.M.S. *Hermes* was sunk by Japanese carrier-based aircraft south of Ceylon. PLYMOUTH NAVAL MEMORIAL. [L/WMC]

**FENTON Herbert**, Pte. 14611262 1st Bn. The King's Shropshire Light Infantry. Killed in Italy 8 February 1944. Aged 35. *His family connections were with Hindley.* CASSINO MEMORIAL. [X]

**FENTON John Richard,** Sailor. Merchant Navy s.s. *Gazcon.* 2 September 1942. Aged 20. In the Gulf of Aden, this cargo ship en route from U.S.A. to the Middle East, was sunk by Japanese submarine *I-29. s of Nancy.* TOWER HILL MEMORIAL. [W/WPC]

**FERGUSON Robert Alfred,** Gnr. 1623465 240 Bty., 77 H.A.A. Regiment, Royal Artillery. Killed 29 November 1943. Aged 33. *s of Robert Thomas & Elizabeth; h of Elizabeth, Appley Bridge.* SINGAPORE MEMORIAL. [AP/APC]

**FERGUSON William Jeffrey,** Sjt. 7399426 Royal Army Medical Corps. Lost while serving as a member of a ship's staff, 12 September 1942. Aged 25. *s of James & Annie, Wigan.* BROOKWOOD MEMORIAL. [WGS]

**FERRY Thomas,** A.B. D/JX175245 R.N. H.M.S. *Erne.* 28 December 1942. Aged 23. *s of Lawrence & Annie; h of Florence Ruby, Wigan.* PLYMOUTH NAVAL MEMORIAL. [X]

**FIELDHOUSE Leonard Anthony,** A.C.2. 1137454 R.A.F.(V.R.) Died 23 September 1943. Aged 33. *h of Agnes, Orrell.* ORRELL (ST JAMES) R.C.CHURCHYARD. [X]

**FILLINGHAM William Vernon,** Sgt. 977754 R.A.F. (V.R.) 21 Sqdn. 15 May 1941 Aged 21. His Blenheim IV bomber from Watton was engaged on anti-shipping operations but was shot down into the sea off Heligoland. All three members of the crew were lost without trace. *s of William & Florence, Wigan.* RUNNYMEDE MEMORIAL. [W/WGS/WPC]

**FINCH James,** Sqd. Ldr. 26th County of Lancaster (Wigan) Bn. Home Guard. Fatally injured in an armoury, 24 February 1941. WIGAN CEMETERY. [BHC/W]

**FINCH James Thomas,** Fus. 13023057 1/8th Bn The Lancashire Fusiliers. 28 April 1944 in India. Aged 24. *s of James & Hannah, Standish.* KOHIMA WAR CEMETERY, INDIA. [ST/STC]

**FINCH William Martlew Miller,** L.Sjt. 3855775 2nd Bn. Coldstream Guards. Died of Wounds in North Africa, 25 December 1942. Aged 25. *s of James & Frances.* MEDJEZ-EL-BAB WAR CEMETERY. [HC]

**FINLAYSON Robert Allan,** 2nd. Officer. *A.M.* Merchant Navy, m.v. *Scottish Prince.* Died 31 May 1941. Aged 25. His ship was bombed and he lost his life rescuing shipmates from the hold. He was awarded a posthumous Albert Medal. *s of Charles & Christina Russell, Newton-le-Willows.* ALEXANDRIA (CHATBY) BRITISH PROTESTANT CEMETERY, EGYPT. [AGS]
[The Albert Medal was awarded for saving life and acts of bravery. In later years, all surviving holders of this medal (and also the Empire Gallantry Medal and the Edward Medal ) exchanged the decorations for the George Cross.]

**FINNEY Charles Milton,** Cpl. 199078 R.A.F. Died 13 March 1943. Aged 42. *h of Lillian Audrey.* WIGAN CEMETERY. [SAC/W]

**FINNEY Robert,** A.B. D/JX305778 R.N. H.M.S. *Charybdis.* 23 October 1943. Aged 21 This cruiser was sunk by German torpedo boats off Northern France. Some sources believe that the body of this seaman was washed ashore and buried on the Atlantic coast. If so, the site has not been identified and he has no known grave. PLYMOUTH NAVAL MEMORIAL. [SCC/W/WSB]
(See also: William Burke; William Clayton; Kenneth Gibson; Richmond Smalley.)

**FISHER Handel Ashton,** Cpl. 552619 Royal Army Veterinary Corps. Killed 19 December 1941 in Hong Kong. Aged 26. *s of Joshua & Edna; h of Nancy.* STANLEY MILITARY CEMETERY, HONG KONG. [ABC]

**FISHER James,** Gnr. 1424378 'Z' Bty., 112 A.A. Regiment, Royal Artillery. Died 4 February 1943. Aged 37. *h of Alice.* INCE-IN-MAKERFIELD CEMETERY. [X]

**FISHER John,** Pte. 3604012 2$^{nd}$ Bn. The Border Regiment. Died sometime between 1-14 April 1944 in Burma. Aged 29. He has no known grave and therefore he is commemorated on the Rangoon Memorial. *s of William & Catherine; h of Gladys.* RANGOON MEMORIAL. [W]

**FISHER John,** Flt. Lt. (Pilot) 130071 R.A.F. (V.R.) 233 Sqdn. Killed in a Dakota while dropping supplies in the Far East 27 September 1945. Aged 25. *s of John James & Winifred Kathleen, Lowton.* TAUKKYAN WAR CEMETERY, BURMA. [BDC/L/LTC]

**FISHER Joseph,** Gnr. 856824 8 Coast Regiment, Royal Artillery. Captured at the surrender of Hong Kong 25 December 1941 and perished 2 October 1942 with the sinking of s.s.*Lisbon Maru* which the Japanese were using to transport prisoners-of-war. Aged 24. SAIWAN BAY MEMORIAL. [A]

**FISHER William,** Pte. 4127575 2$^{nd}$ Bn. The Cheshire Regiment. Killed sometime between 31 October 1942 - 10 November 1942 in the Middle East. Aged 24. *s of William & Charlotte.* ALAMEIN MEMORIAL. [SCC/W/WSB]

**FISHWICK Harold Henry,** Pte. 3861326 2$^{nd}$ Bn. The Loyal Regiment (North Lancashire) Died while a PoW of the Japanese 16 October 1942. Aged 29. *His wife lived in Atherton.* YOKOHAMA BRITISH COMMONWEALTH WAR CEMETERY, JAPAN.[X]

**FISHWICK Thomas,** Pte. 2184082 Corps of Military Police. 30 September 1942. Aged 28. *s of William & Ellen, Appley Bridge.* UP HOLLAND (ST THOMAS) CHURCHYARD. [X]
(His brother William Gaskell also died on service.)

**FISHWICK William Gaskell,** Pte. 157305 Army Catering Corps attd. 17 Field Regiment Royal Artillery. Died 14 September 1947. Aged 29. *s of William & Ellen, Appley Bridge; h of Edna May.* UP HOLLAND (ST THOMAS) CHURCHYARD. [X]
(His brother Thomas also died on service. It is particularly surprising that neither of the two brothers is commemorated locally)

**FITZPATRICK John, Pte.** 14647194 1st (Airborne) Bn. The Border Regiment. 25 September 1944. Aged 19. ARNHEM OOSTERBEEK WAR CEMETERY, HOLLAND. [S]

**FITZPATRICK Joseph, Pte.** 4198452 13th Bn. The King's Regiment (Liverpool). Killed 21 October 1944 while operating behind enemy lines with General Wingate's Chindits. Aged 24. *s of Stephen & Alice, Appley Bridge.* RANGOON WAR CEMETERY, BURMA [X]

**FITZIMMONS James,** Fireman. Merchant Navy s.s. *Avila Star.* 5 July 1942. Aged 28. North-east of the Azores, this passenger-cargo liner en route from South America to U.K., was sunk by the U-boat *U-201. h of Margaret, Orrell.* TOWER HILL MEMORIAL. [X]

**FLANNERY Peter,** A.B. D/SSX20842 R.N. H.M.S. *Orion.* 29 May 1941. Aged 22. *s of Patrick & Elizabeth, Leigh.* PLYMOUTH NAVAL MEMORIAL. [L]

**FLEMING Charles Bernard,** Pilot Offr. (Nav.) 132773 R.A.F. (V.R.) 100 Sqdn. 12 June 1943. Aged 27. The Lancaster III on a raid on Dusseldorf was shot down by a night-fighter over Holland. *s of Charles & Julia, Wigan.* VOORST (TERWOLDE) GENERAL CEMETERY, HOLLAND. [W]

**FLEMING James,** L.A.C. 1764015 R.A.F. (V.R.) Killed in a motor accident in the South of England, 20 April 1943. Aged 21. *s of James & Emily, Atherton.* ATHERTON CEMETERY. [A]

**FLEMING William Joseph Dudley,** Flt. Lt. 100686 R.A.F. (V.R.) 2771 Sqdn. R.A.F. Regiment. Killed in action in North Africa 5 April 1943. Aged 35. *s of the Vicar of Tyldesley, Rev S.J. Fleming & Mrs Fleming.* MEDJEZ-EL-BAB WAR CEMETERY. [X]

**FLETCHER Francis (Frank) Duncan,** Spr. 4698085 1045 Port Operating Coy. Royal Engineers. Died 16 December 1944 in Belgium. Aged 22. *s of William Newsham & Mary Jane, Platt Bridge.* SCHOONSELHOF CEMETERY, ANTWERP. [PBC]

**FLETCHER Gladys,** Ldg. Wren D/WRNS/9426 Womens Royal Naval Service. H.M.S. *Tana.* Presumed killed at sea 12 February 1944. Aged 26. *d of William & Martha of Atherton & Leigh.* PLYMOUTH NAVAL MEMORIAL. [HBC/L/LMC]

**FLETCHER William,** A.B. D/SSX25784 R.N. H.M.S. *Juno.* 21 May 1941. Aged 20. During the Battle of Crete, the destroyer was sunk by German aircraft south-east of Crete. *s of Mrs. M., Pemberton.* PLYMOUTH NAVAL MEMORIAL. [W]

**FLETCHER William,** Sgt.(Flt. Eng.) 2209502 R.A.F. (V.R.) 640 Sqdn. 25 May 1944. Aged 19. A Halifax III bomber left Leconfield to raid Aachen but it crashed near Geilenkirchen where the initial burials of five crew-members took place. Since 1945 they have been reinterred. *s of Thomas & Elizabeth, Bryn.* RHEINBERG WAR CEMETERY. [AMS/BNC]

**FLYNN William**, Pte. 7264789 Royal Army Medical Corps. Killed 12 June 1944 in Italy. Aged 25. *s of William & Anne.* BOLSENA WAR CEMETERY, ITALY. [G/GOC]

**FORKIN Joseph Michael**, Fus. 406165 11th Bn. The Lancashire Fusiliers. Killed in Italy 16 October 1944. Aged 34. *s of John Thomas Herbert & Annie; h of Ruby May.* FAENZA WAR CEMETERY, ITALY. [W]
(The Cenotaph shows him as serving in the Royal Electrical & Mechanical Engineers. CWGC and other records give his regiment as Lancashire Fusiliers.)

**FOSTER Charles Arnold**, Tpr. 7913182 40th (7th Bn. The King's Regiment [Liverpool]) Royal Tank Regiment, R.A.C. Killed 22 July 1942 in the Middle East. Aged 28. EL ALAMEIN WAR CEMETERY. [W]

**FOSTER Harold**, Dvr. 14603586 Royal Corps of Signals, XIII Corps Signals. Killed in Italy 29 June 1945. Aged 39. *s of Moses & Ellen; h of Amelia, Orrell.* UDINE WAR CEMETERY, ITALY. [PC]

**FOSTER James**, Pte. T/14602781 701 Army Transport Coy. Royal Army Service Corps. 14 November 1944. Aged 21. *s of Lewis & Mary, Standish.* LEOPOLDSBURG WAR CEMETERY, BELGIUM. [SSM/ST]

**FOSTER James Gerard**, L.Cpl. 3852794 1st Bn. The Loyal Regiment (North Lancashire) Killed in action in France 1 June 1940 during the retreat to Dunkirk. Aged 30. *s of Francis & Ann, Billinge; h of Monica.* DUNKIRK MEMORIAL. [BC]

**FOSTER John**, Sgt.(Flt. Eng.) 985156 R.A.F. (V.R.) 460 (R.A.A.F.) Sqdn. 25 March 1944. Aged 20. A Lancaster III bomber from Binbrook on a Berlin raid, crashed near Salzuflen. There was one survivor from a crew of seven - six of whom were Australians. *s of John Henry & Ellen, Goose Green.* HANOVER WAR CEMETERY, GERMANY. [W/GGC]

**FOSTER John**, Lieut. 360108 2nd Bn. The Lancashire Fusiliers. Died 21 May 1947 in Austria. Aged 20. *s of George & Sybil, Wigan.* KLAGENFURT WAR CEMETERY, AUSTRIA. [X]

**FOSTER John Thomas**, L.Cpl. 3968947 1st Bn. The Dorsetshire Regiment Died of wounds 9 September 1944 in Belgium. Aged 28. *s of Thomas & Annie, Billinge; h of Violet Minnie.* SCHOONSELHOF WAR CEMETERY, ANTWERP. [BC]

**FOSTER Joseph**, Gnr. 1114278 1 Regiment, Royal Horse Artillery. Killed in action 30 May 1942. Aged 22. He has no known grave. *s of Joseph & Amelia, Ince.* ALAMEIN MEMORIAL. [IN]

**FOSTER Richard**, Tpr. 3865414 18th (5th Bn. The Loyal Regiment [North Lancashire]) Regiment, Reconnaissance Corps. Died while a PoW of the Japanese 14 September 1944. Aged 24. *s of Mr. & Mrs. Jack; h of Alice, Hindley.* SINGAPORE MEMORIAL. [HC]

**FOSTER Robert**, Gnr. 11262702 58 H.A.A. Regiment, Royal Artillery. Lost at sea while serving in North Africa, 7 January 1943. Aged 41. He has no known grave and is thus commemorated on the appropriate memorial. *s of John & Mary; h of Mary Elizabeth, Wigan.* MEDJEZ-EL-BAB MEMORIAL, TUNISIA. [W]

**FOSTER William**, Pte. 3527049 2nd Bn. The Manchester Regiment. Killed in action in Burma, 20 March 1944. Aged 28. *s of Elias & Annie, Newtown; h of Sarah, Wigan.* TAUKKYAN WAR CEMETERY, BURMA. [W]

**FOSTER William Henry**, Pte. 3453092 2nd Bn. King's Shropshire Light Infantry. Died of wounds in Normandy 7 June 1944. Aged 26. *s of James & Mary.* HERMANVILLE WAR CEMETERY. [L/LPC]

**FOWLER Thomson**, Tpr. 3859770 45th Regiment, Reconnaissance Corps. Killed 26 March 1944 in Burma. Age 27. He has no known grave. RANGOON MEMORIAL. [OC]

**FOX Thomas**, Gnr. 852337 Royal Artillery. Accidently shot and killed 6 May 1941. Aged 26. ATHERTON CEMETERY. [X]

**FOX William**, Pte. 13061812 Corps of Military Police. Died 22 May 1942. Aged 26. *h of Ellen.* WIGAN CEMETERY. [W]

**FRANCE-SERGEANT Stanley**, Gnr. 1618578 69 Lt. A.A.Regiment, Royal Artillery. Killed 23 March 1945 in India. Aged 34. *s of Stanley & Elizabeth Ellen; h of Elizabeth, Hindley.* MAYNAMATI WAR CEMETERY, PAKISTAN. [X]

**FRANCIS James**, Pte. 3792904 13th Bn. The King's Regiment (Liverpool) and Commando. Died 7 August 1944 while a PoW of the Japanese. Aged 28. RANGOON WAR CEMETERY. [JC]

**FRANCIS Walter**, Greaser. Merchant Navy s.s. *Otaio* 28 August 1941. Aged 37. In an area west of Ireland, the cargo liner was en route from Liverpool to Australia when it was attacked and sunk by the German U-boat *U-558*. *s of Mr. & Mrs. Walter, Orrell..* TOWER HILL MEMORIAL. [X]

**FROST Leslie Arthur**, Pte. 3858746 1st Bn. The Loyal Regiment (North Lancashire). Killed in action in Italy 16 March 1944. Aged 25. *s of Arthur Frederick & Alice Annie.* CASSINO MEMORIAL. [AIM]

**FRYERS Jack Douglas**, Sto. 1st Class. C/KX96893 R.N. H.M.S. *Achates* 25 July 1941. Aged 22. *s of James & Helena, Leigh.* CHATHAM MEMORIAL. [L/LTC]

**FULLERTON Elliot**, Sgt. (Flt. Eng.) 2204572 R.A.F. (V.R.) 9 Sqdn. 10 May 1944. Aged 19. This Lancaster III from Bardney was tasked to attack railway yards at Lille, but the aircraft exploded in flight near the target. It was the crew's first sortie since arriving at Bardney. Four members of the crew lie in Lille, two in Forest-sur-Marque and one has no known grave. *s of Robert George & Elizabeth Ellen.* HELLEMMES-LILLE COMMUNAL CEMETERY. [L]

**FUREY Martin,** W.O.II (B.S.M.) 779011 3 Regiment, Royal Horse Artillery. Killed 15 May 1945 in Germany. Aged 39. *s of Martin & Bridget, Tyldesley; h of Louise Victoria.* KIEL WAR CEMETERY. [T]

**FUREY Thomas,** Gnr. 1794139 78 Bty., 35 Lt. A.A. Regiment, Royal Artillery. Released from a Japanese PoW camp (as one of only two survivors of the camp) but died 12 September 1945 aged 24. LABUAN WAR CEMETERY, NORTH BORNEO. [L]

**FYLES James,** Tpr. 3858524 4th/7th Royal Dragoon Guards, R.A.C. Killed in Holland, 19 November 1944. Aged 25. BRUNSSUM WAR CEMETERY, HOLLAND. [UPC]

**GADD Harry Albert George,** Flying Offr. (Air Bmr.) 152574 R.A.F. (V.R.) 550 Sqdn. 3 November 1944. Aged 23. The Lancaster I bomber from North Killingholme was lost on a raid on Dusseldorf. *s of George & Sarah.* HEVERLEE WAR CEMETERY, BELGIUM. [L/LPC]

**GALLACHER John,** Gnr. 14560140 59 (6th Bn. The Hampshire Regiment) Anti-Tank Regiment, Royal Artillery. Killed 10 July 1944 in France. Aged 19. *s of Patrick & Sarah, Lowton.* ST MANVIEU WAR CEMETERY. [X]

**GALLACHER Thomas,** Spr. 2111219 Royal Engineers Died 14 October 1942. Aged 26. *h of Doris, Pemberton.* WIGAN CEMETERY. [X]

**GALLIMORE Ernest,** Pte. 11421065 1st Bn. Argyll & Sutherland Highlanders. Killed in Italy 8 April 1945. Aged 34. *h of Ann Jane, Astley.* RAVENNA WAR CEMETERY, ITALY. [T]

**GALVIN John,** Pte. 3523297 2nd Bn. The Loyal Regiment (North Lancashire). Captured at the fall of Singapore and died as a PoW of the Japanese 30 May 1943, aged 33. *s of Christopher & Sarah; h of Marian, Lowton St Mary's.* KANCHANABURI WAR CEMETERY. [X]

**GANNON Patrick J.,** Sjt. 3453689 1/8th Bn. The Lancashire Fusiliers. Killed in India 28 April 1944. Aged 24. *s of John & Mary; h of Irene, Wigan.* KOHIMA WAR CEMETERY, INDIA. [W]

**GARFIN Francis,** A.B. C/JX152178 R.N. H.M. Submarine *Thistle*. 10 April 1940. Aged 26. The submarine was torpedoed and sunk by the German U-boat *U-4* off Skudenes. All 53 crew members perished. *s of George William & Nellie.* CHATHAM NAVAL MEMORIAL. [L]

**GARFIN Michael Terence,** Flt. Sgt. 1002281 R.A.F. (V.R.) 139 Sqdn. Died in a flying accident, December 18 1941. Aged 20. LEIGH CEMETERY. [L/LTA]

**GARNER Sydney,** Pte. S/238113 Royal Army Service Corps. Died 27 December 1942 as the result of a road accident in the Middle East. Aged 32. *s of William & Jane; h of Evelyn.* BENGHAZI WAR CEMETERY, LIBYA.[SAC/W]

**GARVIN Arthur,** Gnr. 1514978 223 Bty., 56 (4ᵗʰ Bn. The King's Own Royal Regiment [Lancaster]) Anti-Tank Regiment, Royal Artillery. The exact date of his death is not known, but he was killed sometime between 27 May and 23 June 1940 in France during the withdrawal to Dunkirk and the subsequent successful evacuation of over 300,000 troops. Aged 21. *s of William & Edith, Wigan.* CASSEL COMMUNAL CEMETERY. [W]

**GARRITY John,** Pte. 3780213 2/7ᵗʰ Bn. The Queen's Royal Regiment (West Surrey). Killed in action in Italy 13 September 1944. Aged 24. *s of Thomas & Anne; h of Kathleen.* CORIANO RIDGE WAR CEMETERY, ITALY. [L]

**GASKELL Alfred Ronald,** Flying Offr. 162083 R.A.F. (V.R.) 18 Sqdn. Killed 9 August 1944 in Italy. Aged 21. *s of Ernest & Ellen Ann.* CESENA WAR CEMETERY, ITALY. [SAC/W/WGS/WPC]

**GASKELL Allan V.** Sgt. 970129 R.A.F. (V.R.) Killed in a flying accident in Scotland 10 March 1941. Aged 25. *s of James & Mary, Highfield, Wigan.* HIGHFIELD (ST MATTHEW) CHURCHYARD. [AGS/HIC/W]

**GASKELL John,** Pte. 3654798 1ˢᵗ Bn. The South Lancashire Regiment (Prince of Wales's Volunteers) Killed in Belgium between 31 May and 4 June 1940 during the withdrawal to Dunkirk Aged 21. OOST-DUINKERKE COMMUNAL CEMETERY, BELGIUM. [GGC/HIC/W]

**GASKELL Joseph,** Pte. 7616967 Royal Army Ordnance Corps. Lost in the sinking of s.s. *Lancastria* which was attempting to evacuate over 9000 troops and civilians from France 17 June 1940. Aged 23. He has no known grave. *s of Harry & May.* DUNKIRK MEMORIAL. [L]
(Twelve other local men perished when this ship was sunk. See the **Herbert Cunliffe** entry for names and details of the sinking)

**GASKELL Joseph,** L.Cpl. 3861616 1ˢᵗ Bn. The Loyal Regiment (North Lancashire) Died of wounds in North Africa 30 April 1943. Aged 29. *h of Ellen, Wallgate, Wigan.* OUED ZARGA WAR CEMETERY, TUNISIA. [W]

**GASKELL Norman,** Sgt. (W.Op./Air Gnr.) 646822 R.A.F. Drowned whilst on duty, 28 November 1940. Aged 22. RUNNYMEDE MEMORIAL. [NC/W/WGS]

**GASKELL Robert,** Pte. 3526448 2ⁿᵈ Bn. Argyll & Sutherland Highlanders. Killed in action Belgium, 18 September 1944. Aged 29. *s of Thomas & Margaret, Orrell.* KASTERLEE WAR CEMETERY, BELGIUM. [UPH/UPC]

**GASKELL William,** Pte. 2121736 Army Catering Corps Killed in a road accident in Austria 22 August 1945. Aged 36. KLAGENFURT WAR CEMETERY, AUSTRIA. [X]

**GATLEY Peter,** W.O. (Pilot) 1072709 R.A.F. (V.R.) 242 Sqdn. Killed in a Spitfire during air operations in Italy, 9 September 1943. Aged 20. *s of George & Nellie, Leigh.* CATANIA WAR CEMETERY, ITALY. [L/LGS/LPC]

GAUNT Albert Charles, Gnr. 1119411 118 Field Regiment, Royal Artillery. Died of beriberi while a PoW of the Japanese in Thailand 26 October 1943. Aged 35. *s of John & Mary.* CHUNGKAI WAR CEMETERY, THAILAND. [AC/AGS/NAV]

GAYNARD Robert, Pte. 3866203 1st Bn. The Loyal Regiment (North Lancashire) Killed 23 April 1943 in North Africa. Aged 22. *s of Joseph & Martha, Ashton-in-Makerfield.* MASSICAULT WAR CEMETERY, TUNISIA. [X]

GEE Ernest, A.B. D/JX221179 R.N. H.M.S. *Sultan.* He died in Singapore 16 February 1942 during the fierce fighting during the attempted defence of the colony. He has no known grave. H.M.S *Sultan* was the major shore base. PLYMOUTH NAVAL MEMORIAL [HIY]

GEE Harold, Cpl. 3864592 The Loyal Regiment (North Lancashire) and No.2 Commando. Killed 10 October 1944. Aged 24. *s of James & Jane, Billinge.* PHALERON WAR CEMETERY (SPECIAL MEMORIAL) [BC]
(He was buried at the time in Albania but his grave is now lost.)

GEE John, Sto. 1st. Class. D/SKX1266 R.N. H.M. Submarine *P. 311.* 8 January 1943. Aged 29. This submarine was lost (possibly mined) off Maddelena. *s of William & Margaret, North Ashton.* PLYMOUTH NAVAL MEMORIAL. [AC/AMS/NAV]

GEORGESON Leonard, Gnr. 1139528 151 (The Ayrshire Yeomanry) Field Regiment, Royal Artillery. Killed in France, 19 July 1944. Aged 28. *s of William & Annie; h of Phyllis Georgeson, Worsley Mesnes.* BANNEVILLE-LA-CAMPAGNE CEMETERY, FRANCE. [JC/WGS]

GERAGHTY Thomas, Pte. 3976457 Durham Light Infantry. Died 6 June 1946. Aged 34. *s of Thomas & Rebecca; h of Ruth, Ince.* INCE-IN-MAKERFIELD CEMETERY. [X]

GERRARD James Henry, A.B. D/SX193683 R.N. H.M.S. *Barham.* 25 November 1941. Aged 21. In the eastern Mediterranean, this battleship was torpedoed by U-boat *U-331* and blew up with the loss of 862 crew. *s of Ernest & Betsy, Pemberton.* PLYMOUTH NAVAL MEMORIAL. [HIY/PC/W]
(See also: J.T. Mills; Joseph O'Brien; John Robinson.)

GERRARD Thomas, Gdsmn. 2722984 2nd Bn. Irish Guards. Killed 4 August 1944 in France. Aged 28. *s of John & Annie, Orrell.* ST CHARLES DE PERCY WAR CEMETERY. FRANCE. [X]

GIBSON Charles, Pte. 2188590 46 Coy., Auxiliary Military Pioneer Corps. Lost in the sinking of s.s. *Lancastria* which was attempting to evacuate troops and civilians after the fall of France. 17 June 1940. Aged 25. *s of Charles & Annie; h of Ellen, Wigan.* DUNKIRK MEMORIAL [X]
(Twelve other local men perished when this ship was sunk. See the **Herbert Cunliffe** entry for their names and service details, along with information concerning the events surrounding the sinking)

**GIBSON Horace**, Dvr. 14513282 Royal Corps of Signals, 5 Wireless Group. Killed in France 5 July 1944. Aged 35. *s of William & Mary Alice, Ince; h of Ellen.* BAYEAUX WAR CEMETERY. [IN/SCC]

**GIBSON James**, Gnr. 1114332 69 Anti-Tank Regiment, Royal Artillery. Killed in England 7 December 1941. Aged 30. LEIGH CEMETERY. [L]

**GIBSON Kenneth**, Ord. Seaman. D/JX396042 R.N. H.M.S. *Charybdis.* 23 October 1943. Aged 19. The cruiser was sunk by German torpedo boats off Northern France. *s of Elias & Agnes.* PLYMOUTH NAVAL MEMORIAL. [L/LPC]
(See also: William Burke; William Clayton; Robert Finney; Richmond Smalley.)

**GIBSON Thomas**, Pte. 14432216 2nd Bn. Seaforth Highlanders, (Ross-shire Buffs, The Duke of Albany's) Killed in action, 23 June 1944. Aged 18. *s of Michael & Catherine, Wigan.* RANVILLE WAR CEMETERY, FRANCE. [W]

**GILES Sidney**, Pte. 14512779 2nd Bn. The East Lancashire Regiment. Killed in Burma, 5 November 1944. Aged 31. *s of William Henry & Sarah, Leigh; h of Marian.* TAUKKYAN WAR CEMETERY, BURMA. [L/LTC]

**GILL Harold**, L.Sjt. 3660359 2nd Bn. The East Lancashire Regiment. Died in Burma 18 April 1945. Aged 32. *s of Frank & Jane; h of Gladys, Atherton.* TAUKKYAN WAR CEMETERY, BURMA. [A/L]

**GILL John**, Pte. 14584175 2nd Bn. The Loyal Regiment (North Lancashire). Died of wounds 2 October 1944 in Italy. Aged 19. FLORENCE WAR CEMETERY. [L]

**GLADWIN William**, Gnr. 843099 4 Bty., 1 Lt. A.A. Regiment, Royal Artillery. Killed in action, 10 February 1942 in the Middle East. Aged 26. *s of James & Martha; h of Sarah, Wigan.* KNIGHTSBRIDGE WAR CEMETERY, ACROMA, LIBYA. [W]

**GLASSBROOK Gerald**, Sgt.(Air Gnr.) 649748 R.A.F. 61 Sqdn. 3 June 1942. A Lancaster, on an operation to bomb Essen, crashed near Wesel. Six of the crew of seven were killed and these were originally buried at Dusseldorf, but subsequently they have been reinterred in Reichswald Forest. *Family connections in Orrell.* REICHSWALD FOREST WAR CEMETERY, GERMANY. [X]

**GLOVER Harry**, Tpr. 14828909 11th Hussars (Prince of Albert's Own), R.A.C. Died 30 May 1947 while in the Occupation Forces in Germany. Aged 20. *s of Frederick & Margaret, Up Holland.* MUNSTER HEATH WAR CEMETERY. [UPH/UPC]

**GLOVER James**, Gdsmn. 2662442 Coldstream Guards Died 17 March 1941. Aged 30. WIGAN CEMETERY. [X]

**GLOVER John**, Pte. 4038895 6th Bn. Durham Light Infantry. Killed in action in Italy 17 July 1943. Aged 23. *s of George & Florence, Spring View, Ince.* CATANIA WAR CEMETERY, ITALY. [IN/ISM]

**GLOVER William,** A.B. D/JX567123 R.N. H.M.S. *Afrikander.* 1 November 1945. Aged 20. *s of William & Mary Alice, Hindley.* DOUGLAS CHURCH OF THE PROVINCE OF SOUTH AFRICA CEMETERY. HERBERT DISTRICT. [X]

**GLOVER William,** L.Cpl. 2365051 Royal Corps of Signals, 10<sup>th</sup> Armd. Div. Sigs. (The Middlesex Yeomanry). Killed 12 June 1942 in the Middle East. Aged 25. *s of Joseph & Elizabeth May, Hindley.* ALAMEIN MEMORIAL. [X]

**GOLDEN Henry,** Spr. 1874304 41 Fortress Coy. Royal Engineers. Died 21 July 1945. Aged 26. *s of Luke & Elizabeth Ellen, Ince.* LABUAN WAR CEMETERY, BORNEO. [X]

**GOLDTHORPE George,** Pte. 4539353 1<sup>st</sup> Bn. The York & Lancaster Regiment. Killed 12 January 1944 in Italy. Aged 24. *s of Joseph & Ellen; h of Monica, Up Holland.* MINTURNO WAR CEMETERY, ITALY. [X]

**GOLLOP Robert,** Flt. Sgt. (Nav./W.Op.) 152257 R.A.F. (V.R.) 211 Sqdn. Killed 27 July 1944 in Burma. Aged 29. *s of George & E.M.* TAUKKYAN WAR CEMETERY, BURMA. [W]

**GOODACRE Ralph,** Sgt. (Flt. Engr.) 2209795 R.A.F. (V.R.) 103 Sqdn. 29 July 1944. Aged 19. A Lancaster III bomber from Elsham Wolds, on a raid on Stuttgart, crashed with the loss of all the crew near Freudenstadt. *s of Mr. & Mrs. W.R., Wigan.* DURNBACH WAR CEMETERY, GERMANY. [SMC/W/WGS]

**GORDON Thomas,** Cpl. 7262343 Royal Army Medical Corps. Killed 15 February 1942. Aged 27. SINGAPORE MEMORIAL. [W]

**GORE George Leslie,** Ldg. Mechanic. FAA/FX85859 R.N. H.M.S. *Avenger* 15 November 1942. Aged 19. West of Gibraltar, the German U-boat *U-155* attacked a convoy and torpedoed this escort aircraft carrier which blew up with the loss of over 600 crew. *s of Edward & Agnes, Standish.* LEE-ON-SOLENT MEMORIAL. [SSM/ST/STC]

**GORMALLY Kevin,** Sgt. 2204564 R.A.F. (V.R.) Killed 15 January 1945. Aged 19. The wreckage of his aircraft was found in Israel. *s of John & Kathleen.* ALAMEIN MEMORIAL. [W/WGS]

**GORMAN Joseph,** Pte. 3457766 10<sup>th</sup> Bn. Highland Light Infantry (City of Glasgow Regiment.). Accidently shot while on night patrol in Germany 8 September 1945. Aged 32. He was a D-Day veteran. HAMBURG WAR CEMETERY. [L]

**GORTON John Frederick,** Flt. Sgt. 357798 R.A.F. Lost in the sinking of H.M.S. *Glorious* 10 June 1940. Aged 43. This aircraft carrier was sunk by the battlecruisers *Gneisenau* and *Scharnhorst* 300 miles west of Narvik. There were only 43 survivors. Flt. Sgt. Gorton had joined the R.A.F. in 1924. *s of Albert George & Amelia; h of Winifred, Leigh.* RUNNYMEDE MEMORIAL. [L/LMC]
(See also: Samuel Alker; W.L.Duckworth; John Jameson; Edward Knight; Peter McNicholas; B.T. Starkie; F. Swan.)

**GOULDING Albert E.** A.C.2. 978247 R.A.F. (V.R.) 35 Sqdn. Killed 23 December 1940. *s of Richard & Elizabeth.* WIGAN CEMETERY. [W]

**GOULDING Joseph Thomas,** L.Cpl. 14583668 1st Bn. The Loyal Regiment (North Lancashire) Died of wounds in Italy 8 September 1944. *s of Harriet, Standish.* NAPLES WAR CEMETERY, ITALY. [SSM/ST/STC]

**GOULDING William,** Fus. 3451447 1st Bn. The Lancashire Fusiliers. Killed in action 12 April 1944 in Burma. Aged 25. *s of James & Ann, Orrell.* TAUKKYAN WAR CEMETERY, BURMA. [W/PC]

**GRAHAM Granville,** Sgt.(W.Op.) 970896 R.A.F. (V.R.) 58 Sqdn. He was killed in action 6 November 1940. Aged 22. A Whitley V bomber on a raid on Hamburg was heard calling for assistance but no trace was found of the aircraft or the crew. It was probably Sgt. Graham's first operational flight. *s of William & Nellie, Leigh.* RUNNYMEDE MEMORIAL. [L/LGS/LMC/WMC]

**GRAY William John Alexander,** Lieut. 123245 713 General Construction Coy., Royal Engineers. Killed during the evacuation of Dunkirk 29 May 1940 when the destroyer H.M.S. *Wakeful* was torpedoed. Aged 33. *s of John Alex & Mary Ellen, Ashton-in-Makerfield; h of Peggy.* DUNKIRK MEMORIAL. [AGS/BNC]

**GREEN Arthur James,** Lieut. 299730 The York & Lancaster Regiment. Killed in Normandy. 9 July 1944 Aged 21. *s of Alfred & Elsie, Leigh.* ST MANVIEU WAR CEMETERY. [L/LGS]
(His brother Flt. Lt. John Frederick Green, *D.F.C.* was killed in a flying accident in 1945.)

**GREEN Cornelious,** Dvr. 2367257 Royal Corps of Signals; H.Q. Eigth Army Group, Royal Artillery Signals Section. Killed in action in Normandy 15 July 1944. Aged 23. *s of Peter & Sarah Elizabeth, Orrell; h of Mary Ellen.* RYES WAR CEMETERY, FRANCE. [OC]

**GREEN Harold,** Pte. 325360 9th Bn. (The Queen's Own Yorkshire Dragoons) King's Own Yorkshire Light Infantry. Killed in action 24 April 1943. Aged 23. MEDJEZ-EL-BAB WAR CEMETERY. [W]

**GREEN Henry,** L.A.C. 1105550 R.A.F. (V.R.) Died in North Borneo while a PoW of the Japanese, 16 March 1945. Aged 24. *s of Peter & Mary Alice, Pemberton.* SINGAPORE MEMORIAL. [HIC/HIY/W]

**GREEN James,** Pte. 3858850 2nd Bn. The Loyal Regiment (North Lancashiure) Killed in Singapore 23 January 1942. Aged 22. *s of Thomas & Sarah Ellen, Pemberton.* SINGAPORE MEMORIAL. [W]

**GREEN John Frederick,** Flt. Lt. 128350 *D.F.C.* R.A.F. (V.R.) 248 Sqdn. Killed in a flying accident during a training flight off Plymouth. 23 August 1945. Aged 26. *s of Alfred & Elsie, Leigh.* RUNNYMEDE MEMORIAL. [L/LGS]
(His brother Lieut. Arthur James Green was killed in Normandy in 1944.)

**GREEN Richard,** Cpl. 3458021 11<sup>th</sup> Bn. The Lancashire Fusiliers. Killed 15 November 1944. Aged 31. *s of Richard & Mary; h of Gladys, Ince.* FAENZA WAR CEMETERY, ITALY. [IN]

**GREEN Robert Richard,** Pte. 1674572 7<sup>th</sup> Bn. Argyll & Sutherland Highlanders. Killed in France 8 August 1944. Aged 32. *s of Mary Alice, Wigan.* BANNEVILLE-LA-CAMPAGNE WAR CEMETERY. [SAC/W]

**GREEN Samuel Edwin,** Pte. 3857674 2<sup>nd</sup> Bn. The Loyal Regiment (North Lancashire) Died 21 September 1944 while a PoW of the Japanese. Aged 23. *s of Samuel & Sophia Agnes, Beech Hill.* SINGAPORE MEMORIAL. [W]

**GREEN Walter,** Spr. 2184332 170 Tunnelling Coy. Royal Engineers. Died of wounds 2 May 1945. Aged 39. Captured and became a PoW at Dunkirk in 1940. As the war was drawing to an end he completed a forced march from Poland only for the column to be strafed by Allied aircraft in North West Germany. He is buried in Holland. *h of Lily.* VENRAY WAR CEMETERY, HOLLAND. [L]

**GREEN William,** Pte. 3858531 1<sup>st</sup> Bn. The Loyal Regiment (North Lancashire) Died 9 June 1940 following the evacuation of Dunkirk. Aged 21. *s of Richard & Mary, Leigh.* ST VALERY-EN-CAUX CEMETERY. [T/HGC/LMC]

**GREEN William,** Sgt. (W.Op./Air. Gnr.) 1081353 R.A.F. 467 (R.A.A.F.) Sqdn. 28 July 1943. Aged 34. A Lancaster III bomber from Bottesford was shot down by a night-fighter over Germany. Two of the crew of seven became prisoners of war. *s of Samuel & Jane, Bryn.* HAMBURG WAR CEMETERY. [AGS/BNC]

**GREEN William,** Gdsmn. 2619379 6<sup>th</sup> Bn. Grenadier Guards Killed in action 17 March 1943. Aged 23. *s of Mrs. E., Orrell.* SFAX WAR CEMETERY, TUNISIA. [OC]

**GREEN William,** Sgt. (Air Gnr.) 1129659 R.A.F. 149 Sqdn. 24/25 August 1942. Aged 22. His Stirling I bomber was tasked to bomb Frankfurt but it developed an engine fire and crashed soon after taking-off from R.A.F. Lakenheath in Suffolk. All seven members of the crew perished. IRLAM (ST JOHN THE BAPTIST) CHURCHYARD. [AS]

**GREENALL Eric,** Teleg. P/SSX288810 R.N. *H.M.M.L. 155* 9 April 1942 Aged 21. *s of Francis & Elizabeth.* WIGAN CEMETERY. [SCC/W/WSB]

**GREENALL Leslie,** Sto. P/KX136777 R.N. H.M.S. *Sikh.* Died of wounds 25 September 1942. Aged 20. During the attack on Tobruk, this destroyer sank after being damaged by shore batteries. *s of Edward & Sarah, Bryn.* TOBRUK WAR CEMETERY, LIBYA [AMS/BNC]

**GREENALL Robert,** Sto. 1<sup>st</sup> Class. D/SS123822 R.N. H.M.S. *Hecla.* 12 November 1942. Aged 42. West of Gibraltar, the depot ship was sunk by the German U-boat *U-515. s of John & Elizabeth; h of Elizabeth Mary.* PLYMOUTH NAVAL MEMORIAL. [PC]

**GREENHALGH James,** Pte. 3530498 5th Bn. The Manchester Regiment. Died 16 June 1941. *He had close family connections in both Ince & Wigan.* WIGAN CEMETERY. [X]

**GREENHALGH Leslie,** L.A.C. 1137149 R.A.F. (V.R.) Killed in a flying accident in Ireland 30 December 1942. Aged 22. LEIGH CEMETERY. [L/LGS/LTC]

**GREENHOUGH Jesse French,** Pte. 4461529 Army Catering Corps attd. 2nd. Bn. Durham Light Infantry. Fatally injured in India 5 July 1945. Aged 30. RANGOON WAR CEMETERY. [A/T]

**GREGORY Arthur,** L.A.C. 1098505 R.A.F. (V.R.) Died 2 February 1946. Aged 40. *s of Joseph & Caroline.* ATHERTON CEMETERY. [CUC]

**GREGORY Frank,** L.Sjt. 3854916 2nd Bn. The Loyal Regiment (North Lancashire) Died 20 March 1944. Aged 36. *s of Samuel & Mary; h of Esther Helen.* COPPULL PARISH CHURCHYARD. [ABC]

**GREGORY Frederick,** A.B. D/JX241366 R.N. H.M.S. *Hurworth.* 22 October 1943. Aged 27. This destroyer ran into a minefield east of Kalymnos and was sunk. *s of Richard & Mary Jane; h of Hilda.* PLYMOUTH NAVAL MEMORIAL. [L]

**GREGORY John,** Cpl. 3964302 1st Bn. The Welch Regiment. Killed 11 September 1944 in Italy. Aged 26. *s of Walter & Annie, Aspull.* CORIANO RIDGE WAR CEMETERY, ITALY. [AS/ASC]

**GREGORY Robert Edward,** Pte. 3526539 2nd Bn. The King's Own Royal Regiment (Lancaster). Killed 5 December 1941 in the Middle East. Aged 25. He has no known grave. *s of William & Elizabeth; h of Annie, Wigan.* ALAMEIN MEMORIAL. [W]

**GREGORY Thomas Joseph,** Sgt. (Air Bmr.) 996725 R.A.F. (V.R.) 57 Sqdn. 12/13 May 1943. Aged 31. A Lancaster I bomber on a raid to Duisburg, crashed on the Dutch/German border near Emmerich. *s of Harry & Annie; h of Vera, Leigh.* GENDRINGEN R.C.CEMETERY, HOLLAND. [L/LGS/LMC]

**GREGORY William,** Fus. 1699702 2nd Bn. The Lancashire Fusiliers. Killed 27 October 1944 in Italy. Aged 31. *s of Jack & Ellen; h of May.* FAENZA WAR CEMETERY, ITALY. [SCC/W]

**GRICE Ronald William,** A.C.2. 994444 R.A.F. (V.R.) He was captured at the fall of Batavia, Java and died whilst being held as a PoW of the Japanese 30 March 1945. Aged 24. *s of James John & Ada Alice.* SINGAPORE MEMORIAL. [KMC/W/WGS]

**GRIFFIN Martin John,** A.B. D/JX334408 R.N. H.M.S. *President III,* but lost in s.s. *Empire Heath* which was sunk 11 May 1944 by U-boat *U-129* as the cargo ship was east of Brazil en route to U.K. Aged 23. *s of Mr. M.* PLYMOUTH NAVAL MEMORIAL. [W]

**GRIFFITHS Robert,** Dvr. 14702777 Royal Army Service Corps. Died 7 May 1946 Aged 38. *s of Joseph & Mary Elizabeth, Ince.* INCE-IN-MAKERFIELD CEMETERY. [IN/SCC]

**GRIME Frank,** W.O. III 3529624 5th Bn. The Manchester Regiment. Killed 25 May 1940 during the withdrawal to Dunkirk. Aged 33. LILLE SOUTHERN CEMETERY, FRANCE. [A/CUC]

**GRIME James Albert,** Ldg. S.B.A. P/MX65841 R.N. H.M.S. *Assegai* Died in a military hospital in South Africa 29 May 1944. Aged 26. *s of James & Clara; h of Elsie May, Atherton.* JOHANNESBURG (WEST PARK) CEMETERY, SOUTH AFRICA. [A]

**GRIME William** A.B. P/JX392596 R.N. H.M.S. *President III* Killed 26 September 1943. Aged 20. *s of Albert & Mary, Westleigh.* PORTSMOUTH NAVAL MEMORIAL. [L]

**GRIMES Ernest,** Ldg. S.B.A. D/X7376 R.N. H.M.S. *Drake.* Died 20 November 1944. WIGAN CEMETERY. [X]

**GRIMES James,** Fus. 3451727 1/8th Bn. The Lancashire Fusiliers. Died of wounds 2 June 1940. Aged 21. *s of James & Jane, Wigan; h of Laura, Wigan..* WIGAN CEMETERY. [W/WSB]

**GRIMSHAW Francis,** Pte. 6093560 1/6th Bn. Queen's Royal Regiment (West Surrey). 17 October 1943. Age 26. NAPLES WAR CEMETERY. [ISM/W]

**GRINDLEY Robert,** Pte. 5961595 1st Bn. Bedfordshire & Hertfordshire Regiment. Killed 19 October 1944 in Italy. Aged 22. *s of Albert & Annie, Wigan.* FAENZA WAR CEMETERY, ITALY. [W]

**GRINDLEY Robert,** 2622549 5th Bn. Grenadier Guards. Killed in action 27 April 1943 in North Africa. Aged 20. *s of William & Ellen, Kitt Green.* MEDJEZ-EL-BAB WAR CEMETERY, TUNISIA. [W]

**GRUNDY Albert,** Teleg. D/JX309196 R.N. H.M.S. *Kite.* 21 August 1944. Aged 42. While escorting a convoy off north Norway, the sloop was sunk by *U-334. s of John & Abigail; h of Mary Elsie.* PLYMOUTH NAVAL MEMORIAL. [BDC/L] (See also: Thomas Aldred; Edward Nelson; Thomas Payne.)

**GRUNDY Eric,** Pilot Offr.(Nav.) 195679 R.A.F. (V.R.) 21/22 February 1945. Aged 33. His Lancaster I bomber took-off to attack the Mittelland Canal but was shot down with the loss six of the seven members of the crew. *s of Mr. & Mrs. T.W. Leigh.* REICHSWALD FOREST WAR CEMETERY, GERMANY. [BDC/L/LGS]

**GRUNDY Frederick,** Pilot Offr. 155369 R.A.F. (V.R.) 158 Sqdn. 3 October 1943. Aged 21. A Halifax II bomber was hit by flak and crashed into the sea off Texel. *s of John & Frances, Astley; h of Gladys, Hindsford.* RUNNYMEDE MEMORIAL. [A/HAC/T]

**GRUNDY George,** Pte. 3861331 1st Bn. Royal Norfolk Regiment. Killed in action in Holland, 14 October 1944. Aged 21. OVERLOON WAR CEMETERY, HOLLAND. [L]

**GRUNDY George Clifford,** A.C.2. 1051471 R.A.F. (V.R.) 239 Sqdn. Died 27 April 1941. Aged 27. *h of Margaret.* STANDISH (ST WILFRID) CHURCHYARD. [ST/STC/W/WGS]

**GRUNDY James,** L.Cpl. 3855223 Corps of Military Police. Captured at the fall of Singapore and died as a PoW of the Japanese, 1 October 1942. Aged 27. *s of Richard & Elizabeth, Wrightington.* KRANJI WAR CEMETERY, SINGAPORE. [X]

**GRUNDY Peter,** Fus. 14664340 11th Bn. The Lancashire Fusiliers. Killed 16 October 1944 in Italy. Aged 36. *s of Thomas & Harriet; h of Elizabeth, Hindley.* FAENZA WAR CEMETERY, ITALY. [HC]

**GRUNDY Wilfred James,** P.O. Radar Mech. P/MX575794 R.N. H.M.S. *Goodall.* 29 April 1945 Aged 22. This frigate was torpedoed by U-boat *U-968* off Murmansk and had to be sunk. PORTSMOUTH NAVAL MEMORIAL. [ACC/AGS]

**GRUNDY William,** Gnr. 14347132 32 Heavy Regiment, Royal Artillery. Killed in action 19 October 1944 in Italy. CESENA WAR CEMETERY, ITALY. [W/GGC]

**GUTHRIE Joseph Michael,** Pte. 14202972 1st Bn. The Loyal Regiment (North Lancashire). Killed in action in Italy 28 January 1944. Aged 21. *s of Patrick & Elizabeth Ann, Wigan.* ANZIO WAR CEMETERY, ITALY. [W]

**GUY Kenneth,** Teleg. D/JX401508 R.N. H.M.S. *Mourne.* 15 June 1944. This frigate was sunk off the Lizard by German U-boat *U-767. s of Henry & Ada, Wigan.* PLYMOUTH NAVAL MEMORIAL. [IN]
(See also: Henry Makinson.)

**HADDOCK Sydney,** A.B. D/JX223508 R.N. H.M.S. *Drake IV.* Died 14 June 1942. PLYMOUTH NAVAL MEMORIAL. [AS]

**HAGUE Cyril** Gnr. 948338 153 (The Leicestershire Yeomanry) Field Regiment, Royal Artillery. Died in Germany as a member of the Occupation Forces 1 January 1946. Aged 26. *s of W.B. and Jane, h of Alice, Crooke.* COLOGNE SOUTHERN CEMETERY. [S]

**HAILWOOD John,** Gnr. 1123015 118 Field Regiment, Royal Artillery. Captured in May 1943 and died whilst being held as a PoW of the Japanese 9 April 1945. Aged 29. *s of John & Henrietta; h of Louisa.* KRANJI WAR CEMETERY, SINGAPORE. [L/LMC]

**HAINES Alfred James Charles,** Pte. 3781461 13th Bn. The King's Regiment (Liverpool) Killed in India, 7 April 1942. Aged 29. *s of Alfred James Charles & Ethel; h of Mildred.* MADRAS WAR CEMETERY, INDIA. [BNC]

**HALL Frank,** Flt. Lt.(Pilot) 100566 R.A.F. (V.R.) 60 Sqdn. Killed while piloting a Hurricane on an operation in India 8 March 1944. Aged 24. CHITTAGONG WAR CEMETERY, INDIA. [LGS/T/TC]

**HALL Frederick Grundy,** L/Sjt. 2720871 2<sup>nd</sup> Bn. Irish Guards Killed 11 September 1944. Aged 24. *s of Richard B. & Matilda, Wigan; h of Margaret Bell, Wigan.* LEOPOLDSBURG WAR CEMETERY, BELGIUM. [W/WGS/WPC]

**HALL John,** Marine PLY/X110425 No. 45 Royal Marine Commando. Died of wounds in France 25 August 1944. BEUZEVILLE COMMUNAL CEMETERY. [AS/ASC/NSC]

**HALLINAN John,** Bdr. 1106957 13 (Honourable Artillery Coy.) Royal Horse Artillery. Killed in action 27 June 1944. Aged 35. *h of Mary, Wigan.* BAYEAUX MEMORIAL. [W/GGC]

**HALLIWELL Henry,** Gnr. 1830982 401 (5<sup>th</sup> Bn. Royal Warwickshire Regiment) Bty. 100 Lt. A.A. Regiment, Royal Artillery. Killed in Burma 28 March 1944. Aged 33. *s of Henry & Elizabeth, Newtown.* KOHIMA WAR CEMETERY, INDIA. [NC/W]
(Some sources give his regiment as The Gordon Highlanders and indeed he is shown on the Wigan memorial as serving with this regiment at the time of his death. Official records and the CWGC give the details above.)

**HALLIWELL James,** Gnr. 1082736 5 Field Regiment, Royal Artillery. Killed 5 February 1942 in Singapore. Aged 27. *His family connections were with Ince & Wigan.* SINGAPORE MEMORIAL. [W]

**HALLIWELL J.T.** Pte. 14092176 1<sup>st</sup> Bn. The Loyal Regiment (North Lancashre) Died 25 October 1946 in Palestine. *He had family connections with Hindley.* KHAYAT BEACH WAR CEMETERY, ISRAEL. [X]

**HALLIWELL Kenneth Thomas,** Pilot Offr.(Nav./W.Op) 134702 R.A.F.(V.R.) Died 21 March 1943. Aged 23. *s of James Unsworth & Emily, Swinton.* CARLISLE (DALSTON ROAD) CEMETERY. [LGS]

**HAMILTON Claude William,** Capt. 250986 Royal Army Medical Corps. 18 May 1944 in Italy. Aged 24. *s of Robert & E.A., Golborne; h of Anne, Golborne.* CASERTA WAR CEMETERY, ITALY. [LGS]

**HAMPSON Arthur,** Pte. 7639277 Royal Army Ordnance Corps Died of dysentry in a Japanese PoW camp, 1 December 1942. Aged 31. *s of Peter & Mary.* LABUAN WAR CEMETERY, NORTH BORNEO. [X]

**HAMPSON Arthur Noel,** Sgt. 946762 R.A.F. (V.R.) 149 Sqdn. 13 August 1941. Aged 21. A Wellington I bomber on a raid on Hanover was hit by flak which killed Sgt. Hampson. Another member of the crew died after the aircraft crash-landed in Suffolk. *s of Fred W. & E.A., Wigan.* STANDISH (ST WILFRID) CHURCHYARD. [SMC/STC/W/WGS]

**HAMPSON James Douglas**, Lieut. 193825 1st Bn. The Loyal Regiment (North Lancashire) Killed in action in North Africa, 23 April 1943. Aged 22. *s of James & Nellie, Atherton.* MEDJEZ-EL-BAB WAR CEMETERY, TUNISIA. [A/LGS]

**HAMPSON James Henry**, Lieut. 267991 7th Bn. The South Staffordshire Regiment. Killed in Normandy 8 July 1944. *s of John Wilson & Louisa Marion; h of Hilda May.* CAMBES-EN-PLAINE WAR CEMETERY, FRANCE. [A]

**HAMPSON Maurice**, Flt. Sgt. 1231035 R.A.F. (V.R.) 51 Sqdn. 4 December 1943. Aged 22. The Halifax II was lost without trace on a raid over Leipzig and all seven members of the crew are commemorated on the Runnymede Memorial. *s of Maurice & Esther; h of Edna.* RUNNYMEDE MEMORIAL. [A/HBC]

**HAMPSON Stanley**, Tpr. 3391514 11th Hussars (Prince Albert's Own), R.A.C. Killed in action in Italy, 2 October 1943. Aged 31. *s of Samuel & Eliza; h of Lily.* SALERNO WAR CEMETERY, ITALY. [T]

**HAMPSON Thomas Frederick**, Chief Offr. Merchant Navy s.s. *Leadgate.* 11 March 1943. Aged 39. The cargo ship on convoy from New York to the United Kingdom was sunk in the North-west Approaches by German U-boats. *s of George & Hannah, Winstanley; h of Margaret Alice.* TOWER HILL MEMORIAL. [HIC/W/WGS]

**HAMPSON William**, Engineman LT/KX101097 R.N. Patrol Service H.M.S. *Van Meerlant.* Died 4 June 1941. Aged 22. *s of Fred & Mary Jane.* LOWESTOFT MEMORIAL. [W/WPC]

**HAMPSON William**, Pte. 3654997 1st Bn. The South Lancashire Regiment (The Prince of Wales's Volunteers) Killed D-Day, 6 June 1944. Aged 31. *s of James & Elizabeth; h of Irene, Ashton-in-Makerfield.* HERMANVILLE WAR CEMETERY, FRANCE. [AIM]

**HANKINSON George**, Pte. 3528829 1st Bn. The Manchester Regiment. Died whilst being held as a PoW of the Japanese, 13 March 1944. Aged 27. *s of Anne Jane, Ashton-in-Makerfield. It is not known why he is not commemorated on any local memorial.* KANCHANABURI WAR CEMETERY, THAILAND. [X]

**HANNAH Norman**, A.B. D/JX 346261 R.N. H.M.S. *Lochailort* Killed while operating a tank landing craft during the invasion of France on D-Day 6 June 1944. Aged 20. *s of William Arthur & Annie, Leigh.* PLYMOUTH NAVAL MEMORIAL. [L/LGS/LTC]

**HARCOURT Joseph**, Gnr. 979929 Royal Artillery. Died 14 February 1945. Aged 34. HINDLEY CEMETERY. [X]

**HARDMAN Harold**, Fus. 3658907 10th Bn. The Lancashire Fusiliers. Died in a military hospital in India, 10 September 1943. Aged 28. *Fus. Hardman's father, who was awarded the Military Medal, was killed in the First World War just two weeks before the armistice.* DELHI WAR CEMETERY, INDIA. [T/TC]

**HARDMAN Leonard**, Spr. 1649041 Royal Engineers. Died 13 May 1945 in hospital one day after his return from service in Italy. Aged 28. *s of Richard & Ethel; h of Bertha.* WORSLEY (ST MARK) CHURCHYARD. [T]

**HARDMAN Norman**, Gnr. 13056409 8 Medium Regiment, Royal Artillery. Died of wounds in India. 17 March 1944. Aged 27. *s of Norman & M.A., Atherton.* IMPHAL WAR CEMETERY, INDIA. [A]

**HARGREAVES John**, Coder P/JX229764 R.N. H.M.S. *Cossack* 23 October 1941. Aged 30. This destroyer on convoy duty was torpedoed by U-boat *U-563* in the North Atlantic. *s of John & Emma, Worsley Mesnes.* PORTSMOUTH NAVAL MEMORIAL. [JC/W]
(See also: James Atherton; Thomas Ralph Rainford.)

**HARLEY Alfred**, Pte. 14376254 General Service Corps. Died 7 January 1943. Aged 33. *h of Florence May.* HINDLEY CEMETERY. [PBC]

**HARMER Thomas**, Pte. 14827912 13th. (2/4th Bn. The South Lancashire Regiment) Bn. The Partachute Regiment. Killed 3 April 1945. Aged 18. *He had family connections with Wigan.* REICHSWALD FOREST WAR CEMETERY, GERMANY. [X]

**HARRIS George Edmund**, Pte. 3778667 2nd Bn. The King's Regiment (Liverpool) Killed 12 May 1944 in Italy. Aged 31. *h of Ellen, Kitt Green.* CASSINO MEMORIAL. [W/WPC]

**HARRISON Graham**, Sgt. (Flt. Engr.) 2203348 R.A.F. 149 Sqdn. 24 June 1944. Aged 24. A Stirling III took-off from Methwold to attack a flying bomb site. It was shot down by a night-fighter and crashed at Lisbourg in the Pas-de-Calais. *s of John & Ruth M., Wigan.* FRUGES COMMUNAL CEMETERY, FRANCE. [SMC/W]

**HARRISON Jack Eckersley**, Pilot Offr. J/26639 Royal Canadian Air Force. Killed in a flying accident in Scotland 25 November 1943. Aged 31. ATHERTON CEMETERY. [A/LGS]
(Educated at Leigh Grammar School, P.O. Harrison emigrated to Canada before the war and joined the R.C.A.F. in 1942.)

**HARRISON John**, Fus. 3447211 2/6th Bn. The Lancashire Fusiliers. Died in a military hospital 20 June 1943. Aged 31. *h of Mary Ethel, North Ashton.* ASHTON-IN-MAKERFIELD (ST THOMAS) CHURCHYARD. [X]

**HARRISON William**, Sgt. 1514814 R.A.F. (V.R.) Killed in a mid-air collision whilst engaged on a training flight over London, 2 September 1943. Aged 22. *s of Mr. & Mrs. T., Ashton-in-Makerfield.* ASHTON-IN-MAKERFIELD (ST THOMAS) CHURCHYARD. [AGS/AIM]

**HART Christopher James**, Gnr. 1626516 H.Q. 48 Lt. A.A. Regiment, Royal Artillery. Killed 4 April 1945 in the Far East. Aged 34. *h of Gladys Eveline, Wigan.* DJAKARTA WAR CEMETERY. [X]

**HART James**, L.Cpl. 2762223 1st Bn. The Black Watch (Royal Highland Regiment) Died 9 October 1941. Aged 25. LEIGH CEMETERY. [X]

**HART John Cecil**, Major 92125 53 Field Regiment, Royal Artillery. Killed in action in Italy 25 July 1944. Aged 32. *s of Col. John (Managing Director of Bickershaw Colleries) & Isabella; h of Barbara Joan.* BOLSENA WAR CEMETERY, ITALY. [B]

**HART Richard**, Pte. 3857543 2nd Bn. The Loyal Regiment (North Lancashire). He was killed 23 January 1942 in the Far East but he has no known grave and is therefore commemorated on the Singapore Memorial. Aged 21. *s of Richard & Sarah Ellen, Wigan.* SINGAPORE MEMORIAL. [SCC/W]

**HARTLEY Jack**, Sgt. 1620932 R.A.F. (V.R.) Died 17 December 1944. Aged 20. *s of Mrs. H. Lower Ince.* INCE-IN-MAKERFIELD CEMETERY. [IN]

**HARVEY Fred**, Cpl. 982444 R.A.F. (V.R.) Died while on demobilisation leave 17 February 1946. Aged 30. *s of Edward & Florence, Atherton; h of Margaret, Howe Bridge, Atherton.* ATHERTON CEMETERY. [X]

**HARVEY Harold**, Fus. 3451923 2/5th Bn. The Lancashire Fusiliers. Killed in France 31 July 1944. Aged 25. *s of William Richard & Frances, Leigh.* FONTENAY-LE-PESNEL, CEMETERY. [L]

**HASLAM James Frank**, Dvr. T/14705949 Royal Army Service Corps. Killed in Germany 17 April 1945. Aged 19. *s of Edward & Maggie, Leigh.* REICHSWALD FOREST WAR CEMETERY, GERMANY. [L/LPC/LMC]

**HATTON George William**, Sgt. (Air Gnr.) 1535749 R.A.F. (V.R.) 21 Sqdn. Died 10 December 1942. Aged 20. *s of Edward & Elizabeth, Leigh.* A Ventura aircraft crashed near Thetford in Norfolk. All six airmen on board were killed. GLAZEBURY (ALL SAINTS) CHURCHYARD. [L/LTC]

**HATTON Horace**, Pte. 10545352 Royal Army Ordnance Corps. Died 5 July 1941 Aged 20. *s of Thomas & Margaret Ann, Bickershaw.* BROOKWOOD MEMORIAL, SURREY. [B]

**HAWTHORN Joseph**, Sto. 1st Class. D/KX102765 R.N. H.M.S. *Repulse* 10 December 1941. Aged 25. This battle cruiser was sunk by Japanese aircraft off Kuantan, Malaya. *s of Henry & Sarah Ann, Ince.* PLYMOUTH NAVAL MEMORIAL. [IN]

**HAYES William**, A.B. D/JX567879 R.N. H.M.S. *Arbiter.* Died 19 March 1944. *s of Robert & Martha.* PLYMOUTH NAVAL MEMORIAL. [T]

**HAZLETT Maxwell**, Fireman. Merchant Navy s.s. *Turakina* 20 August 1940. Aged 30. The cargo liner, en route to the U.K., was sunk by the German commerce raider *Orion* north-west of New Zealand. *s of Samuel & Agnes; h of Florence, Golborne.* TOWER HILL MEMORIAL. [X]

**HEAP Arthur,** Fus. 3461130 1/8th Bn. The Lancashire Fusiliers. Died of malaria in India 25 January 1945. Aged 37. *His wife lived in Astley.* CALCUTTA (BHOWANIPORE) WAR CEMETERY [T]

**HEATH John,** Sjt. 3655176 1st Bn. The King's Royal Rifle Corps Killed 19 September 1944 in Italy. Aged 24. *s of Harold & Margaret E. Ashton-in-Makerfield.* CORIANO RIDGE WAR CEMETERY, ITALY. [AIM]

**HEATON David,** Pte. 3856916 2nd Bn. The Border Regiment. Killed 31 March 1944 in Burma. Aged 24. *s of Peter & Elizabeth.* IMPHAL WAR CEMETERY, INDIA. [IN]

**HEATON Eric William,** Sgt. 1494490 R.A.F. (V.R.) Died 4 December 1944 Aged 21. *s of W.M.F. & Annie, Orrell.* ORRELL (ST LUKE) CHURCHYARD. [PC]

**HEATON Francis Patrick,** Sgt.(Air Gnr.) 1699714 R.A.F.(V.R.) 57 Sqdn. 3 November 1943. Aged 20. A Lancaster I bomber on a raid on Dusseldorf was attacked by a night-fighter and crashed near Hechtel, Belgium. Three members of the crew of eight survived and the dead were originally buried at St-Truiden. *s of John Fancis & Ellen.* HEVERLEE WAR CEMETERY, BELGIUM. [W]

**HEATON Henry,** Pte. 6093620 4th Bn. The Buffs (Royal East Kent Regiment) Killed in action 14 November 1943 on Leros. Aged 23. *s of Thomas & Cicely, Pemberton.* LEROS WAR CEMETERY, GREECE. [NC/W]

**HEATON James,** L.A.C. 1475397 R.A.F. (V.R.) Killed 4 December 1943 in North Africa. Aged 22. *s of Herbert & Charlotte, Landgate, Ashton-in-Makerfield.* DELY IBRAHIM WAR CEMETERY, ALGERIA. [AIM]

**HEATON Reginald,** C.S.M. T/44136 Royal Army Service Corps. Died 14 April 1946 while on demobilisation leave. WIGAN CEMETERY. [X]

**HEATON Richard,** Sjt. 3594911 The Manchester Regiment. Died 4 August 1947 Aged 40. *s of Richard & Ellen; h of Ethel, Atherton.* ATHERTON CEMETERY. [X]

**HEATON Robert Douglas,** L.Cpl. 3533894 1st Bn. The Manchester Regiment. Captured at the fall of Singapore and died in Thailand as a PoW of the Japanese 26 May 1943. Aged 25. *s of Mr. & Mrs. Samuel H., Wigan.* THANBYUZAYAT WAR CEMETERY. [W/WGS]

**HEATON William Pilkington,** Sgt. 1685597 R.A.F.(V.R.) Killed 15 January 1945. Aged 21. *s of Levi & Mary Louise, Westhoughton.* ALAMEIN MEMORIAL, EGYPT. [HGS]

**HENRY Alan Paul Telford,** Sgt.(W.Op/Air Gnr.) 2204861 R.A.F. (V.R.) Died 11 December 1944. Aged 19. *s of Stephen & Hannah, Shevington.* SHEVINGTON (ST ANNE) CHURCHYARD. [S]

**HERSNIP Harry,** Sgt. 1356681 R.A.F. (V.R.) R.A.F. Regiment. Killed 21 November 1942, in North Africa. Aged 35. *s of Harry & Alice; h of Nellie, Newtown.* BONE WAR CEMETERY, ALGERIA. [NC/W]

**HESKETH Albert Gaskell,** A.B. D/JX339058 R.N. H.M.S. *President III* but lost in m.v. *Rosewood.* 9 March 1943. Aged 20. South of Iceland, the tanker, which was en route from New York to the Clyde, was sunk by the U-boat *U-409. s of Albert A. & Ethel, Orrell.* PLYMOUTH NAVAL MEMORIAL. [PC]

**HESKETH Henry,** Dvr. T/174835 Royal Army Service Corps. 25 April 1942 Aged 26. *h of Doris, Kitt Green.* PEMBERTON CEMETERY. [X]

**HESKETH Joseph Kershaw,** Pte. 14408534 4th Bn. The Queen's Own Royal West Kent Regiment. Killed 7 April 1944 in Burma. Aged 19. *s of Thomas N. & Jane.* KOHIMA WAR CEMETERY. [X]

**HESKETH Norman,** Pte. 4922983 2nd (Airborne) Bn., The South Staffordshire Regiment. Killed 9 July 1943 during the airborne landings in Sicily which preceded the main attack. Aged 27. *s of William & Mary, Wallgate, Wigan.* CASSINO MEMORIAL. [W]

**HESKETH William,** Gnr. 779893 60 Field Regiment, Royal Artillery. Killed sometime between 30 May and 2 June 1940 during the Dunkirk evacuation. Aged 30. He has no known grave. *s of Charles and Alice; h of Clarice, Orrell.* DUNKIRK MEMORIAL. [PC]

**HEWITT James Hems,** L.Cpl. 3782436 6th Bn. The Royal Lincolnshire Regiment. Killed 18 September 1944 in Italy. Aged 22. *s of Joseph & Florence, Poolstock, Wigan.* MONTECCHIO WAR CEMETERY, ITALY. [W]

**HEWITT William,** Pte. 14234845 1st Bn. The Duke of Wellington's Regiment (West Riding). Killed in action in Italy, 12 September 1944. Aged 20. *s of William & Ann, Billinge.* FLORENCE WAR CEMETERY, ITALY. [HIY/OC]

**HEYES Henry,** L.Cpl. T/107863 Royal Army Service Corps. Killed 8 February 1943 in Italy. Aged 23. *s of George & Alice, Billinge.* ANCONA WAR CEMETERY. [BC]

**HEYES James Edward,** Pte. Auxiliary Military Pioneer Corps. Died 9 June 1940 Aged 21. WIGAN CEMETERY. [X]

**HEYES Joseph Theodore,** Sto. 1st Class. D/KX136725 R.N. H.M.S. *Panther.* 9 October 1943. Aged 20. Off Rhodes, this destroyer was sunk by German aircraft. *s of John Henry & Mary Elizabeth, Wigan.* PLYMOUTH NAVAL MEMORIAL. [W]

**HEYES Thomas,** Gnr. 14671595 65 (The Norfolk Yeomanry) Anti-Tank Regiment, Royal Artillery, Killed in action 29 May 1945 in Holland. Aged 19. *s of Thomas & Margaret Heyes, Frog Lane, Wigan..* JONKERBOS WAR CEMETERY, HOLLAND. [W/WPC]

**HEYES William**, Gnr. 1082738 70 Field Regiment, Royal Artillery. Killed in action in Italy 7 January 1944. Aged 29. *s of Joseph & Mary Jane, Aspull; h of Mary Elizabeth, Wigan.* CASSINO WAR CEMETERY. [AS/HDC/W]

**HEYWOOD Joseph**, Sub Lieut. R.N.V.R. H.M.S. *Capel* 26 November 1944. Aged 28. Off Cherbourg, this frigate was sunk by the German U-boat *U-486. h of Frances, Tyldesley.* PORTSMOUTH NAVAL MEMORIAL. [T/TC]

**HIBBS Samuel**, Fus. 3654369 2nd Bn. The Lancashire Fusiliers. Killed in Italy 9 August 1943. CATANIA WAR CEMETERY, ITALY. [W]

**HICKEY James**, Sto. 1st Class. D/KX128774 R.N. H.M.S. *Bideford.* 22 July 1944. Aged 29. *s of William & Alice Hickey, Wigan.* PLYMOUTH NAVAL MEMORIAL. [X]

**HICKSON Herbert**, L.A.C. 1132097 R.A.F. (V.R.) Died in Ormskirk Military Hospital, 21 February 1946. Aged 37. ASHTON-IN-MAKERFIELD (HOLY TRINITY) CHURCHYARD. [BNC]

**HIGGINSON Joseph**, A.B. D/JX257045 R.N. H.M.S. *President III.* Lost in s.s. *Rhona* 26 November 1943. Aged 22. *h of Edna.* PLYMOUTH NAVAL MEMORIAL. [L/LPC]

**HIGHAM Bernard Ralph**, Sjt. 3714069 1st Wing, Glider Pilot Regiment, A.A.C. Killed at Arnhem, Holland, 25 September 1944. Aged 26. *s of John Joseph & Florence Brigham, Billinge.* ARNHEM OOSTERBEEK WAR CEMETERY. [BC] (His brother, Phillip Geoffrey, also died on active service.)

**HIGHAM Clifford**, Tpr. 305635 2nd Royal Horse Guards (The Blues). Killed in Belgium, 7 September 1944 Aged 24. *s of William & Margaret, Wigan; h of Ivy.* LEOPOLDSBURG WAR CEMETERY, BELGIUM. [BHC/W]

**HIGHAM Frank**, Midshipman. R.N.V.R. H.M.S. *Macaw.* Accidently drowned in the River Thames, 31 May 1944. Aged 19. *s of Alfred & Margaret Ann, Astley.* LEIGH CEMETERY. [LGS/T]

**HIGHAM Joseph Patrick**, Spr. 1875766 35 Fortress Coy., Royal Engineers. Captured at the fall of Singapore and died 1 October 1943 as a PoW of the Japanese while working on the Burma-Siam railway. Aged 22. *s of Joseph & Ann.* CHUNGKAI WAR CEMETERY, THAILAND. [W]

**HIGHAM Phillip Geoffrey**, Sgt. 1132896 R.A.F. (V.R.) 104 Sqdn. Killed 30 October 1943 in Italy. Aged 21. *s of John Joseph & Florence Brigham, Billinge.* BOLSENA WAR CEMETERY, ITALY. [BC] (His brother, Bernard Ralph, also died on active service.)

**HIGHTON Frank Walker**, Engine Room Artificer. C/MX77166 R.N. H.M.S. *Sultan.* Died in Singapore 16 February 1942 but has no known grave. Aged 26 *s of James & Annie, Shevington.* CHATHAM NAVAL MEMORIAL. [S]

**HIGHTON James,** A.C.1. 1111403 R.A.F. (V.R.) 242 Sqdn. Died as a PoW of the Japanese 18 September 1944. Aged 24. *s of William & Annie, Atherton; h of Clarice.* SINGAPORE MEMORIAL. [A]

**HIGHTON John,** Pte. 3521196 32 Coy. Auxiliary Military Pioneer Corps. Accidentally killed in France, 29 January 1940 Aged 33. JANUAL CEMETERY, DIEPPE. [W]
(Some sources - including the Wigan memorial - give this soldier as serving in the Royal Engineers at the time of his death. Commonwealth War Graves Commission records give the detail shown here.)

**HIGSON Robert,** Pte. 14420535 2nd Bn. The Gordon Highlanders Killed in action 30 October 1944 in Holland. Aged 20. MIERLO WAR CEMETERY. [W]

**HILL Eric,** Sub Lieut.(A) R.N.V.R. H.M.S. *Victorious* 17 October 1944. Aged 22. Killed in the Far East during an attack on the Car Nicobar Islands by aircraft from the aircraft-carriers H.M.S. *Victorious* and H.M.S. *Indomitable. s of Charles Richard & Lillie., Orrell.* FLEET AIR ARM MEMORIAL, LEE-ON-SOLENT. [OC/OCY/WGS]

**HILL Gordon Leslie,** Flt. Sgt. (Air Gnr.) 1350603 R.A.F. (V.R.) 50 Sqdn. 26 July 1943. Aged 23. The Lancaster III bomber from Skellingthorpe was shot down during an operation to bomb Essen and crashed near Nijmegen. Three members of the crew became PoWs.; the five who died are buried in Uden War Cemetery. *s of Sydney & Minnie Hill; h of Alice Hill, Wigan.* UDEN WAR CEMETERY, HOLLAND. [AS/HDC]

**HILL John Edward,** A.C.2. 1050687 R.A.F. (V.R.) Lost in s.s. *Laconia* 12 September 1942. This was sunk by the German U-boat *U-156* north-east of Ascension Island. The troopship, en route from the Middle East to the U.K., was carrying 1793 Italian PoWs but over 2200 people on board died. *s of Thomas William & Lily Beatrice.* ALAMEIN MEMORIAL. [W]

**HILL Norman Clifford,** A.C.2. 2207345. R.A.F. (V.R.) 5013 Airfield Construction Sqdn. He died suddenly 8 December 1943 in a Cambridgeshire hospital. Aged 36. *h of Alice Hill, Ashton-in-Makerfield, Lancashire.* ASHTON-IN-MAKERFIELD (ST THOMAS) CHURCHYARD. [AIM]

**HILL Thomas,** Gnr. 1426716 9 Coast Regiment, Royal Artillery. Died as a PoW of the Japanese 5 March 1943. Aged 29. *s of Mr & Mrs William, Platt Bridge; h of Annie, Hindley.* SINGAPORE MEMORIAL. [X]

**HILTON Edward,** Cpl. 2886684 1st Bn. The Gordon Highlanders. Died of wounds 18 August 1944 in Normandy. Aged 28. *s of John & Ellen, Leigh.* RYES WAR CEMETERY, FRANCE. [L/LPC]

**HILTON Frank,** Flying Offr. 118642 R.A.F. (V.R.) 295 Sqdn. Died 19 May 1943. Aged 29. *s of William & Martha, Ince; h of Alice, Hindley Green.* INCE CEMETERY. [IN]

**HILTON Frank Basil Edge**, Sjt. 1895161 Royal Engineers. Died of diptheria in a Middle East hospital 28 October 1943. Aged 29. *s of Frank & Alice Ann*. RAMLEH CEMETERY, ISRAEL. [T/TMC]

**HILTON George Sanders**, A.C.1. 1403363 R.A.F. (V.R.) Died 13 August 1941. Aged 20. *s of Henry & Ellen, Bickershaw*. ABRAM (ST JOHN) CHURCHYARD. [B]

**HILTON John**, Sgt (Flt. Engr.) 1496574 R.A.F. (V.R.) 51 Sqdn. 9 June 1944. Aged 22. This Halifax III took-off from Snaith to bomb lines of communication. It crashed on return near the airfield at Holme-on-Spalding Moor, Yorkshire, with the loss of the entire crew. *s of George & Ethel, Orrell; h of Brenda Joy, Trysull*. TRYSULL (ALL SAINTS) CHURCHYARD, TRYSULL & SEISDON, STAFFORDSHIRE. [OC]

**HILTON John**, Fus. 14550545 2/5th Bn. The Lancashire Fusiliers. Killed in action in Normandy, 17 July 1944. Aged 19. *s of Wilfred & Ethel, Pemberton*. FONTENEY-LE-PESNEL CEMETERY. [HIY]

**HILTON John**, Spr. 14594042 Royal Engineers. Died in a Liverpool hospital, 9 January 1946. Aged 39. *s of J. & M.Hilton; h of E Hilton*. ABRAM (ST JOHN) CHURCHYARD. [ABC]

**HILTON Robert**, Spr. 1873626 240th Army Field Coy., Royal Engineers. Died 13 April 1941. Aged 25. *h of Annie, Higher Ince*. INCE-IN-MAKERFIELD CEMETERY. [IN]

**HILTON Ronald**, Sgt. 581219 R.A.F. 10 Sqdn. 7 September 1940. Aged 21. A Whitley V on an operation to bomb the Salzhot Oil Depot in Berlin was lost without trace. The five members of the crew have no known graves. *s of William & Amelia, Leigh*. RUNNYMEDE MEMORIAL. [L/LGS/LTC]

**HILTON Thomas**, A.C.2. 1535907 R.A.F. (V.R.) Died 7 March 1942. Aged 20. *s of Thomas & Mary, Standish*. STANDISH (OUR LADY) R.C. CHURCHYARD. [SSM/ST]

**HINCHCLIFFE Alexander Herbert**, Gunner 1131693 76 (The Shropshire Yeomanry) Medium Regiment., Royal Artillery. Killed 27 March 1944 in Italy. Aged 33. *s of Joseph & Jennie, Chorley. (Gnr. Hinchcliffe was Chief Assistant Librarian at Leigh from 1933 until he joined the army in October 1941)*. CASSINO WAR CEMETERY, ITALY. [X]

**HINDLEY Frederick**, A.B. D/JX290093 R.N. H.M.S. *President III*. 21 December 1943. Aged 22. MALTA (CAPUCCINI) NAVAL CEMETERY. [L/LMC]

**HINDLEY James**, A.B. (Radar) D/JX420121 *Mentioned in Despatches* R.N. *H.M.M.T.B. 673* 27 June 1944 Aged 19. Killed during naval action in the English Channel. *s of James & Lily Mary, Leigh*. DARTMOUTH (LONGCROSS) CEMETERY. [L/LGS/LTA]

**HINDLEY John,** Sgt. (W.Op/Air Gnr.) 1035580 R.A.F. (V.R.) 621 Sqdn. Killed in an air accident in East Africa, 23 November 1943. Aged 22. *s of William & Minnie, Astley.* HARGEISA WAR CEMETERY, SOMALI REPUBLIC. [T]

**HISLOP Edward,** Pilot Offr. (Pilot) 187942 R.A.F. (V.R.) 24 December 1944. Aged 29. This Halifax III from Pocklington attacked targets in Mulheim and was caught in a barrage, was then abandoned and crashed near Krefeld. Two of the crew were killed; five became PoWs. *s of Edward & Jane; h of Ellen, Newtown.* REICHSWALD FOREST WAR CEMETERY, GERMANY. [X]

**HITCHEN Thomas,** Gnr. 934135 137 Field Regiment, Royal Artillery. Killed 23 November 1944 in the Far East. He has no known grave. Aged 26. *s of Samuel & Ellen,Pemberton.* RANGOON MEMORIAL. [W/PC]

**HOCKEN Harold Barlow,** A.C.2. 549560 R.A.F. Lost in the sinking of H.M.S. *Courageous* by German U-boats west of Ireland 17 September 1939. Aged 18. RUNNYMEDE MEMORIAL. [A/HBC]
(See also: Horace Barker and Percival Waldron.)

**HODGE Donald Hartley,** Sgt. (Pilot) 1104390 R.A.F. (V.R.) 99 Sqdn. 1 September 1941. Aged 20. While attempting to land on return from a raid over Germany, the Wellington bomber of which Sgt. Hodge was pilot was shot down by a German Ju 88 intruder and it crashed near Mildenhall, Suffolk. There was only one survivor from a crew of six. LEIGH CEMETERY. [BDC/L/LGS]

**HODGE Frederick,** Pilot Offr. 135701 R.A.F. (V.R.) Killed in a flying accident in California 5 February 1943 when two Spitfires crashed during a training exercise. Aged 22. *s of Thomas & Margaret Jane, Leigh.* SACRAMENTO (EAST LAWN) CEMETERY, CALIFORNIA, U.S.A. [BDC/L/LGS]

**HODGKINSON Frank Edward,** Pte. K/10173 Seaforth Highlanders of Canada. Killed in Italy 9 August 1944. Aged 21. *s of Frank & Violet, Prince Rupert, Canada. His parents were married in Leigh in 1922 and he was born in the town. The family subsequently emigrated to Canada but clearly still had relatives and connections in the area.* FLORENCE WAR CEMETERY [L/LTC]

**HODGKINSON Herbert Eric,** L.Bdr. 1578153 17 Coast Regiment, Royal Artillery. Died as a PoW of the Italians 11 January 1943. Aged 25. *Elder s of Cllr. Herbert Hayward & Annie, Bickershaw; h of Mary Patricia.* CASERTA WAR CEMETERY, ITALY. [B/W]

**HODGKINSON William,** Pte. 4121734 The Cheshire Regiment, attd. to H.Q.I. Corps. Killed in Belgium during the fall back to Dunkirk sometime between 27 May 1940 - 2 June 1940. Aged 30. *s of John &Maria; h of Lily.* DUNKIRK MEMORIAL. [A/HBC]

**HODGSON John,** Pte. 1695570 2/6th Bn. Queen's Royal Regiment (West Surrey) Killed 19 December 1944 in Italy. Aged 30. *s of William James & Cecilia; h of Gwendoline Marie, Wigan.* FORTI WAR CEMETERY, ITALY. [X]

**HODSON Fred,** Sjt. 1114307 81 Anti-Tank Regiment, Royal Artillery. Killed 19 February 1944 in Italy. Aged 27. *s of Jack & Florence; h of Annie, Atherton.* CASSINO MEMORIAL [HAC]

**HODSON Frederick,** Gnr. 967075 106 (The Lancashire Hussars) Lt. A.A. Regiment, Royal Artillery. Killed in action at sea during the evacuation of Greece, 26/27 April 1941. Aged 24. *s of Mr & Mrs A., Westleigh; h of Edna, Leigh.* ATHENS MEMORIAL. {L/LGS/T]

**HODSON Thomas,** Tpr. 3458675 Royal Wiltshire Yeomanry, R.A.C. Killed in Italy 20 June 1944. Aged 32. *s of Harold & Helen; h of Margaret.* ASSISI WAR CEMETERY. [BDC/L]

**HODSON William,** Pilot Offr.(W.Op/Air Gnr.) 185072 R.A.F. (V.R.) 226 Sqdn. Killed 19 November 1944 in a Mitchell aircraft. JONKERBOS WAR CEMETERY, HOLLAND. [G/GOC]

**HOGAN Joseph,** Sjt. 3442645 2<sup>nd</sup> Bn. The Lancashire Fusiliers. Died of wounds in a Brussels hospital, 8 September 1940. As this was several months after the surrender of Belgium, he would have been a PoW of the Germans. Aged 37. *s of Thomas & Susan; h of Annie.* BRUSSELS TOWN CEMETERY. [W]

**HOLCROFT John,** Tpr. 3850655 18<sup>th</sup> (5<sup>th</sup> Bn. The Loyal Regiment [North Lancashire] ) Regiment, Reconnaissance Corps. Captured at the fall of Singapore and died while a PoW of the Japanese working on the Burma-Siam railway. 7 June 1943. Aged 43. *s of Thomas & Elizabeth; h of Alice, Hindley.* THANBYUZAYAT WAR CEMETERY. [X]

**HOLCROFT John Henry,** Sjt. T/121069 Royal Army Service Corps. Died 31 December 1943 as a PoW of the Japanese. Aged 25. *s of Robert Henry & Elizabeth, Appley Bridge.* KANCHANABURI WAR CEMETERY, THAILAND. [S/AP/APC]

**HOLCROFT Joseph Henry,** Pte. 3856322 2<sup>nd</sup> Bn. The Loyal Regiment (North Lancashire) Posted missing in March 1942 and died as a PoW of the Japanese 16 June 1943. Aged 23. *s of Joseph & Frances Elizabeth.* KANCHANABURI WAR CEMETERY, THAILAND. [L/LTA]

**HOLDCROFT William,** Pte. 3391403 The East Lancashire Regiment. Killed in a motor accident 30 August 1941. Aged 28. *h of Mary, Platt Bridge.* HINDLEY CEMETERY. [PBC]
(Some sources give the spelling as *Holcroft*)

**HOLDEN Frank,** Fus. 3453100 1/8<sup>th</sup> Bn. Lancashire Fusiliers. Killed 7 May 1944 in India. Aged 25. *He had family connections in Ashton-in-Makerfield.* KOHIMA WAR CEMETERY, INDIA. [ACC/AMS]

**HOLDEN Kenneth,** Pte. 14641776 1/7<sup>th</sup> Bn. Royal Warwickshire Regiment. Died of wounds in France, 31 July 1944. Aged 19. *s of Samuel & Alice.* RYES WAR CEMETERY, FRANCE. [L]

**HOLDEN Kenneth David**, Sgt.(Flt. Egr.) 2209331 R.A.F. (V.R.) Killed in a flying accident in Yorkshire, 15 April 1944. Aged 20. TYLDESLEY CEMETERY. [A/HAC]

**HOLDEN Stanley**, L.A.C. 1381908 R.A.F. (V.R.) Killed in the U.S.A. 10 December 1941. Aged 30. *s of Mr. & Mrs. James, Pemberton; h of E.M.J.* MONTGOMERY (OAKWOOD) CEMETERY ANNEXE, ALABAMA. [W/WGS]

**HOLDEN Thomas**, L.A.C. 1141226 R.A.F. (V.R.) 32 Sqdn. Died in the Middle East, 6 September 1945. Aged 36. *s of Issac & Annie; h of Doris, Ashton-in-Makerfield.* KHAYAT BEACH WAR CEMETERY, ISRAEL. [ACC]

**HOLDEN William**, Pte. 3856655 9th Bn. Durham Light Infantry. Killed in Sicily, 17 July 1943. Aged 24. CATANIA WAR CEMETERY, ITALY. [A]

**HOLDING Allan**, Ldg. Seaman. P/JX186811 R.N. H.M.S. *President III* . Lost in s.s. *River Afton* 4 July 1942. Aged 27. The s.s. *River Afton* was part of the ill-fated Russia-bound convoy PQ-17 which suffered terrible losses. This ship was sunk by U-boat *U-703*. *s of James & Elizabeth; h of Myra T.* PORTSMOUTH NAVAL MEMORIAL. [W]

**HOLDING James Anthony**, Sgt. 3527184 2nd Bn. Grenadier Guards. Died of pneumonia 26 October 1939 Aged 22. *s of Joseph & Sarah.* WIGAN CEMETERY. [WPC]

**HOLDING Leslie**, Sgt. 1672421 R.A.F. (V.R.) Died 5 September 1943. Aged 20. *s of Thomas & Florence, Beech Hill, Wigan.* STANDISH (ST WILFRID) CHURCHYARD. [BHC/STC/W]

**HOLDING Thomas**, Dvr. T/50235 Royal Army Service Corps. Killed in a road accident, 9 September 1940 Aged 31. *s of Reubin & Margaret; h of Alice.* PEMBERTON (ST JOHN'S) CHURCHYARD. [W/PC]

**HOLLAND Arthur**, W.O. 1028124 R.A.F. (V.R.) 44 Sqdn. 7 July 1944. Aged 29. A Lancaster I bomber from Dunholme Lodge attacked a flying-bomb storage depot at St-Le-d'Esserent. It came down at Equennes-Eramecourt and the whole crew was laid to rest in the local churchyard. *h of Joan.* EQUENNES CHURCHYARD, FRANCE. [AIM/AMS]

**HOLLAND Norman**, Pte. 3533023 1st Bn. The Manchester Regiment. Died as a PoW of the Japanese, 21 September 1944. Aged 25. *Foster s of Joseph & Jane Ann Naylor, Golborne.* SINGAPORE MEMORIAL [AIM]

**HOLLAND Philip** Sgt. 2614992 1st Bn. Grenadier Guards. Killed in action at Arnhem, 26 September 1944. BERGEN-OP-ZOOM CEMETERY, HOLLAND. [W]

**HOLLAND Thomas**, Pte. 4465149 9th Bn. Durham Light Infantry. Killed in action in North Africa, 22 March 1943. Aged 29. *His parents lived in Ince; h of Florence.* ENFIDAVILLE WAR CEMETERY, TUNISIA. [IN/ISM]

**HOLLINSHEAD James Frederick,** Gnr. 14951399 56 Medium Regiment, Royal Artillery. He died in Dereham (Norfolk) Hospital, 16 August 1945. Aged 18. *s of J.W. & E.E. Hollinshead, Pemberton.* WIGAN CEMETERY. [W]

**HOLLIS Thomas,** Cpl. 1875764 Royal Engineers Killed in Burma 25 May 1944. Aged 29. RANGOON MEMORIAL. [PBC]

**HOLLOWAY Victor Douglas, (See DOUGLAS Victor)**

**HOLMAN Leonard,** Pte. 14663426 The Cheshire Regiment. Died 11 June 1946 Aged 31. *s of Edgar & Lizzie Holman; h of Dora Holman, Leigh.* ATHERTON CEMETERY. [L]

**HOLME Albert,** Cpl. 618398 R.A.F. Died of wounds in Italy. 18 February 1944. Aged 28. *s of John & Margaret, Lower Ince.* SALERNO WAR CEMETERY, ITALY [IN/ISM]

**HOLME Harry Pears,** Sgt.. (Air Gnr.) 1301281 R.A.F. (V.R.) 75 Sqdn. 28 April 1943. Aged 35. A Stirling III bomber on a minelaying operation was hit by flak and crashed into the Baltic with the loss of all seven members of the crew – five having no known grave. This squadron lost four bombers on this particular operation and twenty-eight aircrew died. On this night, Bomber Command lost twenty-four aircraft and one hundred and forty-five aircrew died. *s of Thomas & Sarah; h of Eveline, Lower Ince.* SVINØ CHURCHYARD, DENMARK. [IN/ISM]

**HOLT Arthur,** Spr. 216716 1015 Port Operating Coy. Royal Engineers. Killed in Italy 29 May 1945. Aged 33. *s of Daniel & Margaret; h of Margaret Emily.* BARI WAR CEMETERY, ITALY. [L]

**HOLT Frank,** Sgt. 1163169 R.A.F. (V.R.) 3 Sqdn. Killed 14 August 1941 aged 25. He left Biggin Hill in his Hurricane fighter aircraft, but failed to return from an intruder sortie to Le Touquet. *s of Charles & Margaret, Orrell.* RUNNYMEDE MEMORIAL. [OC/OCY/WGS]

**HOLT Herbert Collier,** Pte. 3531411 5th Bn. The Manchester Regiment. He became a PoW at Dunkirk in May 1940 and subsequently contracted tubercolosis in a German camp. He was a patient in various hospitals after the war and was allowed home shortly before he died 20 March 1947. Aged 26. ATHERTON CEMETERY. [A/HBC]

**HONDERWOOD William Stewart,** L.A.C. 569469 R.A.F. 73 Sqdn. Lost in the sinking of s.s. *Lancastria,* 17 June 1940. Aged 20. RUNNYMEDE MEMORIAL. [G/GOC]
(Twelve other local men perished when this ship was sunk. See the **Herbert Cunliffe** entry for names and details of the loss.)

**HOOSON Stanley,** L.Cpl. 3781210 9th Bn. The Royal Fusiliers (City of London Regiment.) Killed 5 September 1944. Aged 34. *h of Annie.* CASSINO MEMORIAL. [SGC/W]

**HOOTON Ernest,** Cpl. 3968732 1/5<sup>th</sup> Bn. The Welch Regiment. Killed in action in Holland 23 September 1944. Aged 28. BERGEN-OP-ZOOM WAR CEMETERY, HOLLAND. [W]
(Cpl. Hooton is listed on the Wigan memorial as serving in the Army Air Corps. His service number and CWGC records show he was with the Welch Regiment.)

**HOOTON Francis,** Sgt. 1381953 R.A.F. (V.R.) 405 (R.C.A.F.) Sqdn. 29 November 1942. Aged 31. Sgt. Hooton and fourteen R.C.A.F. airmen died when a Halifax bomber on a ferrying flight to Beaulieu crashed near Melberley, Yorkshire. This was amongst the worst of the non-operational accidents of the Second World War. *s of Peter & Ann; h of Elizabeth.* STANDISH (OUR LADY) R.C. CHURCHYARD. [SSM/WGS]

**HORNBY James,** Pte. 2188588 Auxiliary Military Pioneer Corps. Killed by enemy action 31 October 1940 in the U.K. Aged 37. WIGAN CEMETERY. [W]
(He is shown on the Wigan Cenotaph as serving in the Royal Engineers at the time of his death. His service number indicates that, for a time at least, he served in the Royal Engineers.)

**HORNBY Walter G.** Fus. 3525780 2<sup>nd</sup> Bn. The Lancashire Fusiliers. Killed during the evacuation of Dunkirk. 26 May 1940. Aged 24. *s of James & Mary, Wallgate, Wigan.* HALLUIN COMMUNAL CEMETERY, FRANCE. [W]

**HORRABIN John,** Tpr. 3856744 18<sup>th</sup> (5<sup>th</sup> Bn. The Loyal Regiment [North Lancashire] ) Regiment, Reconaissance Corps. Died 22 July 1943 whilst being held as a PoW of the Japanese in a Thailand camp. Aged 24. THANBYUZAYAT WAR CEMETERY. [A]

**HORROCKS David Wilson,** Pilot Offr. (Pilot) 74653 R.A.F. (V.R.) 40 Sqdn. 27 June 1941. Aged 23. His Wellington bomber crashed near Eeklo, Belgium with the loss of all the members of the crew. *s of John & Agnes, Leigh; h of Gladys Audrey, Salisbury, Southern Rhodesia. P.O. Horrocks was in the Colonial Service before the war. He was married only thirteen days before his death.* RUNNYMEDE MEMORIAL. [L/LMC]

**HORROCKS Kenneth,** A.C.1. 1511178 R.A.F. (V.R.) Killed 9 July 1943 in the Middle East. Aged 20. *s of James & Amy.* ALEXANDRIA (HADRA) WAR MEMORIAL CEMETERY, EGYPT. [L/LMC]

**HORROCKS Thomas,** Flt. Sgt. 650027 R.A.F. (V.R.) 617 Sqdn. 7 October 1944. Aged 22. A Lancaster I bomber from Woodhall Spa attacked the Kembs Dam but was hit by flak near the target. It flew on before being put down in the Rhine near the border town of Chalampe. He has no known grave. RUNNYMEDE MEMORIAL. [L/LAS/LTC]

**HOSLER Albert,** Pte. M/16880 The Royal Canadian Infantry Corps (Edmonton Regiment) 26 February 1941. Aged 31. *s of Thomas & Elizabeth, Newtown. Pte Hosler emigrated to Canada in 1929.* HIGHFIELD (ST MATTHEW) CHURCHYARD. [W]

**HOUGH Martin,** L.Cpl. T/202444 Royal Army Service Corps. Died as a PoW of the Japanese. 18 December 1944. Aged 49. *L.Cpl Hough was considerably older than the average for soldiers serving in H.M.F. He was a First World War veteran.* KANCHANABURI WAR CEMETERY, THAILAND. [W]

**HOUGH Ralph,** Pte. 14662764 2$^{nd}$ Bn. The Bedfordshire & Hertfordshire Regiment. Killed in Italy 25 November 1944. Aged 27. *s of Richard & Margaret; h of Hilda.* FORLI WAR CEMETERY, ITALY. [W]

**HOUGHTON Arthur,** Cpl. 3656349 2$^{nd}$ Bn. The Lancashire Fusiliers. Killed 17 May 1944, in Italy. CASSINO WAR CEMETERY. [L]

**HOUGHTON Jack,** A.B. P/JX219794 R.N. H.M.S. *Grasshopper.* Died 5 February 1945 as a PoW of the Japanese. Aged 31. He had been captured in December 1942 when the gunboat H.M.S *Grasshopper* was driven ashore on Sianpeng Island, Sumatra. *s of Robert & Ellen Ann, Hindley Green.* PORTSMOUTH NAVAL MEMORIAL. [X]

**HOUGHTON James,** Dvr. 2359679 Royal Corps of Signals, 'N' Corps Signals. Died whilst being held as a PoW of the Japanese 16 December 1943. Aged 38. *s of John & Helen; h of Beatrice Gladys.* KANCHANABURI WAR CEMETERY, THAILAND. [JC/W/WPC]

**HOUGHTON James William Harold,** A.B. D/MD/X2976 R.N.V.R. H.M.S. *Lively.* 11 May 1942. Aged 28. This destroyer was sunk after being attacked by German Ju-88 aircraft south of Crete. *s of Albert & Margaret Alice, Pemberton.* PLYMOUTH NAVAL MEMORIAL. [HIC/W]

**HOUGHTON John,** L.Cpl. 3525406 1$^{st}$ Bn. The Manchester Regiment. Died whilst being held as a PoW of the Japanese. 13 July 1943. Aged 32. *s of George & Harriet, Wigan.* THANBYUZAYAT WAR CEMETERY, BURMA. [SCC/W]

**HOUGHTON Walter,** Engine Room Artificer. D/SMX225 R.N. H.M.S. *Bramble.* 31 December 1942. Aged 28. While on escort duty to Russia, this minesweeper was sunk by the German heavy cruiser *Admiral Hipper* north of North Cape. *s of George Arthur & Elizabeth Alice, Leigh.* PLYMOUTH NAVAL MEMORIAL [L/LTC] (See also: John Winstanley.)

**HOUGHTON William,** A.C.2. 1019729 R.A.F. (V.R.) 16 August 1941 in Egypt.. Aged 29. *s of Henry & Elizabeth Ellen, Hindley; h of Annie, Hindley.* ISMAILIA WAR MEMORIAL CEMETERY, EGYPT. [HC]

**HOUSLEY Stanley,** A.B. P/JX177831 R.N. H.M.S. *Arrow.* 4 August 1943. Aged 23. A.B. Housley was killed when the destroyer on which he was serving was severely damaged by the explosion of an ammunition ship at Algiers. *s of John & Rose Ann, Pemberton.* PORTSMOUTH NAVAL MEMORIAL. [W/GGC]

**HOWARD James,** Spr. 14762528 Royal Engineers. Died 4 June 1947. Aged 31. *s of Moses & Ellen; h of Florence Millicent, Wigan.* WIGAN CEMETERY. [W]

**HOWARD Thomas,** Dvr. 2019927 9 Bomb Disposal Coy., Royal Engineers. Killed by enemy action in the Midlands, 12 December 1940. Aged 26. PEMBERTON (ST JOHN'S) CHURCHYARD [W/PC]

**HOWARD William,** L.A.C. 993714 R.A.F. (V.R.) Died of pneumonia 21 March 1943. Aged 27. *h of Kathleen, Kitt Green.* UP HOLLAND CEMETERY. [X]

**HOWARTH Harry,** Sgt. (Air Gnr.) 1509468 R.A.F. (V.R.) 191 Sqdn. Died in India, 2 October 1943. Aged 21. *s of Walter & Annie, Newtown.* KARACHI WAR CEMETERY. [W]

**HOWARTH Jack,** Pte. 3455018 2nd Bn. The Essex Regiment. Killed in action in Holland, 23 February 1945. Aged 28. *s of John & Mary; h of Ann.* JONKERBOS WAR CEMETERY, HOLLAND. [L]

**HOWARTH James,** Pte. 3526669 5th Bn. The Manchester Regiment Killed 28 May 1940 during the withdrawal to Dunkirk. Aged 27. REXPOEDE COMMUNAL CEMETERY, FRANCE. [SCC/W]

**HOWE William Henry,** Gdsmn. 2664481 2nd Bn. Coldstream Guards. Killed 26 February 1944. Aged 22. *s of Joseph C. & Sarah, Westhoughton.* NAPLES WAR CEMETERY. [HGS]

**HUGHES Gilbert,** Pte. 3859534 1st Bn. The Gordon Highlanders Killed in action 23 October 1942 in the Middle East. Aged 26. *s of Edward & Emma; h of Edna Elizabeth, Newtown.* EL ALAMEIN WAR CEMETERY, EGYPT. [SGC/W]

**HUGHES Harold,** Pte. 3859504 1st Bn The Loyal Regiment (North Lancashire). Died 2 March 1946 in Italy. Aged 26. *s of Nathaniel & Alice, Bryn.* BOLOGNA WAR CEMETERY, ITALY. [AMS/BNC]

**HUGHES James,** Sgt. 2206716 R.A.F. (V.R.) 408 Sqdn. 25 April 1945. He was a member of the crew of a Halifax bomber which left Linton-on-Ouse to bomb gun positions at Wangerooge. It collided in the target area with another Halifax resulting in the deaths of all fourteen airmen from both aircraft. Aged 28. *s of Edwin & Annie, Bamfurlong.* RUNNYMEDE MEMORIAL. [ABC/AIM/BMC]

**HUGHES James Henry,** Pte. 4924328 The South Staffordshire Regiment. Died 29 November 1945. Aged 33. *h of Olive.* LEIGH CEMETERY. [X]

**HUGHES John,** A.B. D/SSX28252 R.N. H.M.S. *Neptune.* 19 December 1941. Aged 23. This cruiser ran on to a minefield while hunting an Italian convoy and sank with the loss of all but one of her entire crew. *s of John & Mary Ellen.* PLYMOUTH NAVAL MEMORIAL. [HGC/T]
(See also: Colin F. Coppock; Douglas Pilling; Joseph Simm.)

**HUGHES John,** Fus. 3451736 1/8th Bn. The Lancashire Fusiliers. Killed in Belgium, 10 May 1940. Aged 21. WORMHONDT COMMUNAL CEMETERY, DUNKIRK. [AS/ASC]

**HUGHES John,** Craftsman 2014217 Royal Electrical & Mechanical Engineers. Killed in Italy 1 August 1944. Aged 28. *s of John & Elizabeth; h of Dorothy, Astley.* AREZZO WAR CEMETERY. [X]

**HUGHES Jonathan,** Pte. 3530101 6th Bn. The York & Lancaster Regiment. Killed in action in Italy 13 September 1944. Aged 25. *s of Mr. & Mrs. E., Tyldesley.* CORIANO RIDGE WAR CEMETERY, ITALY. [X]

**HUGHES Robert Owen,** Sub. Lieut.(A) R.N. H.M.S. *Triumph.* He was a pilot in the Fleet Air Arm and was killed 7 March 1947 while operating from this aircraft carrier. Age 21. He has no known grave. *s of Albert E. & Ethel B., Wigan.* LEE-ON-SOLENT MEMORIAL. [BHC]

**HUGHES Thomas,** Gnr. 1823563 55 H.A.A. Regiment, Royal Artillery. Died of wounds, 6 October 1942. RAMLEH WAR CEMETERY. [W]

**HULME Herbert H.** Pte. 3451927 1st Airborne Bn. The Border Regiment. Killed in Sicily, 10 July 1943. Aged 24. *s of Robert & Hilda; h of Ellen Mary.* SYRACUSE WAR CEMETERY. [B]

**HULME John,** Dvr. T/272664 Royal Army Service Corps attd. Royal Artillery. Died whilst being held as a PoW of the Japanese 15 July 1945. Aged 31. *s of William & Alice Hulme; h of Phyllis Hulme.* LABUAN WAR CEMETERY, NORTH BORNEO. [L/LMC]

**HULME John Ernest,** Spr. 1892812 54 Field Coy., Royal Engineers. Killed in the Middle East 23 November 1941. KNIGHTSBRIDGE WAR CEMETERY, LIBYA. [AC/NAV]

**HULME Robert,** A.B. D/JX399799 R.N. H.M.S. *President III* but lost in m.v. *Derrycunihy* 26 June 1944. Aged 30. The cargo ship was sunk by a mine off the Normandy beaches. *s of Robert & Hilda, Bickershaw.* PLYMOUTH NAVAL MEMORIAL. [B]

**HUNT John William,** Sgt. (Air Gnr.) 615956 R.A.F. 102 Sqdn. 26 February 1943. Aged 35. The Halifax II bomber was shot down over Cologne. All eight members of the crew perished. RHEINBERG WAR CEMETERY. [L]

**HUNT Oswald,** Sgt. 1515438 R.A.F. (V.R.) 23 September 1943. Aged 26. *h of Marion May.* HIGHFIELD (ST MATTHEW) CHURCHYARD. [W]

**HUNTER Alexander Smith,** Pte. 3657542 1st Bn. The South Lancashire Regiment (The Prince of Wales's Volunteers). Died of wounds in France 15 August 1944. Aged 28. *h of Ellen.* BAYEAUX WAR CEMETERY, FRANCE. [T/TC]

**HUNTER Hamish Macbean,** Lieut. 156640 18th Bn. Reconnaissance Corps. Died in England, 24 September 1941 Aged 24. *s of Dr. James & Margaret.* ASHTON-IN-MAKERFIELD (ST THOMAS) CHURCHYARD. [AIM/WGS]

**HUNTER James**, Sjt. 5835260 3 Bty., 6 H.A.A. Regiment, Royal Artillery. Died 3 March 1943 whilst being held as a PoW of the Japanese. He has no known grave.. Aged 28. *s of Richard & Mary; h of Isabel, Wigan.* SINGAPORE MEMORIAL. [W/WPC]

**HUNTER Joseph**, Gnr. 919590 240 Bty., 77 H.A.A. Regiment, Royal Artillery. Died whilst being held as a PoW of the Japanese 6 June 1943. Aged 21. AMBON WAR CEMETERY, INDONESIA. [X]

**HURST George**, Pte. 4978033 1st Bn. The York & Lancaster Regiment. Killed 16 October 1943 in Italy. Aged 29. *s of Mr. & Mrs. Albert, Wigan.* BARI WAR CEMETERY, ITALY. [X]

**HURST George Frederick**, Pte. 3861868 The Loyal Regiment (North Lancashire) Died 10 October 1947. *h of Ellen.* HINDLEY CEMETERY. [X]

**HURST Herbert Kitchener**, Sgt. 1588410 R.A.F. (V.R.) 463 (R.A.A.F.) Sqdn. Died 26 March 1945. Aged 28. *h of Winifred.* WIGAN CEMETERY. [X]

**HURST John**, Pilot Offr. 121463 *D.F.C.* R.A.F. (V.R.) 603 Sqdn. Killed 2 July 1942 while flying a Spitfire during the defence of Malta. Aged 24. *s of James & Annie; h of Winifred Maud.* MALTA MEMORIAL. [X]

**HURST John Charles**, Sgt. 745671 R.A.F. (V.R.) Died 30 September 1940 Aged 20. *s of Ernest & Edith, Billinge.* BILLINGE (ST AIDAN) CHURCHYARD. [W/WGS/WPC]

**HUXLEY Joseph**, L.Cpl. 3717506 Movement Control Group, Royal Engineers. Died of wounds 28 March 1945 in Belgium. Aged 26. *h of Winifred, Wigan.* SCHOONSELHOF CEMETERY, ANTWERP. [SCC/W/WSB]

**HYLAND Kenneth Arthur**, A.C.2. 1545648 R.A.F. (V.R.) Killed 25 June 1942 in the Middle East. Aged 19. *s of John & Annie, Wigan.* EL ALAMEIN WAR CEMETERY, EGYPT. [W]

**HYLAND Lawrence**, Cpl. 3527162 2nd Bn. The York & Lancaster Regiment, attd. H.Q. 14th. Infantry Brigade. Died of typhus in India, 12 June 1944. Aged 27. *s of Mr. & Mrs. James Hyland, Wigan; h of D. Hyland.* GAUHATI WAR CEMETERY, INDIA. [X]

**INGHAM Arthur**, Spr. 1912431 663 Artisan Works Coy., Royal Engineers. Died during the evacuation of St Nazaire, sometime between 6 and 10 July 1940. Aged 24. *s of James Maden & Mary Jane.* ESCOUBLAC-LA-BAULE CEMETERY, FRANCE. [L/LAS/LTC]

**INGHAM William**, Gnr. 1087197 178 Field Regiment, Royal Artillery. He died of wounds in Burma 7 March 1944. Aged 31. *s of William & Jesse Ingham; h of Hannah Ingham, Toplock, Wigan.* TAUKKYAN WAR CEMETERY, BURMA. [AS/ASC]

**INGRAM John,** Sgt. 784432 4 H.A.A. Regiment, Royal Artillery. Killed in Malta, 7 March 1942. Aged 33. *s of Mr. & Mrs. J; h of Mary C.* PEMBROKE MILITARY CEMETERY, MALTA. [AS]

**IRVING Clifford,** Pte. 3858821 1<sup>st</sup> Bn. The Loyal Regiment (North Lancashire) Killed in Italy 14 February 1944. Aged 26. *s of John & Ellen, Ashton-in-Makerfield.* ANZIO WAR CEMETERY, ITALY. [ACC/AMS]

**IRVING Thomas Malcolm,** 3<sup>rd</sup> Radio Officer, Merchant Navy s.s. *Fort Missanabie.* He died 19 May 1944 on only his second voyage when this cargo ship was sunk shortly after leaving the port of Taranto by the German U-boat *U-453. s of Mr & Mrs Robert W., Worsley.* TOWER HILL MEMORIAL [LGS]

**ISHERWOOD Ernest,** Spr. 2002126 256 Field Coy., Royal Engineers. 27 November 1942. Aged 24. *s of Mr. & Mrs. Ernest; h of Clarice.* ASPULL (ST ELIZABETH) CHURCHYARD. [BCC/BL/AS/ASC]

**ISHERWOOD Mary,** L.A.C.W. 2085214 W.A.A.F. Killed in a motor accident at St Eval, Cornwall, 7 November 1945. Aged 22. She was to have been married the following month. *d of Frank & Alice, Leigh.* LEIGH CEMETERY. [L]

**ISHERWOOD Samuel,** Flt Sgt. (Air Gnr.) 634050 R.A.F. 617 Sqdn. 24 June 1944. Aged 22. He took-off from Woodhall Spa in a Lancaster I armed with a Tallboy bomb in an attempt to destroy a flying-bomb site at Wizernes. His aircraft was hit by flak and crashed near St Omer with the loss of five members of the crew. *s of Lucy; h of Mary Alice, New Springs.* LEULINGHEM CHURCHYARD, FRANCE. [X]

**JACKSON Clifford,** Sjt. 3443426 2<sup>nd</sup> Bn. The Glasgow Highlanders, Highland Light Infantry (City of Glasgow Regiment.) Killed 22 September 1944 in Holland. Aged 25. *s of Mr. & Mrs. T; h of Anne, Wigan.* MIERLO WAR CEMETERY, HOLLAND. [SSC/W]

**JACKSON Edward Earle,** Gnr. K/75081 Royal Canadian Artillery. Died 4 February 1942. *He had local family connections and presumably emigrated to Canada before the war.* WIGAN CEMETERY. [X]

**JACKSON Frederick,** L.A.C. 1957570 R.A.F. (V.R.) 2735 Sqdn. R.A.F. Regiment. Died 14 July 1942. Aged 36. *s of Levi & Mary Ellen, Astley; h of Annie.* ATHERTON CEMETERY. [X]

**JACKSON George,** Telegraphist D/SSX28723 R.N. H.M.S. *Diamond.* 27 April 1941. Aged 21. While leaving Nauplia, this destroyer was sunk by German Stuka dive-bombers. It was carrying survivors from ships sunk in a previous action. *s of Joseph & Hannah, Tyldelsley.* PLYMOUTH NAVAL MEMORIAL [T/TC] (See also: Thomas Lawrenson.)

**JACKSON John,** Pte. 3528007 1<sup>st</sup> Bn. The Manchester Regiment. 19 January 1942. Aged 23. SINGAPORE MEMORIAL. [W]

**JACKSON John Edward,** Gnr. 11005382 25 Coast Regiment, Royal Artillery. Died 2 July 1943. Aged 37. *h of May.* BROOKWOOD MEMORIAL. [L]

**JACKSON John Henry,** A.B. D/JX306000 R.N. H.M.S. *President III* 8 March 1943. Aged 19. *s of William Henry & Margaret Ann, Orrell.* BUCEO BRITISH CEMETERY, MONTEVIDEO. [OC]

**JACKSON Thomas,** Pte. 2762200 1st Bn. The Black Watch (Royal Highland Regiment) Killed 2 November 1944 in Holland. Aged 28. *s of Herbert & Mary; h of Jane.* VENRAY WAR CEMETERY, HOLLAND. [L]

**JACKSON Thomas,** Pte. 3529270 1st Bn. The Manchester Regiment. 5 September 1943. Aged 26. Died whilst he was being held as a PoW of the Japanese. THANBYUZAYAT WAR CEMETERY. [W/HC]

**JAGGER Donald,** Sgt. (W. Op./Air Gnr.) 2205762 R.A.F. (V.R.) 101 Sqdn. 22 June 1944. Aged 19. A Lancaster I from Ludford Magna crashed at the village of Drunen, Holland. Four of the eight members of the crew were killed. *s of Frederick William & Mary.* JONKERBOS WAR CEMETERY, HOLLAND. [LGS/T/TC]

**JAMESON Benjamin,** Gnr. 1808854 1 Maritime Regiment, Royal Artillery. Killed at sea 31 August 1942. Aged 21. *s of James & Mary Ann.* PORTSMOUTH NAVAL MEMORIAL. [L]

**JAMESON John,** A.B. D/SSX22763 R.N. H.M.S. *Glorious.* 9 June 1940. Aged 23. This aircraft carrier was sunk by the German battlecruisers *Gneisenau* and *Scharnhorst* 300 miles west of Narvik. There were only 43 survivors. *s of Samuel & Margaret, Leigh.* PLYMOUTH NAVAL MEMORIAL. [L/LTA]
(See also: Samuel Alker; Walter L. Duckworth; Edward Knight; Peter McNicholas; John F. Gorton; Benjamin T. Starkie; Frederick Swan.)

**JAMESON Norman,** Sgt. 973079 R.A.F. (V.R.) 90 Sqdn. Died of wounds 26 August 1944. Aged 23. *h of Kathleen Jameson, Wigan.* WIGAN CEMETERY. [JC/W]

**JAQUES Arthur,** Sqdn. Ldr. 128978 *D.F.C. and Bar.* R.A.F. (V.R.) Died 25 October 1945. Aged 30. *s of William & Mary Ellen, Wigan; h of Jean, Wigan.* KILARROW NEW PARISH CHURCHYARD, ISLE OF ISLAY. [STC/WGS]
(His brother Henry Stephen also died on active service.)

**JAQUES Henry Stephen,** Sgt. 968333 R.A.F. (V.R.) Died 29 July 1941. Aged 24. *s of William & Mary, Wigan.* WIGAN CEMETERY. [ST/STC/WGS]
(His brother Arthur also died on active service.)

**JENKINS Harold,** A.B. D/JX221167 R.N. H.M.S. *Prince of Wales.* 10 December 1941. Aged 24. The battleship was sunk by Japanese aircraft off Kuantan, Malaya with the loss of 337 members of the crew. *s of Alfred & Mabel, Hindley.* PLYMOUTH NAVAL MEMORIAL. [HC]
(See also: Jack Ainscough; Stanley Carter.)

**JENKINSON James Arthur**, L.Cpl. 3860170 2nd Bn. The York & Lancaster Regiment; attd. 2nd. Bn. The Royal Leicestershire Regiment. Died in India 29 March 1944. Aged 27. *s of Herbert Richard & Bertha Lilian; h of Barbara.* RANGOON MEMORIAL. [G/GOC]

**JENKINSON James Wilfred**, Telegraphist D/J79620 R.N. H.M. Submarine *Seahorse.* 12 January 1940. Aged 37. This submarine was sunk whilst on patrol in the Heligoland Bight. *s of John Richard & Jane Hannah; h of Martha Elizebeth.* PLYMOUTH NAVAL MEMORIAL. [L]

**JENNINGS Frederick B**. Pte. 14420282 2nd Bn. The Gordon Highlanders. Died of wounds received in action 11 November 1944. Aged 19. His parents were resident in Belfast, but he had lived with his grandmother in Bickershaw for twelve years. ABRAM (ST JOHN) CHURCHYARD. [B]

**JERVIS Frederick Joseph**, Flt. Sgt. 979438 *D.F.M.* R.A.F. (V.R.) Died 25 January 1944. Aged 23. *h of Rosaline.* WIGAN CEMETERY. [W]

**JEX Arthur**, Pte. 3968800 15th Bn. The Welch Regiment. Died 3 November 1940 *h of Annie, Orrell.* ORRELL (ST LUKE) CHURCHYARD. [OC/OCY]

**JOHNSON Alfred**, Marine. PO/104059 Royal Marines. H.M.S. *Glasgow* Died 30 March 1942. Aged 29. *s of Henry & Mary; h of Edith Betty.* PORTSMOUTH NAVAL MEMORIAL. [JC/W]

**JOHNSON Bernard Reginald**, P.O. Motor Mechanic D/MX77669 R.N. *H.M.L.C.F. 1* Killed 17 August 1944. Aged 22. *s of Joseph Reginald & Julia Dorothy.* PLYMOUTH NAVAL MEMORIAL. [LGS]

**JOHNSON Charles Edward**, Marine. PO/X120122 Royal Marines. Killed in Normandy on D-Day, 6 June 1944. Aged 20. *s of Robert & Ann, Hindley.* BAYEAUX WAR CEMETERY. [X]

**JOHNSON Clifford**, Pte. T/157223 51 Division Supply Coy., Royal Army Service Corps. 11 June 1940 Aged 23. He has no known grave. *s of John Henry & Jane; h of Jean May, Wigan;* DUNKIRK MEMORIAL [W]

**JOHNSON Harold**, Fus. 3445894 1/5th Bn. The Lancashire Fusiliers. Killed during the evacuation of Dunkirk sometime between 30 May 1940 and 2 June 1940. He has no known grave. Aged 26. *s of Joseph & Elizabeth; h of Annie, Pemberton.* DUNKIRK MEMORIAL. [W]

**JOHNSON Horace**, Dvr. 1889318 256 Field Coy., Royal Engineers. Killed in action in Italy, 30 October 1944. Aged 25. *s of Herbert & Mary, Leigh; h of Elsie, Lowton-St-Marys.* SANTENO VALLEY WAR CEMETERY, ITALY. [L/LAS/LTC]

**JOHNSON Hugh**, Fus. 3130967 2nd Bn. Royal Scots Fusiliers. Killed 10 July 1943 in Sicily. *s of William & Mary Alice, Darlington Street East, Wigan.* SYRACUSE WAR CEMETERY, SICILY. [WSB]

**JOHNSON Jack,** Sto. 2nd. Class. C/KX100380 R.N. H.M.S. *Kelly.* 9 May 1940. Aged 21. Stoker Johnson was one of twenty crewmen killed when H.M.S. *Kelly* was torpedoed by German E-boats in the North Sea. *s of Samuel & Betsy.* HEBBURN CEMETERY, DURHAM. [X]

**JOHNSON John Bernard,** Flt. Sgt. 1488398 R.A.F. (V.R.) 296 Sqdn. Killed 12 July 1944. Aged 20. *s of John & Sarah, Wigan.* RUNNYMEDE MEMORIAL. [W/WGS]

**JOHNSON Norman Gerrard,** Pte. 3865902 1$^{st}$ Bn. The Loyal Regiment (North Lancashire) He was killed 30 April 1943 while serving somewhere in North Africa.. Aged 20. *His mother lived in Scholes, Wigan.* MASSICAULT WAR CEMETERY, TUNISIA. [X]

**JOHNSON William,** Pte. 3603540 1$^{st}$ (Airborne) Bn. The Border Regiment. Killed during the invasion of Sicily 10 July 1943. Aged 28. *s of William & Nancy, Standish.* CASSINO MEMORIAL. [IN/ST/STC]

**JOHNSON William,** Pte. 3603356 4$^{th}$ Bn. The Border Regiment. Killed 5 December 1941 in the Middle East. *He had family connections in Pemberton.* TOBRUK WAR CEMETERY. [W]

**JOLLEY Joseph Vincent,** L.Cpl. 5682537 *Mentioned in Despatches* 8th. Bn The Royal Fusiliers (City of London Regiment). Died of wounds in Italy, 21 January 1944. Aged 21. *s of Joseph & Mary Elizabeth, Higher Ince.* CASSINO MEMORIAL. [X]

**JONES Arthur,** Sgt. 1297209 R.A.F. (V.R.) 97 Sqdn. He was killed 4 July 1943. Aged 23. His Lancaster bomber left Bourn to bomb Cologne but was shot down. Six of the crew of seven, including Sgt. Jones, have no known grave. RUNNYMEDE MEMORIAL. [AGS]

**JONES Charles Edwin,** Flying. Offr. (Pilot) 130652 R.A.F. (V.R.) 12 Sqdn. 23 November 1943. Aged 24. His Lancaster III bomber was on a bombing raid to Berlin. It crashed at Vrees where all seven members of the crew were buried on 26 November. They have been subsequently laid to rest in Reichswald Forest War Cemetery. *s of William & Elizabeth Ellen, Wigan; h of Muriel, Pemberton.* REICHSWALD FOREST WAR CEMETERY, GERMANY. [JC/W/WGS]

**JONES David,** Tpr. 3715805 1$^{st}$ Royal Tank Regiment, R.A.C. Killed in action in France, 22 August 1944. Aged 30. ST DESIR WAR CEMETERY, FRANCE. [HC]

**JONES Edward,** Tpr. 3522434 7$^{th}$ Royal Tank Regiment, R.A.C. attd. H.Q. 7$^{th}$ Armoured Division. Died 10 May 1942 '...at sea' according to PRO records. Aged 32. *h of Elizabeth and with family connections in the Wigan area.* ALAMEIN MEMORIAL. [X]

**JONES Edward,** Gnr. 11416169 6 Maritime Regiment, Royal Artillery. Lost at sea 8 March 1943. Aged 20. *s of John Harrison & Mary, Tyldesley.* PLYMOUTH NAVAL MEMORIAL. [T]

**JONES Edward**, Flt. Sgt. (Air Bomber) 548901 R.A.F. 37 Sqdn. Killed in action 26 June 1944. *s of Richard & Dora, Ashton-in-Makerfield; h of Lena.* BUDAPEST WAR CEMETERY, HUNGARY. [AIM/AMS]

**JONES Frank**, Fus. 3195221 1st Bn Royal Inniskilling Fusiliers Killed in action in the Far East, 31 March 1943. Aged 27. *s of Thomas & Florence; h of Mary Josephine.* RANGOON MEMORIAL. [L/LTA]
(His brother, Pte. John Thomas Jones was also killed on active service. Both brothers were killed in the Far East; they have no known graves, and both are commemorated on the Rangoon Memorial.)

**JONES Fred Uriah Cook**, A.C.2. 1029526 R.A.F. (V.R.) 118 Sqdn. Died 2 February 1942. Aged 21. *s of William & Sarah, Ashton-in-Makerfield.* ASHTON-IN-MAKERFIELD (ST THOMAS) CHURCHYARD. [ACC]

**JONES George Mathias**, Sgt. 1083449 R.A.F. (V.R.) 270 Sqdn. Killed in a flying accident in West Africa 13 January 1944. Aged 23. YABA CEMETERY, LAGOS. [T/TC]

**JONES James**, Coder P/JX252016 R.N. H.M.S. *Penelope.* 18 February 1944. Aged 35. Off Anzio, this cruiser was sunk by the German U-boat *U-410.* *s of Absolem & Margaret, Atherton; h of Ellen.* PORTSMOUTH NAVAL MEMORIAL. [A/HAC]

**JONES John Edward**, Cpl. 3857370 18th (5th Bn. The Loyal Regiment [North Lancashire]) Regiment, Reconnaissance Corps. Captured in the Far East and died 25 August 1943 whilst being held as a PoW of the Japanese. Aged 26. *s of Ernest & Annie, Blackrod; h of Kathleen Elizabeth.* THANBYUZAYAT WAR CEMETERY, BURMA. [ASC/BCC/BL]

**JONES John Thomas**, Pte. 3531251 1st Bn. West Yorkshire Regiment (The Prince of Wales's Own). Killed in Burma 7 June 1944. Aged 25. *s of Thomas & Florence, Lowton St Mary's.* RANGOON MEMORIAL. [X]
(His brother Frank was killed on active service 15 months earlier. Both brothers were killed in the Far East; they have no known graves, and are both commemorated on the Rangoon Memorial. Although Frank's name is to be found on two local memorials, brother John surprisingly is not commemorated locally.)

**JONES Norman**, Dvr. T/192105 Royal Army Service Corps. After being a PoW for five years, he died in a U.K. hospital 20 June 1945. Aged 29. GOLBORNE (ST THOMAS) CHURCHYARD. [G/GOC]

**JONES Robert**, A.C.1. 2203913 R.A.F.(V.R.) Killed in a accident involving a motor-cycle and a lorry in France. 1 January 1945. Aged 19. *s of Robert & Elizabeth Ann.* CAMBRIA COMMUNAL CEMETERY. [L]

**JONES Roger**, L.Sgt. 3855630 3 Medium Regiment, Royal Artillery. Killed during the withdrawal to Dunkirk, 21 May 1940. Aged 21. *s of James & Ann, Hindley.* TOURNAI COMMUNAL CEMETERY, BELGIUM. [X]

**JONES Stanley,** Sgt.(Flt. Engr.) 1038767 R.A.F. (V.R.) 76 Sqdn. 4 December 1943. Aged 20. His Halifax V bomber on a raid on Leipzig was shot down by a German night-fighter and crashed at Achteburg. All members of the crew perished but three have no known graves. *s of Enoch & Martha, Newtown.* HAMBURG CEMETERY, OHLSBURG. [GGC/HIY/W]

**JOYCE Stanley William,** Gnr. 1537045 171 Bty, 57 Lt. A.A. Regt., Royal Artillery. 29 January 1943 in the Middle East. Aged 25. *s of James & Lilian, Atherton.* BENGHAZI WAR CEMETERY, LIBYA. [X]

**JUKES Leslie,** Ldg. Seaman. C/SSX17273 R.N. H.M.S. *Goodson.* 21 May 1945. Aged 29. *s of J & Lily Jukes, Ince.* WIGAN CEMETERY. [IN]

**JURY John,** Flt. Sgt.(W.Op/Air Gnr.) 1072406 R.A.F. (V.R.) Died in a Calcutta hospital 24 November 1943. Aged 30. *s of John William & Jesse; h of Edith Mary, Leigh.* BHOWANIPORE CEMETERY, CALCUTTA. [L/LGS/LMC/WMC]

**KANE James,** A.C.2. 967134 R.A.F. (V.R.) Died 29 October 1944 as a PoW of the Japanese while being transported from Ambon to Java. He was buried at sea. Aged 29. SINGAPORE MEMORIAL. [A]

**KAY Arthur,** Spr. 3389940 Royal Engineers. Killed in Germany 19 March 1945. Aged 28. *s of George & Mary Ann, Ince.* REICHSWALD FOREST WAR CEMETERY, GERMANY. [IN]

**KAY Douglas Arthur,** Mess Room Boy. Merchant Navy, s.s. *Darcoila* 28 September 1940. Aged 18. This cargo ship was sunk by the U-boat *U-32* south of Iceland. Thirty-one members of the crew perished. *s of Samuel & Ethel, Leigh.* TOWER HILL MEMORIAL. [L/LMC]
(See also: William James Strong.)

**KAY Horace,** Pte. 3461646 6th Bn. Durham Light Infantry. Killed 17 June 1944 in France. Aged 22. *s of Ernest & Eliza, Up Holland.* TILLY-SUR-SEULLES WAR CEMETERY. [UPC/UPH]

**KEARSLEY Ernest,** L.Cpl. 14373273 87 Assault Squadron, Royal Engineers. Killed 7 November 1944 in Holland. Aged 35. *s of Henry & Elizabeth, Wigan; h of Dorothy, Beech Hill, Wigan.* BERGEN-OP-ZOOM WAR CEMETERY, HOLLAND. [W]

**KEARSLEY Harold,** Pte. 4919745 2nd Bn. The Monmouthshire Regiment. 22 October 1944. Aged 28. UDEN WAR CEMETERY, HOLLAND. [SGC/W]

**KEE James,** Flying Offr. 42713 R.A.F. (V.R.) 219 Sqdn. Died 28 October 1941. Aged 24. *s of Robert & Janet.* WORSLEY (ST MARK) CHURCHYARD. [T]

**KEENAN Robert George,** L.A.C. 552083 R.A.F. Killed 30 May 1941 in the Middle East. Aged 20. *s of Mr. & Mrs. W.M., Hindley.* ALEXANDRIA(CHATBY) MILITARY & WAR MEMORIAL CEMETERY, EGYPT. [X]

**KELLY George,** Sjt. 3529525 13<sup>th</sup> (2/4<sup>th</sup> Bn. South Lancashire) Bn. The Parachute Regiment, A.A.C. Killed in action 22 August 1944 in France. Aged 23. *s of John & Annie; h of Hilda Eileen.* RANVILLE WAR CEMETERY. [L/LTC]

**KELLY James,** Cpl. 3964288 1/5<sup>th</sup> Bn. The Welch Regiment. Died of wounds in France 1 July 1944. Aged 25. *s of Luke & Rose, Platt Bridge; h of May, Wigan.* ST MANVIEU WAR CEMETERY. [IN/PBC]

**KELLY John,** Gnr. 14372975 Royal Artillery. Died 5 February 1946. Aged 22. *h of Annie.* TYLDESLEY CEMETERY. [X]

**KELLY John,** Pte. 3649439 1<sup>st</sup> Bn. The South Lancashire Regiment (The Prince of Wales's Volunteers.) Killed in action on D-Day 6 June 1944. Aged 40. *s of John & Ann, Wigan; h of Elizabeth, Hindley.* BAYEAUX WAR CEMETERY. [X]

**KELLY John Kenneth,** Pte. 3861132 2<sup>nd</sup> Bn. The West Yorkshire Regiment (The Prince of Wales's Own) Died 15 February 1944 in Burma. Aged 30. *s of William & Elizabeth; h of Florence, Wigan.* TAUKKYAN WAR CEMETERY, BURMA. [W]

**KELLY William Leonard,** Sgt. (W.Op/Air Gnr.) 1000480 R.A.F. (V.R.), 455(R.A.A.F.) Sqdn. 13 February 1942. Aged 21. All members of the crew died when this Hampden bomber from Wigsley abandoned its minelaying operation and crashed near Lincoln. *s of Edward & Ellen, Ashton-in-Makerfield.* ASHTON-IN-MAKERFIELD (ST THOMAS) CHURCHYARD. [AGS/AIM]

**KENNEDY James Daniel,** L. Sjt. 319498 *M.M.* 5<sup>th</sup> Royal Inniskilling Dragoon Guards, R.A.C. 26 September 1944. Aged 23. *s of Patrick & Sarah Margaret.* UDEN WAR CEMETERY, HOLLAND. [W]

**KENNEDY Sylvester,** Pte. 14668933 2<sup>nd</sup> Bn. Royal Lincolnshire Regiment. Killed in Holland 9 March 1945. Aged 19. *s of William & Mary.* GROESBEEK CANADIAN WAR CEMETERY. [W]

**KENYON Charles,** Pte. 3865475 1<sup>st</sup> Bn. Royal Norfolk Regiment. Killed 14 October 1944 in Holland. Aged 37. *s of Charles & Esther; h of Mary Ann, Platt Bridge.* OVERLOON WAR CEMETERY, HOLLAND. [PBC]

**KENYON Harry,** A.B. C/JX299418 R.N. H.M.S. *Boadicea.* 13 June 1944. Aged 35. Off Portland Bill, this destroyer was sunk by German aircraft. *s of Laban & Ellen.* CHATHAM NAVAL MEMORIAL. [L/WMC]
(See: Eric Abbott and John Moores who also died in this action.)

**KENYON Norman,** Pte. 3974944 Parachute Regiment, A.A.C. Killed 5 February 1943, in North Africa. Aged 20. He has no known grave. *s of Walter & Rebecca, Pemberton.* MEDJEZ-EL-BAB MEMORIAL, TUNISIA. [W]

**KENYON Vincent,** Pte. 3530217 1<sup>st</sup> Bn. The North Staffordshire Regiment (Prince of Wales's) Died in India 18 July 1945. Aged 24. RANCHI WAR CEMETERY, INDIA. [T]

**KIDD Ernest**, L.Bdr. 3864546 4 Maritime Regiment, Royal Arrtillery. Lost at sea 7 March 1943. Aged 25. *s of Louis H. & Ellen Ann, Wigan.* PLYMOUTH NAVAL MEMORIAL. [WSB]

**KIERAN James Christopher**, L.Cpl. 3454275 2/5th Bn. The Lancashire Fusiliers. Died of wounds in France, 9 July 1944. Aged 27. *s of Patrick & Mary Ann, Tyldesley.* RANVILLE WAR CEMETERY, FRANCE. [T]

**KING J.** Pte. 4861413 Army Catering Corps. Died in Germany 20 July 1945 whilst serving as a member of the Occupying Forces.. Aged 29. *s of George H. & Martha King; h of Elizabeth King, Whelley, Wigan.* MUNSTER HEATH WAR CEMETERY [W]

**KIRKWOOD Alfred**, Dvr. T/293579 Royal Army Service Corps. Died as a result of a road accident in Italy, 23 September 1945. Aged 23. *h of Sarah Alice.* BARI WAR CEMETERY, ITALY. [L]

**KNIGHT Edward**, A.B. D/SSX 20672 R.N. H.M.S. *Glorious* 9 June 1940. Aged 21. This aircraft carrier was sunk by the German battlecruisers *Gneisenau* and *Scharnhorst* 300 miles west of Narvik. There were only 43 survivors. *s of Christopher & Azillah, Astley.* PLYMOUTH NAVAL MEMORIAL. [X]
(See the following who were also lost in the same action: Samuel Alker; Walter L. Duckworth; John F. Gorton; John Jameson; Peter McNicholas; Benjamin T. Starkie; Frederick Swann.)

**KNIGHT Frederick**, Ldg. Airman FAA/FX90731 R.N. H.M.S. *Goshawk* 30 October 1942 Aged 20. *s of Leonard James & Lily.* FLEET AIR ARM MEMORIAL, LEE-ON-SOLENT. [A]

**KNIGHT John Joseph**, Fus. 3453478 1/8th Bn. Lancashire Fusiliers. Killed in Burma 8 June 1944. Aged 26. *s of James & Martha Knight; h of Louise Knight. Fus. Knight's father was killed in the First World War.* KOHIMA WAR CEMETERY, INDIA. [T]

**KNOWLES Eric**, Gnr. 959871 152 (The Ayrshire Yeomanry) Field Regiment, Royal Artillery. Died of wounds in North Africa 7 May 1943. Aged 24. *s of Mrs. M.A Knowles.* MASSICAULT WAR CEMETERY, TUNISIA. [L/LMC]

**KNOWLES James Lawrence**, Rfn. 14302995 1st Bn. The Cameronians (Scottish Rifles). Killed in action 15 May 1944 in Burma. Aged 20. *s of Arthur & Catherine, Wigan.* TAUKKYAN WAR CEMETERY, BURMA. [W]

**KNOWLES Stanley**, A.C.2. 1106586 R.A.F. (V.R.) Killed 3 November 1940 Aged 20. *s of Edward & Jane.* WIGAN CEMETERY. [W]

**KNOWLES Thomas Taylor**, Sto. 1st Class. C/KX84366 R.N. H.M.S *Exmoor*. 25 February 1941. Aged 28. The destroyer was sunk by a mine off Lowestoft. *s of Edward & Mary; h of Elizabeth, Worsley Mesnes, Wigan.* CHATHAM NAVAL MEMORIAL. [JC/W]

**KOPPENS John Martinus,** Rfn. 2247420 2nd Bn. The Cameronians (Scottish Rifles). Killed 27 May 1940 in Belgium during the withdrawal to Dunkirk. Aged 20. *s of John & Maria, Astley.* ESQUELMES WAR CEMETERY, BELGIUM. [X]

**KYTE Harold,** Fus. 3451759 1st Bn. The Lancashire Fusiliers. Killed in action in Burma 18 June 1944. Aged 25. He has no known grave. *s of James & Mary Jane, Lower Ince.* RANGOON MEMORIAL. [IN]

**LACEY Austin,** A.C.1. 1533668 R.A.F. (V.R.) Died 1 December 1942 in the Middle East. Aged 20. *s of Edmund & Lily.* SUEZ WAR MEMORIAL CEMETERY. [W]

**LAKIN James Duncan,** Sgt. (Air Gnr.) 1624474 R.A.F. (V.R.) 104 Sqdn. Killed 11 October 1944 in Italy. Aged 21. *s of George & Minnie.* PADUA WAR CEMETERY, ITALY. [W/WGS]

**LAMB Ian,** Sub Lieut. R.N.V.R. H.M.S. *St. Angelo* 11 January 1943. Aged 22. *s of Harold & Clara. h of Margaret, Blackrod.* FLEET AIR ARM MEMORIAL, LEE-ON-SOLENT. [BCC/BL]

**LAMB James,** Spr. 3531273 561 Field Coy., Royal Engineers. Killed 1 November 1944 in Italy. Aged 29. *s of Henry & Mary; h of Louisa, Crooke.* CORIANO RIDGE WAR CEMETERY, ITALY. [S]

**LAMBERT Walter George Richard,** Chief P.O. P/237997 R.N. H.M.S. *Gosling* 26 December 1943. Aged 52. *s of Walter George Richard & Emily; h of Ada Anne.* LOWTON (ST LUKES) CHURCHYARD, LOWTON ST. MARYS. [X]

**LANDER Robert Otley,** Sgt. (Nav.) 1425942 R.A.F. (V.R.) 15 Sqdn. 4 September 1943 Aged 22. A Stirling III bomber from Mildenhall crashed into the sea off the west coast of Denmark while on a minelaying operation. All the crew died and Sgt. Lander's body along with three others was washed ashore. The rest of the crew have no known graves. *s of Charles Henry & Elizabeth, Hindley; h of Vera Nellie.* FREDERICKSHAVN CEMETERY, DENMARK. [X]

**LANGFORD Norman,** Sgt. 2216243 R.A.F. (V.R.) Killed in a flying accident 2 April 1945. Aged 20. *s of John Richard & Harriet, Hindley Green..* HINDLEY CEMETERY. [X]

**LANGTON Henry,** Fus. 3524491 2nd Bn. The Lancashire Fusiliers. Died 26 October 1946. Aged 35. *s of George & Esther, Standish; h of Edith Lily, Standish.* STANDISH (ST WILFRID) CHURCHYARD. [STC]

**LATHAM Albert,** Tpr. 14258305 13th/18th Royal Hussars, R.A.C. Killed 9 August 1944 in France. He has no known grave. BAYEAUX MEMORIAL [OC]

**LATHAM Frank,** L. Bdr. 987550 11 Field Regiment, Royal Artillery. Lost at sea during the Greece campaign. 1 December 1944. Aged 26. *h of E.* ATHENS MEMORIAL. [L/LTC]

**LATHAM James,** Pte. 14674294 1/7th Bn. The Royal Warwickshire Regiment. Killed in France 8 August 1944. Aged 19. *s of James & Mary Louisa, Lowton St. Marys.* BAYEAUX WAR CEMETERY. [L/LMC]

**LAW Stanley,** L. Cpl. T/3776418 63 (Airborne) Comp. Coy., Royal Army Service Corps. Killed 21 September 1944. Aged 28. During the Arnhem airborne operation his plane caught fire. Aged 28. *s of Percy & Beatrice; h of Constance, Bryn.* ARNHEM OOSTERBEEK WAR CEMETERY, HOLLAND. [AC/NAV]

**LAWLER John James,** Pte. 14628963 6th Bn. The King's Own Scottish Borderers. Killed 17 September 1944. KASTERLEE WAR CEMETERY. [UPC/UPH]

**LAWRENSON John Heaton,** Sgt. (Obs.) 580791 R.A.F. (V.R.) 99 Sqdn. Killed 22 May 1940 when his Wellington bomber from Newmarket crashed near Belval in the Ardennes during a raid on Dinant. Aged 21. BELVAL COMMUNAL CEMETERY, FRANCE. [AGS]

**LAWRENSON Thomas,** A.B. D/SSX18662 R.N. H.M.S. *Diamond.* 27 April 1941. While leaving Nanplia, this destroyer was sunk by German Stuka dive-bombers. The ship was carrying survivors from other ships. *s of James Harold & Mary Alice, Ashton-in-Makerfield.* PLYMOUTH NAVAL MEMORIAL. [AIM]
(See also George Jackson who was lost in the same action.)

**LAWSON Ernest,** Sjt. 133755 2nd Wing, Glider Pilot Regiment, A.A.C. A glider pilot who was killed in action on the first day of Operation Market Garden (Arnhem) 17 September 1944. Aged 28. ARNHEM OOSTERBEEK WAR CEMETERY. [SCC/W/WGS]

**LAWTON Frank,** Chief Engine Room Artificer. P/MX46881 R.N. H.M.S. *Delight.* 29 July 1940. Aged 36. The destroyer was sunk by German Stuka dive-bombers off Portland. *s of Edward & Margaret Ellen; h of Barbara Mary.* PORTSMOUTH NAVAL MEMORIAL. [L]

**LAWTON Kenneth,** Pte. 4758799 16th Bn. The Durham Light Infantry. Killed in action in North Africa 8 April 1943. Aged 20. MEDJEZ-EL-BAB WAR CEMETERY, TUNISIA. [HAC/T]

**LEACH Francis,** Pte. 3856389 2nd Bn. The Loyal Regiment (North Lancashire) Killed in Singapore 12 February 1942. Aged 25. He has no known grave. SINGAPORE MEMORIAL. [W]

**LEADBETTER Joseph,** Sgt. (Air Gnr.) 1237320 R.A.F. (V.R.) 106 Sqdn. 30 May 1943. Aged 19. His Lancaster III bomber was lost during a raid on Wuppertal. *s of Henry & Frances, Bryn.* REICHSWALD FOREST WAR CEMETERY, GERMANY. [X]

**LEARY James,** Fus. 3455984 4th Bn. The Royal Northumberland Fusiliers. Killed in action in Holland, 18 September 1944. Aged 29. VALKENSWAARD WAR CEMETERY, HOLLAND. [X]

**LEE Brian,** Capt. EC/72 4th Bn. 9th Jat Regiment, Indian Army. Killed in the Far East 19 January 1942, aged 24, while serving with the Indian Army which he had joined on the outbreak of war. In 1939 he was working in the textile industry in India. *s of Harry & Ethel.* KRANJI WAR CEMETERY, SINGAPORE, SPECIAL MEMORIAL 'C' 'BURIED NEAR THIS SPOT' (Burials took place from the Singapore Hospital in various cemeteries, but during the occupation the identification of individual graves was lost. Capt. Lee's remains were known to have been transferred to Kranji but it is not possible to locate the actual grave.) [L/LGS]

**LEE James,** Gnr. 14220968 93 (6th Bn. The Argyll & Sutherland Highlanders) Anti-Tank Regiment., Royal Artillery. Killed in action in North Africa, 21 February 1942. Aged 19. *s of William & Martha, Tyldesley.* ENFIDAVILLE WAR CEMETERY, TUNISIA. [W]

**LEE Joseph,** Pte. 14583466 1st Bn. The East Lancashire Regiment. Died of wounds 21 July 1944 in France. Aged 19. BAYEAUX WAR CEMETERY. [UPC/UPH]

**LEE Richard,** Pte. 3390537 1st Bn. The East Lancashire Regiment. Killed 28 March 1945. Aged 28. *s of James & Polly; h of Martha, Wigan.* REICHSWALD FOREST WAR CEMETERY, GERMANY. [IN/W]

**LEE William,** Pte. 3662092 7th Bn. The South Lancashire Regiment (The Prince of Wales's Volunteers) Killed in India 30 June 1943. Aged 33. *s of James & Bertha; h of Florence.* KIRKEE CEMETERY, INDIA. [L/LMC]

**LEECH Joseph Francis,** Dvr. T/10663588. 253 (Airborne) Comp. Coy., Royal Army Service Corps. Killed in Holland 20 September 1944 during the battle for Arnhem. Aged 22. *s of Joseph Thomas & Abigail.* OOSTERBEEK WAR CEMETERY, HOLLAND. [W]

**LEIGH Eric,** Pilot Offr. (Flt. Engr.) 185670 R.A.F. (V.R.) 463 (R.A.A.F.) Sqdn.. Killed in action 23 October 1944. Aged 39. His Lancaster I bomber took-off from Waddington to attack batteries near the port of Vlissingen but crashed in the target area. He was well above the average age of Bomber Command aircrew and was the only member of the crew to be killed. *s of William & Mary Jane; h of Gladys.* BERGEN-OP-ZOOM WAR CEMETERY, HOLLAND. [W]

**LEIGH William,** Fus. 3656357 2nd Bn. The Lancashire Fusiliers. Killed in action in North Africa 26 November 1942. Aged 23. *s of Mr. & Mrs. W.* MEDJEZ-EL-BAB WAR CEMETERY. [L]

**LEIGH William,** Pte. 2886841 2nd Bn. The Gordon Highlanders. Killed in action in France 27 August 1944. Aged 24. *s of William & Ellen, Wigan.* TILLY-SUR-SEULLES WAR CEMETERY. [W]

**LEYLAND John,** L.Cpl. 3391716 4th Royal Tank Regiment, R.A.C. Killed in Germany 26 March 1945. Aged 32. *s of Robert & Elizabeth; h of Mary, Abram.* REICHSWALD FOREST WAR CEMETERY, GERMANY. [AB/B]

**LEYLAND John (Jack** in CWGC) Cpl. 3383508 1st Bn. The East Lancashire Regiment. Killed in Normandy 10 July 1944. Aged 33. *s of Paul & Mary Jane; h of Mary Ellen.* BROUAY WAR CEMETERY. [BC]

**LEYLAND Robert,** L. Bdr. 1803415 267 Bty., 69 Lt. A.A. Regiment, Royal Artillery. Killed 24 May 1944 in the Far East while serving with General Wingate's Chindits. He has no known grave. Aged 31. *h of Jane (Jennie), Wigan.* RANGOON MEMORIAL. [SCC/W]

**LEYLAND William,** Tpr. 7899118 1st Lothian & Border Horse, R.A.C. Killed in Holland 2 November 1944. Aged 26. *s of Mrs. E. and stepson of R. Nicholson, Newtown.* BERGEN-OP-ZOOM WAR CEMETERY, HOLLAND. [W]

**LINDLEY John Hubert,** Sgt. (Pilot) 1673199 R.A.F. (V.R.) 37 Sqdn. Killed in Italy 21 August 1944. Aged 20. *s of John Hubert Lindley (who was Borough Treasurer of Leigh) & Margaret E. Lindley, Leigh.* NAPLES WAR CEMETERY, ITALY. [L/LMC]

**LIPTROT William,** Pte. 13075494 243 Coy. Pioneer Corps. Killed 12 October 1943. Aged 34. *s of Harriet, Wigan.* CATANIA WAR CEMETERY, ITALY [SCC/W]

**LITHERLAND George,** Pte. 3911748 2nd Bn. The Gloucestershire Regiment. Died 17 December 1940. Aged 20. *s of Thomas & Annie, Wigan.* WIGAN CEMETERY. [SGC/W]

**LITTLER George,** Gdsmn. 2662307 3rd Bn. The Coldstream Guards. Killed 23 January 1944 in Italy. Aged 23. s of Henry & Mary. MINTURNO WAR CEMETERY. [BC]

**LIVESAY Hezekiah,** Ldg. Sto. P/KX78377 R.N. H.M. Submarine *Oxley.* 10 September 1939. Aged 29. South-west of Stavanger, the submarine H.M.S. *Triton* accidentally torpedoed and sunk the *Oxley.* Only 2 members of the 54 strong crew survived. *He had been in the Royal Navy for some 12 years and was married to a Portsmouth woman.* PORTSMOUTH NAVAL MEMORIAL. [W]
(War was declared on 3 September 1939 and Ldg. Sto. Livesay was therefore the first fatal casualty of the Second World War who had connections with any of the towns and townships covered by this book. On the Wigan Cenotaph, his surname is incorrectly spelt *Livesey* )

**LLOYD Fred,** Pte. 3386235 The East Lancashire Regiment. Died 10 July 1947. WIGAN CEMETERY. [X]

**LLOYD Harry Oliver,** Gnr. D/10694 1 Survey Regiment, Royal Canadian Artillery. Killed 12 October 1944. Aged 25. *s of Edward Oliver Lloyd DCM & Sarah Elizabeth Lloyd, Toronto, Canada. (It has not been possible to discover his connections with Standish, but it is highly likely that the family emigrated from the area in the pre-war years but still had family members living in Lancashire.)* ANCONA WAR CEMETERY, ITALY. [STC]

**LLOYD John,** Fus. 14245629 2/5<sup>th</sup> Bn. The Lancashire Fusiliers. Killed in action in France, 8 July 1944. Aged 21. *s of Richard & Elizabeth, Pemberton.* CAMBES-EN-PLAINE CEMETERY. [OUC/PC/W]

**LOFTHOUSE Ronald,** Flying Offr. 123585 R.A.F. (V.R.) 114 Sqdn. Killed 5 September 1943 in the Middle East. Aged 24. He has no known grave. *s of James & Elizabeth Annie.* ALAMEIN MEMORIAL. [HGC]

**LORD Allan,** A.C.2. 2208846 R.A.F. (V.R.) Died 25 February 1946. Aged 21. *s of William & Susannah, Aspull.* ASPULL (ST ELIZABETH) CHURCHYARD. [X]

**LORD Robert,** Pte. 3530533 1<sup>st</sup> Bn. Durham Light Infantry. Killed in action in Sicily, 5 August 1943. Aged 22. CATANIA WAR CEMETERY. [T]

**LOVATT Harry,** Dvr. T/10661430 Royal Army Service Corps. Died 6 December 1943 somewhere in the Middle East. Aged 24. *s of Clara.* GAZA WAR CEMETERY, EGYPT. [T]

**LOVE Cyril,** Sgt. 3527527 1<sup>st</sup> Bn. The Manchester Regiment. Died 25 July 1943 while a PoW of the Japanese. Aged 28. *s of Albert & Elizabeth Alice.* KANCHANABURI WAR CEMETERY, THAILAND. [A/HAC/HBC]

**LOWE Charles Leslie,** Ord. Seaman. D/JX538585 R.N. H.M.S. *Chaser.* 18 April 1945. Aged 18. *s of Charles Benjamin & Linda, Chestnut Road, Whelley, Wigan.* PLYMOUTH NAVAL MEMORIAL. [SGC/W/WSB]

**LOWE Frank,** Spr. 121085 24 Field Coy. Royal Engineers. Killed in action 25 March 1945. Aged 25. REICHSWALD FOREST WAR CEMETERY, GERMANY. [IN/ISM]

**LOWE Geoffrey,** 2nd. Lieut. 224572 Royal Engineers Died 23 March 1942. Aged 23. *s of Arnold & Marjorie, Old Hartford, Cheshire.* ATHERTON CEMETERY. [HBC/LGS]

**LOWE George Cyril,** L.A.C. 1113671 R.A.F. Died 28 June 1945. Aged 40. *h of Hilda Mary.* WRIGHTINGTON (ST JAMES) CHURCHYARD. [W]

**LOWE Peter,** L.A.C. 1122679 R.A.F. (V.R.) Died of dysentry in India, 13 August 1944. Aged 21. *s of Mr. & Mrs. J., Leigh.* MAYNAMATI CEMETERY, PAKISTAN. [T]

**LOWE Thomas,** Gnr. 1057271 115 Field Regiment, Royal Artillery. Killed in Capetown 27 April 1942. Aged 36. *h of Florence May, Ashton-in-Makerfield.* CAPETOWN (MAITLAND) CEMETERY, SOUTH AFRICA. [AIM/BMC]

**LOWE Thomas Gibson,** Rfn. 6922310 10th. (2nd. Bn. The Tower Hamlets Rifles) Bn.., The Rifle Brigade, (The Prince Consort's Own). Killed in action in North Africa, 12 April 1943. Aged 37. *s of Mr. & Mrs. Thomas; h of Lily, Pemberton.* ENFIDAVILLE WAR CEMETERY, TUNISIA. [HIY/W]

**LOWE William,** Pte. 3865890 1st Bn. The Loyal Regiment (North Lancashire). Killed in North Africa 23 April 1943. Aged 21. He has no known grave. *s of John Thomas & Martha, Pemberton.* MEDJEZ-EL-BAB MEMORIAL, TUNISIA. [HIC/W]

**LOWTON Robert,** Pte. 3964345 2nd Bn. The Devonshire Regiment. Killed 31 March 1945 in Germany. Aged 26. *s of Robert & Elizabeth, Standish.* REICHSWALD FOREST WAR CEMETERY, GERMANY. [ST/STC]

**LUNN John,** Dvr. T/60662 Royal Army Service Corps. The actual date of his death is unknown, but he was killed sometime between 26 May 1940 and 22 June 1940 during the withdrawal to Dunkirk and the subsequent action. Aged 25. *h of Beatrice Mary, Wigan.* LONGUENESSE (ST OMER) CEMETERY. [NSC/W]

**LYNAM Thomas Leo,** Pte. T/124829 Royal Army Service Corps. Killed 26 March 1942 in the Middle East. *s of James & Emily, Ashton-in-Makerfield.* HALFAYA SOLLUM CEMETERY, EGYPT. [AMS]

**LYNCH John,** Dvr. T/274568 18 Div. Transport Coy., Royal Army Service Corps. Died 8 January 1944 while a PoW of the Japanese. Aged 37. THANBYUZAYAT WAR CEMETERY, BURMA. .[W]

**LYNCH John,** Fus. 3451393 1/5th Bn. The Lancashire Fusiliers. Died 10 November 1940. Aged 22. *s of Thomas & Bertha, Leigh; h of Martha.* LEIGH CEMETERY. [X]

**LYNCH Joseph,** Stoker 1st Class D/KX87933 R.N. H.M.S. *Lapwing.* 20 March 1945. Aged 28. This sloop was sunk by the German U-boat *U-968* in the Kola Inlet. *s of Joseph & Catherine, Leigh. According to local sources he had nine sisters.* PLYMOUTH NAVAL MEMORIAL. [L]

**LYNCH Joseph,** Pte. 3526654 5th Bn. The Manchester Regiment. Killed in action 19 May 1940 during the withdrawal to Dunkirk. Aged 25. *s of Peter & Ellen; h of Mary.* LILLE SOUTHERN CEMETERY. [W]

**LYNCH Patrick Joseph,** Pte. 3527026 14th (HD) Bn. The Argyll & Sutherland Highlanders. Died of pneumonia in Shobhill Hospital, Glasgow, 2 February 1940. Aged 29. WIGAN CEMETERY. [W]
(According to his service number, Pte. Lynch was originally in The Manchester Regiment and is indeed shown on the Wigan memorial and in other local sources as serving in that regiment. CWGC records however give the information used above.)

**LYNN Ronald,** Flt. Sgt. (Pilot) 1451341 R.A.F. (V.R.) 273 Sqdn. Killed in an accident in Ceylon, 30 May 1944. Aged 21. *s of Percy & Margaret, Wigan.* COLUMBO CEMETERY, CEYLON. [NSC/W]

**LYON Eric,** Flying Offr. (Pilot) 104429 R.A.F. (V.R.) Killed while flight-testing a Beaufighter in Scotland, 4 October 1942. Aged 25. *h of Margaret Lillian, Gathurst.* SHEVINGTON CEMETERY. [S]

**LYON Leslie,** Ord. Smn. D/JX195002 R.N. H.M.S. *Drake.* 21 April 1941. Aged 21. *s of Joseph L. & Ivy Bell, Up Holland Moor.* PLYMOUTH (WESTON MILL) CEMETERY. [UPC/UPH]

**LYON Louis,** Gnr. 6100186 12 (Honourable Artillery Company) Regt., Royal Horse Artillery. Killed in action in Italy 16 June 1944. Aged 29. *s of Louis & Mary, Wigan.* ASSISI WAR CEMETERY, ITALY. [SGC/W]

**LYONS Ellis,** Pte. F/10359 The North Nova Scotia Highlanders, Royal Canadian Infantry Corps. 22 February 1945. Aged 26. *s of James & Mary, Atherton.* GROESBEEK CANADIAN WAR CEMETERY, HOLLAND. [X]

**LYTHGOE John,** Dvr. 1950644 962 Port Construction & Repair Coy., Royal Engineers. Accidentally killed 4 July 1945. Aged 23. *s of John & Annie.* REICHSWALD FOREST WAR CEMETERY, GERMANY. [L]

**LYTHGOE Peter,** Cpl. 3390760 144th (8th Bn. East Lancashire) Regiment., R.A.C. The actual date of his death is unknown but it was sometime between 12 and 15 August 1944 in Normandy. Aged 29. He has no known grave. *h of Mary.* BAYEAUX MEMORIAL, FRANCE. [L/LTC]

**LYTHGOE Stanley,** Gnr. 14274779 65 Field Regiment, Royal Artillery. Killed in Italy 11 September 1944. Aged 29. *s of Edward & Elsie; h of Alice.* GRADARA WAR CEMETERY, ITALY. [L]

**LYTHGOE William,** Gnr. 3864615 4/2 Maritime Regiment, Royal Artillery. He is reported to have been lost at sea 15 September 1941. No further detail is available. Aged 25. *s of James & Margaret, Standish.* PORTSMOUTH NAVAL MEMORIAL. [SSM/ST]

**McANDREW Harold,** Dvr. T/3195484 Royal Army Service Corps. Died 9 March 1946. WIGAN CEMETERY. [X]

**McAVOY Eric,** Gnr. 14373059 160 Field Regiment, Royal Artillery. Died 2 December 1944 in India. Aged 20. *s of Oswald & Jane, Higher Ince.* MADRAS WAR CEMETERY, INDIA. [IN]

**McCABE Frederic,** Pte. 14728911 8th Bn. The Royal Scots (The Royal Regiment). Died of wounds 22 February 1945. Aged 19. *s of Frederic & Hannah, Ince.* REICHSWALD FOREST WAR CEMETERY, GERMANY. [IN]

**McCARTER John Leonard,** Bdr. 1077045 102 (The Northumberland Hussars) Anti-Tank Regiment, Royal Artillery. Killed 3 September 1944 in France. Aged 24. *s of John & Mary.* DON COMMUNAL CEMETERY, ANNOEULLIN, FRANCE. [G/GOC]

**McCAUL John Patrick,** A.C.2. 1050678 R.A.F. (V.R.) 219 Squadron. Died 30 September 1940. No detail of the circumstances of his death are available. Aged 28. LEIGH CEMETERY. [T]

**McCORMACK Thomas,** Pte. 2930404 1st (Liverpool Scottish) Bn., Queen's Own Cameron Highlanders & No. 2 Commando. Died 11 April 1942. Aged 25. *s of Jeremiah & Joanna Ramsay, Liverpool. He had family connections in Wigan.* RENNES EASTERN COMMUNAL CEMETERY, FRANCE. [X]

**McCORMICK James,** Spr. 14641375 65 Mechanical Equipment Platoon, Royal Engineers. Died after an accident in Scotland 11 August 1945. Aged 20. *s of Charles & Mary, Whelley, Wigan.* WIGAN CEMETERY. [X]

**McCORMICK William,** Pte. 2188553 46 Coy., Pioneer Corps. Lost in the sinking of s.s. *Lancastria,* 17 June 1940. Aged 28. *h of Maud, Scholes, Wigan.* DUNKIRK MEMORIAL. [W]
(Twelve other local men perished when this ship was sunk. See the **Herbert Cunliffe** entry for names and details of the sinking.

**McCRIRRICK Jack,** Gnr. 903989 132(The Glamorgan Yeomanry) Field Regt., Royal Artillery. Killed in Italy 3 October 1943. Aged 23. *s of Samuel Nivison Stewart & Ellen, Overhulton, Lancashire.* SANGRO RIVER WAR CEMETERY, ITALY. [LGS]

**McDONALD Joseph,** Pte. NX.11951 Australian Imperial Force, 2/4 Bn. Australian Infantry. Died in hospital in the Middle East 10 July 1941. Aged 33. *s of Sarah, Newtown. It is assumed that he emigrated to Australia before the war.* ALEXANDRIA (HADRA) WAR MEMORIAL CEMETERY. [X]

**McENTEE Hugh,** Ldg. Airman FX86884 R.N. H.M.S. *Jackdaw.* Died in an aircraft crash in Scotland, 18 December 1943. Aged 20. *s of Lawrence & Ellen.* LEIGH CEMETERY. [L]

**McGLONE Edward Michael,** Sgmn. 2357334 Royal Corps of Signals, 48 Lt. AA Regt., R.A. Sig. Sec. 9 August 1945. Aged 35. *s of Edward & Margaret Jane; h of Mary, Ireland.* LABUAN WAR CEMETERY, NORTH BORNEO. [HGS]

**McHUGH Stanley Patrick,** Pte. 3652797 2nd Bn. The South Lancashire Regiment (Prince of Wales's Volunteers) 27 November 1941. Aged 27. *s of Andrew & Catherine, Wigan.* WIGAN CEMETERY. [X]

**McHUGH William,** Pte. 3451384 2nd Bn. The North Staffordshire Regiment (The Prince of Wales's). Killed in Italy 14 December 1944. Aged 26. FAENZA WAR CEMETERY, ITALY. [L/LTA]

**McKEE John,** Sgt. 1089032 R.A.F. (V.R.) 467 Sqdn. 19 February 1943. Aged 27. His Lancaster III bomber was lost without trace on a raid to Wilhelmshaven. *s of Robert & Ellen; h of Rita. He had family connections with Hindley & Abram.* RUNNYMEDE MEMORIAL. [X]

**MACKIE Robert,** Marine PO/X123340 Royal Marines. Died 4 May 1945. Aged 19. *s of James & Jesse; h of Ethel Rose, Lowton St. Mary's* ABERDOUR CEMETERY, FIFE. [X]

**McLEOD William,** Sgmn. 14401591 Royal Corps of Signals, 3rd. Division Signals. Killed in Normandy on D-Day, 6 June 1944. Aged 20. *s of Charles & Anne, Wigan.* HERMANVILLE WAR CEMETERY. [W/WGS]

**McNALLY Enoch,** Pte. 3857109 6th Bn. The Durham Light Infantry. The actual date of his death is unknown, but he was killed in action between 21 and 23 March 1943 in North Africa. Aged 21. He has no known grave and therefore he is commemorated on the appropriate memorial. *s of John & Alice, Lower Ince.* MEDJEZ-EL-BAB MEMORIAL, TUNISIA. [ISM]

**McNAMARA Francis (Frank)** Marine. PLY/X100129 Royal Marines H.M.S. *Prince of Wales* Died in Singapore 16 February 1942 during the period leading to the capture of the Colony by the Japanese. He has no known grave. Aged 24. *h of Dorothy, Atherton.* PLYMOUTH NAVAL MEMORIAL. [A]

**McNAMARA William,** L.Cpl. 3860470 1st Bn. The Royal Irish Fusiliers (Princess Victoria's) Died of wounds 13 January 1944 in the Middle East. Aged 28. MASSICAULT WAR CEMETERY, TUNISIA. [PBC]

**McNICHOLAS Peter,** Stoker 1st Class. D/KX89551 R.N. H.M.S. *Glorious.* 9 June 1940. Aged 24. This aircraft carrier was sunk by the German battlecruisers *Gneisenau* and *Scharnhorst* 300 miles west of Narvik. There were only 43 survivors. *s of James & Agnes.* PLYMOUTH NAVAL MEMORIAL. [L]
(Seven other local men perished in this action: Samuel Alker; Walter L. Duckworth; John Jameson; Edward Knight; John F. Gorton; Benjamin T. Starkie and Frederick Swan.)

**McVEIGH Edward,** L. Bdr. 828240 5 Regiment, Royal Horse Artillery. Killed 29 May 1940 during the withdrawal to Dunkirk. Aged 30. *s of Michael & Mary McVeigh; h of Ellen McVeigh, Bryn. It is not known why his name does not appear on any local memorial.* ST. SYLVESTRE-CAPPEL CHURCHYARD. [X]

**MAJOR Thomas,** Pte. 5382995 1st Bn. Oxfordshire & Buckinghamshire Light Infantry. Killed in action during the period of the Dunkirk evacuation, 1 June 1940. Aged 20. He has no known grave. *s of Mr. & Mrs. Thomas, Pemberton.* DUNKIRK MEMORIAL. [W]

**MAKINSON Henry,** A.B. D/JX172423 R.N. H.M.S. *Mourne.* 15 June 1944. Aged 26. Off the Lizard, this frigate was sunk by the German U-boat *U-767. s of Elizabeth & stepson of Thomas Swann.* PLYMOUTH NAVAL MEMORIAL. [AS/ASC]

**MAKINSON James,** Dvr. T/10705247 Royal Army Service Corps attd. 6th Bn. The Lincolnshire Regiment. Killed in action 2 March 1943. Aged 33. *s of James & Mary Hannah, Worthington; h of Edna, Higher Ince.* TABARKA RAS RAJEL WAR CEMETERY, TUNISIA. [AS/HDC]

**MALONE Thomas,** Spr. 2007284 509 Field Coy., Royal Engineers. Killed in action in France, 19 August 1944. Aged 24. BAYEAUX WAR CEMETERY. [W]

**MALONEY John,** Sjt. 3596101 1st Airborne Bn. The Border Regiment. Killed (most probably drowned as many of the gliders landed in the sea) during the first day of the invasion of Sicily 9 July 1943. Aged 31. He has no known grave. *s of Thomas & Mary Ellen; h of Edna.* CASSINO MEMORIAL [L/LTA]

**MALONEY William,** Bdr. 1114368 54 (The Queen's Own Royal Glasgow Yeomanry) Anti-Tank Regiment. Royal Artillery. Killed 29 December 1944 in Holland. Aged 32. *h of Ada, Worsley Mesnes.* BRUNSSUM WAR CEMETERY, HOLLAND. [JC/W]

**MANN Fred,** A.B. D/JX203163 R.N. H.M.S. *Galatea.* 15 December 1941. Aged 24. This cruiser, returning from North Africa, was sunk by U-boat U-557 off Alexandria. *s of William & Mary A., Boothstown.* PLYMOUTH NAVAL MEMORIAL [LGS] (See also: Ernest Cashin and Herbert Worrall.)

**MANN Horace,** Tpr. 4126666 4th Regiment, Recconaissance Corps, R.A.C. Killed 30 April 1944 in Italy. Aged 26. *s of George & Sarah, Bamfurlong.* CASSINO WAR CEMETERY, ITALY. [ABC/BMC]

**MANSLEY James Kendrick,** Pte. 3866087 1st Bn. Royal Norfolk Regiment. Killed 4 October 1944 in Holland. Aged 21. He has no known grave. *s of Mr. & Mrs. T., Astley.* GROESBEEK MEMORIAL, HOLLAND. [X]

**MANSLEY John Kenneth,** Flt. Sgt. 1068163 R.A.F. (V.R.) 57 Sqdn. 1 May 1943. Aged 21. His Lancaster III bomber from Scampton crashed near Amsterdam. None of the seven crew members has a known grave and all are therefore commemorated on the Runnymede Memorial. *s of Harry & Gertrude Margaret.* RUNNYMEDE MEMORIAL. [A/HBC]
(It is reported that in 1978 the Royal Netherlands Air Force recovered human remains which were believed to have originated from Flt. Sgt. Mansley's aircraft. These now lie in Groesbeek Canadian War Cemetery as unknown airmen.)

**MARKLAND Leslie,** Cpl. 3451935 11th Bn. Lancashire Fusiliers. Killed 13 October 1944 in Italy. Age 26. *s of James & Mary Elizabeth.* FAENZA WAR CEMETERY, ITALY. [AMS/SIM]

**MARKLAND William Gibbons,** Sgt. 1055984 R.A.F. (V.R.) 205 Sqdn. Killed 3 March 1942. Aged 20. *s of Henry Richardson & Florence, Bolton.* SINGAPORE MEMORIAL. [HBC]

**MARRON Stephen Joseph,** L.A.C. 536654 R.A.F. 73 Sqdn. Lost in the sinking of s.s. *Lancastria* 17 June 1940. Aged 25. *s of John Joseph & Margaret, Pemberton.* RUNNYMEDE MEMORIAL. [W]
(Twelve other local men perished when this ship was sunk. See the **Herbert Cunliffe** entry for names and details of the sinking.)

**MARSDEN Arthur Raymond,** Pte. 1640689 2/4th Bn. King's Own Yorkshire Light Infantry. Killed 12 September 1944 in Italy. Aged 24. *s of Thomas & Charlotte.* CASSINO MEMORIAL. [SSC/W/WSB]

**MARSDEN Harry,** Pte. 2934418 The Queen's Own Cameron Highlanders. Killed 16 August 1943. Aged 26. *s of Albert & Edith; h of Muriel, Ashton-in-Makerfield.* ALEXANDRIA (HADRA) WAR MEMORIAL CEMETERY, EGYPT. [AIM]

**MARSDEN Herbert,** Tpr. 7882042 4<sup>th</sup>/7<sup>th</sup> Royal Dragoon Guards, R.A.C. Died 25 May 1940 Aged 31. STANDISH (ST WILFRID) CHURCHYARD. [ST/STC]

**MARSDEN William Jack,** Lieut. R.A.N.V.R. H.M.S. *Varbel.* Died 7 February 1944. Aged 26. PLYMOUTH NAVAL MEMORIAL. [W]

**MARSH Donald,** A.B. C/KX143188 *Mentioned in Dispatches.* R.N. H.M.S. *Pembroke.* Died 26 May 1947 Aged 22. *s of John William & Mary Ellen.* ATHERTON CEMETERY. [X]

**MARSH Frank,** Sto. 2nd. Class. P/KX664171 R.N. H.M.S. *Minster.* 8 June 1944. Aged 29. The netlayer H.M.S. *Minster* (ex Southern Railway) was sunk by a mine off the Normandy beaches. *s of Percy & Elizabeth; h of Gladys.* PORTSMOUTH NAVAL MEMORIAL. [A]
(See: George Barton and Colin Daniels who also were lost in the sinking of this vessel.)

**MARSH Harold,** Pte. 3780105 13<sup>th</sup> Bn. The King's Regiment (Liverpool). Drowned in the Far East 26 July 1942. Aged 32. *s of Edward & Margaret.* KIRKEE CEMETERY, INDIA. [A/TMC]

**MARSH Joseph,** Sgt. 1080667 R.A.F. (V.R.) 35 Sqdn. 14 July 1943. Aged 23. The Halifax I bomber was lost on a raid on Aachen. Only one crew member out of the seven on board survived, but those who died have no known graves. *s of Joseph William & Ellen, Up Holland.* RUNNYMEDE MEMORIAL. [UPC/UPH]

**MARSH Ralph,** Pte. D/33824 8<sup>th</sup> (H.D.) Bn. The Cheshire Regiment. Died in the U.K. 22 January 1940. Aged 39. Pte. Marsh was much older than would have been usual for a serving soldier, but he was a First World War veteran. *s of Richard & Esther; h of Mary, Leigh.* LEIGH CEMETERY. [X]

**MARSH Thomas,** L.A.C. 1692504 R.A.F. (V.R.) Died 8 February 1947. Aged 43. *s of John & Jane; h of Elizabeth, Marsh Green.* PEMBERTON (ST JOHN) CHURCHYARD. [X]

**MARSHALL Edward,** Gnr. 1082447 135 (The Hertfordshire Yeomanry) Field Regiment, Royal Artillery. After being captured at the fall of Singapore, he died as a PoW of the Japanese 1 December 1943. Aged 28. *s of William & Clara; h of Winifred.* KANCHANABURI WAR CEMETERY, THAILAND. [G/GOC]
(His brother William Harold also died on active service,.)

**MARSHALL William Harold,** Sgt. (Pilot) 1684879 R.A.F. (V.R.) 69 Sqdn. Died 24 February 1945. Aged 24. *s of William & Clara; h of Gwendoline Joan.* BRUSSELS TOWN CEMETERY. [G/GOC]
(His brother Edward died while a prisoner of war of the Japanese.)

**MARTIN Jack,** Cpl. 1695543 6th Bn. Queen's Own Royal West Kent Regiment. Died of wounds in Italy, 29 April 1945. Aged 28. *s of Hannah; h of Elsie May, Higher Ince.* FORLI WAR CEMETERY. [W/WSB]

**MARTIN Thomas,** Fus. 7044984 6th Bn. Royal Inniskilling Fusiliers. Died 10 February 1942. Aged 19. *s of William & Jane, Tyldesley.* BELFAST CITY CEMETERY. [X]
(The brother of William who died on active service.)

**MARTIN William,** Fus. 7043713 1st Bn. Royal Inniskilling Fusiliers. Killed in Italy 12 August 1943. Aged 25. *s of William & Jane, Tyldesley.* CATANIA WAR CEMETERY, ITALY. [X]
(The brother of Thomas who died while serving with the same regiment.)

**MASON Edward,** Cpl. 978726 R.A.F. (V.R.) Died 15 January 1945 while a PoW of the Japanese. Aged 25. AMBON WAR CEMETERY, INDONESIA. [SMC/W]

**MASON Harry,** Tpr. 7906385 3rd Caribiniers (Prince of Wales's Dragoon Guards), R.A.C. Died in Burma 20 September 1944. Aged 25. *s of James & Eleanor, Bryn; h of Irene.* IMPHAL WAR CEMETERY. [SAC/W]

**MASON James Edward,** Pte. 13103101 Pioneer Corps. Killed in an accident in the United Kingdom, 1 October 1941. Aged 30. *h of Nora Mason.* WIGAN CEMETERY. [PBC/W]

**MASON John Clifford (Jack)** Sgt.(Obs./Nav) 971264 R.A.F. (V.R.) 235 Sqdn. Killed 11 August 1941 during a Blenheim anti-shipping operation from a base in Scotland. Aged 21. *s of James Ernest & Martha, Wigan.* RUNNYMEDE MEMORIAL. [SAC/W]

**MASON Stanley,** Seaman. LT/JX 532715 R.N. Patrol Service. H.M. Trawler *Pine.* 31 January 1944. Aged 19. German E-boats attacked a convoy south-east of Beachy Head and this naval trawler was sunk. *s of Albert & Martha E., Hindley.* LOWESTOFT MEMORIAL. [X]

**MASON William,** Gnr. 1809130 H.Q. 48 Lt. A.A. Regiment, Royal Artillery. Died 5 March 1945 as a PoW of the Japanese. Aged 34. He has no known grave. *s of William & Eleanor, Standish.* SINGAPORE MEMORIAL. [ST/STC]

**MASSEY John James,** Dvr. 10594926 30 H.A.A. Regiment Workshop, Royal Electrical & Mechanical Engineers. 7 January 1943. Aged 20. Lost in s.s. *Benalbanach* , a passenger/cargo liner on its way from the Clyde to Bona carrying ammunition and troops. It was sunk by enemy aircraft off Algiers. *s of Allen & Betty.* BROOKWOOD MEMORIAL. [W/WPC]
(Some sources show him incorrectly as serving in the R.A.S.C.)

**MATHER Clifford,** A.C.2. 1502722 R.A.F. (V.R.) 37 Sqdn. Killed 14 June 1942 in Libya. Aged 19. *s of William Thomas & Beatrice, Whelley, Wigan.* RUNNYMEDE MEMORIAL. [SSC/W/WSB]

**MATHER Roy,** Pte. 3530311 8th Bn. The Argyll & Sutherland Highlanders. Died of wounds in North Africa 19 April 1943. Aged 23. *s of George & Ellen.* BEJA WAR CEMETERY, TUNISIA. [L]

**MATHER Thomas,** Pte. 7926062 1st Bn. The King's Own Royal Regiment (Lancaster) Died in No. 1 General Hospital in the Middle East 24 August 1942. Aged 34. *s of Thomas & Ann.* He was originally buried at Kantara, but after 1945 was reinterred. MOASCAR WAR CEMETERY, EGYPT. [ST/STC]

**MATTHEWS Kenneth Forshaw,** Sgt (Air Gnr.) 1065498 R.A.F. (V.R.) 10 Sqdn. 18 December 1944. Aged 23. His Halifax III bomber took-off from Melbourne to attack Duisburg but crashed in the Ardennes on the border between France and Belgium. Sgt. Matthews was originally buried in the U.S. Military Cemetery at Les Fosses. *s of Samuel & Maggie, Wigan.* LEOPOLDSBURG WAR CEMETERY, BELGIUM. [X]

**MATTHEWS Timothy Hugh,** Fus. 14791051 4th Bn. The Royal Welch Fusiliers. Killed in Germany 5 March 1945. Aged 18. *He had family connections in Ince.* REICHSWALD FOREST WAR CEMETERY. [X]

**MAWDSLEY Harry (Henry),** L.Bdr. 1115122 102 (The Northumberland Hussars) Anti-Tank Regiment, Royal Artillery. Killed in Belgium 11 September 1944. Aged 23. *s of Henry & Sarah, Blackrod.* GEEL WAR CEMETERY, BELGIUM. [BCC/BL]

**MAWDSLEY John,** A.B. C/JX355104 R.N. *H.M.L.S.T. 421* Killed in action during the landings at Anzio 26 January 1944. Aged 20. *s of Thomas & Hannah.* ANZIO WAR CEMETERY, ITALY. [L]

**MAWDSLEY William,** Pte. 14337348 Pioneer Corps. Killed in Belgium 3 May 1945. Aged 21. *s of William & Margaret, Ince.* TURNHOUT COMMUNAL CEMETERY, BELGIUM. [IN]

**MAWDSLEY William Edward,** L. Cpl. 7688864 Corps of Military Police, attd. King's Shropshire Light Infantry. Died 11 November 1940 in a U.K. hospital after an accident. Aged 30. *h of Annie.* INCE CEMETERY. [X]

**MAXWELL Thomas Gerard,** Dvr. 2098893 Royal Army Service Corps. Died 29 August 1941. WIGAN CEMETERY. [X]

**MAY William,** Pte. 3782486 1st Bn. King's Regiment (Liverpool) Killed 5 March 1944. Aged 21. *s of Mr & Mrs John, Atherton; h of Maud Rose.* TAUKKYAN WAR CEMETERY, BURMA. [A]

**MAYER Leonard Aspinall,** Flt. Sgt. (Nav.) 1051991 R.A.F. (V.R.) 218 Sqdn. 5 May 1942. Aged 29. A Stirling I bomber on a raid on Pilsen crashed in Frankfurt. Only one of the eight crew members survived - and he became a PoW. *s of James & Elizabeth; h of Margaret.* DURNBACH WAR CEMETERY, GERMANY. [SMC/W/WGS/WPC]

**MAYERS Harry,** Pte. 3523145 5th Bn. The Manchester Regiment. Killed in a road accident, 28 October 1939. Aged 29. *h of Emily.* SHEVINGTON CEMETERY. [S]

**MAYERS Joseph Henry,** Gdsmn. 2719816 2nd Bn. Irish Guards. Captured in France in May 1940 and died of his wounds in a Lille hospital 31 July 1940. Aged 27. *s of Henry & Mary Ellen, Hindley.* LILLE SOUTHERN CEMETERY. [X]

**MEADOWS Harry,** Pte. 1640721 2nd Bn. The Gloucestershire Regiment. Died 11 September 1944 in Worcestershire Hospital of wounds received in the invasion of France. Aged 24. *s of Thomas & Sarah, Pemberton; h of Margaret Jane.* PEMBERTON (ST JOHN) CHURCHYARD, WIGAN. [W]

**MEADOWS James Gladstone,** Gnr. 3856946 15 Bty., 6 H.A.A. Regiment, Royal Artillery. Died 29 November 1943 while being transported as a PoW of the Japanese. He has no known grave. Aged 23. *He had family connections in Hindley, Wigan and Leigh.* SINGAPORE MEMORIAL. [X]

**MEADOWS Walter,** Sgt. (Obs.) 924395 R.A.F. (V.R.) 18 Sqdn. Killed 20 September 1941 when his Blenheim bomber was shot down off Zandvoort, Holland while attacking a convoy. Aged 26. He had earlier been a member of the crew of the aircraft which had dropped a replacement artificial leg on to St Omer Aerodrome for the famous Wing Commander Douglas Bader who was a PoW. *s of Walter & Hannah.* BERGEN-OP-ZOOM WAR CEMETERY, HOLLAND. [AC/AGS/NAV]

**MELLAN William Patrick Joseph,** Pte. 14376170 1st Bn. The Dorsetshire Regiment. Killed in action in France 11 June 1944. Aged 20. *s of William Patrick & Edith.* HOTTOT-LES-BAGNES CEMETERY. [L]

**MELLING Eric,** L.Cpl. 3866035 1st Airborne Bn., The Border Regiment. Killed at Arnhem 20 September 1944 during Operation Market Garden. He has no known grave. Aged 21. *s of Thomas & Helen; h of Annie, Wigan.* GROESBEEK MEMORIAL, HOLLAND. [SMC/W]

**MELLING James Ronald,** A.C.2. 1073540 R.A.F. (V.R.) Died in Wigan Infirmary, 2 June 1941. Aged 20. WIGAN CEMETERY. [W]

**MELLING Sydney,** Ord. Sig. D/JX250448 Royal Navy. 7 May 1942. Aged 20. Some sources show him serving in H.M.S. *Party Cunning* at the time of his death; others give H.M.S. *Karanja.* *s of Eva Melling.* DIEGO SUAREZ WAR CEMETERY, MADAGASCAR. [W/WGS]

**MELLING William,** Pte. 3597056 1st Airborne Bn., The Border Regiment. Killed at Arnhem 25 September 1944 during Operation Market Garden. Aged 29. *s of Mrs. Annie Wall, Scholes, Wigan.* ARNHEM OOSTERBEEK WAR CEMETERY, HOLLAND. [W]

**MELLING William Joseph,** Pte. 3596801 4th Bn. The Border Regiment. Killed 5 December 1941 in the Middle East. Aged 27. *s of William & Margaret; h of Louisa, Pemberton.* TOBRUK WAR CEMETERY, LIBYA. [W]

**MELLINGS Stanley,** Pte. 3188213 2nd Bn. King's Own Scottish Borderers. Died of wounds in Burma 19 January 1944. Aged 23. *s of Thomas & Alice Ann.* TAUKKYAN WAR CEMETERY, BURMA. [X]

**MELLOR Fred,** Pte. 14210319 1st Bn. The Herefordshire Regiment, The King's Shropshire Light Infantry. Killed in Holland 22 September 1944. Aged 23. *s of Benjamin & Edith, Leigh.* MIERLO WAR CEMETERY, HOLLAND. [L]

**MERCER Thomas,** E.R.A. 4th Class. D/MX74011 R.N. H.M.S. *Whitaker.* Died 1 November 1944. Aged 23. Off Londonderry, this frigate was seriously damaged by a torpedo from the U-boat *U-483* and was towed to Belfast. It was a total loss. *s of James & Margaret, Tyldesley.* PLYMOUTH NAVAL MEMORIAL. [T/TC] (See Frank Pimblett who also died in the same action.)

**MERGA Fred,** Pte. 13073308 Army Catering Corps attd. The Pioneer Corps. Killed in an accident in England 1 May 1943. Aged 22. *s of Arthur & Gertrude; h of Maggie.* ATHERTON CEMETERY. [A]

**MERRICK John,** Spr. 2149755 Royal Engineers. Killed in action in Sicily 14 July 1943. Aged 22. *s of Thomas & Mary.* SYRACUSE WAR CEMETERY. [X]

**MERRILL George,** Sgt. (Flt. Eng.) 1005888 R.A.F. (V.R.) 35 Sqdn. 2 December 1943. Aged 31. A Halifax II bomber from Graveley crashed near Dusseldorf during a raid on Berlin. *s of William & Kate; h of Matildy.* REICHSWALD FOREST WAR CEMETERY, GERMANY. [SAC/W]

**METCALF Leonard,** Cpl. 3663371 1st Bn. The East Lancashire Regiment. 6 April 1945 in Germany. Aged 29. *s of George & Emma; h of Gladys Lyon, Ince.* REICHSWALD FOREST WAR CEMETERY, GERMANY. [HGC]

**MIDDLETON Eric,** Sgt. 1312412 R.A.F. (V.R.) 612 Sqdn. Killed 4 August 1943 while flying in a Wellington aicraft from a base in England. Details are not known but 612 Squadron was not operating in Bomber Command in 1943. Aged 22. He has no known grave. *s of Henry & Lily.* RUNNYMEDE MEMORIAL. [L/LMC]

**MIDDLETON William,** L.Cpl. 3529147 1st Bn. The Manchester Regiment. Killed 14 February 1942 during the unsuccessful battle to save Singapore. Aged 42. *He had family connections with Wigan.* KRANJI WAR CEMETERY, SINGAPORE. [X]

**MILES Joseph,** Sgt. 992871 R.A.F. (V.R.) Killed in a flying accident 4 January 1943. Aged 22. *s of William & Frances.* LEIGH CEMETERY. [L/LAS/LGS/LTC]

**MILLARD Frank,** Ldg. Smn. P/JX182895 R.N. H.M.S. *Formidable.* 4 May 1945. Aged 26. *s of Joseph & Elizabeth.* PORTSMOUTH NAVAL MEMORIAL. [T/TMC]

**MILLARD Samuel,** L. Cpl. 7606798 6th Bn. The Royal Inniskilling Fusiliers. Killed in action in North Africa 22 April 1943. Aged 29. *s of Eli James & Isabella.* MEDJEZ-EL-BAB WAR CEMETERY, TUNISIA. [T]

**MILLIGAN Clifford,** Chief E.R.A. D/MX58933 R.N. H.M.S. *Pickle.* 4 October 1946. Aged 34. s *of Edward & Mary Ellen Milligan, Ince; h of Olive Milligan.* INCE CEMETERY. [X]

**MILLS John Thomas,** E.R.A. 4th Class. P/MX56288 R.N. H.M.S. *Barham.* 25 November 1941. Aged 23. In the eastern Mediterranean, this battleship was torpedoed by the German U-boat *U-331* with the loss of 862 crew. s *of Thomas & Agnes, Bryn; h of Agnes John.* PORSMOUTH NAVAL MEMORIAL. [X] (See also: J.H. Gerrard; Joseph O'Brien and John Robinson.)

**MITCHELL Albion Richard,** Gdsmn. 3rd Bn. The Coldstream Guards. Killed 30 December 1943 in Italy. Aged 33. s *of Albion & Martha; h of Elsie, Leigh.* MINTURNO WAR CEMETERY, ITALY. [L/LGS]

**MITCHELL Francis (Frank),** Pte. 4692254 1st Bn. King's Own Yorkshire Light Infantry. Died in a Scottish hospital 20 August 1940. Aged 22. s *of Patrick & Alice, Ince; h of Violet.* LEEDS (NEW WORTLEY) CEMETERY. [X]

**MITCHELL John,** Pte. 3858862 1st Bn. The Loyal Regiment (North Lancashire). Died in an Eastern Counties hospital 24 August 1942. Aged 23. s *of J & R, Scholes, Wigan.* WIGAN CEMETERY. [W]

**MITCHELL Thomas,** Tpr. 5049491 1st Regiment, The Recconaissance Corps. Died of wounds in North Africa 12 May 1943. Aged 22. s *of Thomas & Mary.* ENFIDAVILLE WAR CEMETERY, TUNISIA. [W]

**MOLYNEUX William,** Gnr. 3709323 120 Field Regiment, Royal Artillery. Died 1 October 1946. Aged 35. *h of Nancy, Pemberton.* WIGAN CEMETERY. [X]

**MONAGHAN Vincent,** L.A.C. 1056266 R.A.F. (V.R.) Died 23 May 1943. Aged 23. s *of Bernard & Margaret.* WIGAN CEMETERY. [W]

**MONEY Ernle William,** Captain. *O.B.E.* R.N. H.M.S. *Cabbala.* He was the Commanding Officer of a naval camp in Lancashire and died 30 September 1943, aged 59. s *of Col. Edward (Central India Horse) and Susan.* LOWTON ST. MARY'S (ST. MARY) CHURCHYARD. [X]

**MONK Arthur Leslie,** Gnr. 11257553 481 Bty., 98 Lt. A.A. Regiment, Royal Artillery. Killed in an accident 5 June 1942. Aged 29. s *of Arthur & Annie; h of Lily.* ATHERTON CEMETERY. [L] (His surname is shown as *Monks* on the Leigh memorial.)

**MONKS John,** Fus. 3649830 2/6th Bn. The Lancashire Fusiliers. Died 11 November 1941. Aged 36. *h of Margaret, Banfurlong.* GOLBORNE (ST THOMAS) CHURCHYARD. [G/GOC]

**MONKS Thomas,** Cpl. 317143 9th Queen's Royal Lancers, R.A.C. Killed 24 April 1943. Aged 29. s *of Mr & Mrs Isaac, Manley Street, Lower Ince.* MEDJEZ-EL-BAB WAR CEMETERY, TUNISIA. [ISM]

**MOODY Leopold,** Flying Offr. (Nav.) 151395 R.A.F. (V.R.) 540 Sqdn. Killed 10 May 1944 while carrying out photo-reconnaissance in a Mosquito aircraft. Aged 32. *s of Leopold & Margaret; h of Winifred Margaret.* KLAGENFURT WAR CEMETERY, AUSTRIA. [X]

**MOODY Thomas,** Musician. RMB/X1528 A member of the Royal Marines Band on H.M.S. *Dunedin.* 24 November 1941. Aged 37. Off St Paul's Rocks, the cruiser was sunk by the U-boat *U-124.* *s of James & Martha; h of Rose, Wigan.* PORTSMOUTH NAVAL MEMORIAL. [W]

**MOORE Andrew,** Fus. 3451499 2/5th Bn. The Lancashire Fusiliers. Died 1 August 1944 in a military hospital in the U.K. of wounds received in the invasion of Europe. WIGAN CEMETERY. [W]

**MOORES John,** A.B. C/JX352463 R.N. H.M.S. *Boadicea* 13 June 1944. Aged 21. This ship was sunk by German aircraft off Portland Bill. *s of Albert & Mary Ellen.* CHATHAM NAVAL MEMORIAL. [W]
(See: Eric Abbott and Harry Kenyon who also died in this attack.)

**MORAN Joseph,** Fus. 3530633 2nd Bn. The Lancashire Fusiliers. Killed in Italy 27 March 1945. Aged 23. *s of Joseph & Mary.* FAENZA WAR CEMETERY. [T]

**MORGAN Alfred,** Pte. 3716963 8th Bn. Durham Light Infantry. He arrived in France on D-Day but died of wounds 14 June 1944. Aged 32. *h of Ruth Morgan.* RYES WAR CEMETERY, FRANCE. [IN/PBC]

**MORGAN Roger,** Pte. 3513210 50 Coy., Auxiliary Military Pioneer Corps. Lost in the sinking of s.s. *Lancastria* 17 June 1940. Aged 49. *h of Margaret, Pemberton.* DUNKIRK MEMORIAL. [W]
(Twelve other local men perished when this ship was sunk. See the **Herbert Cunliffe** entry for names and details of the sinking.)

**MORGAN Thomas,** Pte. 4977740 The Sherwood Foresters (Nottinghamshire & Derbyshire Regiment) Killed 30 June 1942 in the Far East. He has no known grave. *s of Peter & Catherine, Scholes, Wigan.* RANGOON MEMORIAL. [W]

**MORGAN William,** Pte. 3782768 2nd Bn. The Border Regiment. Killed in action in Burma 5 June 1944. Aged 20. *s of James & Mary, Aspull.* IMPHAL WAR CEMETERY, INDIA. [AS]

**MORLEY John,** A.B. D/JX226799 R.N. H.M.S. *Encounter.* This destroyer was attacked by a force of Japanese destroyers and was sunk by gunfire near Sourabaya 1 March 1942. A.B. Morley was captured and died as a PoW of the Japanese 20 April 1945. Aged 24. *s of William & Jane Ann, Bryn.* AMBON WAR CEMETERY, INDONESIA. [X]

**MORLEY John Thomas (Jackie)** Tpr. 3864578 50th Royal Tank Regiment, R.A.C. Killed 19 July 1943 in Sicily. Aged 22. He has no known grave. *s of Michael & Jane.* CASSINO MEMORIAL. [W]

**MORRIS George,** Craftsman 3862619 Royal Electrical & Mechanical Engineers. Died 1 June 1944 as a result of a road accident in Chester. Aged 29. *s of J.W. & M.J., Pemberton.* WIGAN CEMETERY. [W]

**MORRIS George,** Gnr. 868010 3 Regiment, Royal Horse Artillery. Died in an Egypt hospital 28 July 1940. Aged 23. CAIRO WAR MEMORIAL CEMETERY. [IN]

**MORRIS Harry,** Pte. 3530508 2nd Bn. The Loyal Regiment (North Lancashire). Captured in early 1942 and died as a PoW of the Japanese 24 October 1944 following the sinking of a Japanese PoW transport ship en route from Thailand to Japan. Aged 24. He has no known grave. *s of Thomas & Mary Ann Morris.* SINGAPORE MEMORIAL. [T/TMC]

**MORRIS Richard,** Marine PLY/X1808 Royal Marines H.M.S. *Stronghold.* 2 March 1942. Aged 24. This destroyer was withdrawing from Java when it was sunk by Japanese ships. *s of Meshach & Bertha, Lowton St. Marys.* PLYMOUTH NAVAL MEMORIAL. [X]

**MORRIS Wilfred,** Pte. 13045356 Auxiliary Military Pioneer Corps. Missing at sea when on board s.s. *Mohamed Ali El-Kabir.* 7 August 1940. Aged 26. Off the Irish coast, this passenger liner en route from Bristol to Gibraltar with nearly 700 troops was sunk by the German U-boat *U-38.* 120 crew and troops died. *s of Albert & Mary Ellen; h of Edith, Atherton.* BROOKWOOD MEMORIAL, SURREY. [A/HAC]

**MORRISON Daniel,** L.A.C. 968334 R.A.F. (V.R.) Killed 20 September 1940. Aged 20. *s of James Roy & Mariden. He had family connections in Standish and Tyldesley.* DEANE (ST MARY) CHURCHYARD, BOLTON. [LGS/ST/STC]

**MORT Thomas,** A.B. D/JX156010 R.N. H.M.S. *Matabele.* 17 January 1942. Aged 20. This destroyer, while escorting a Russia-bound convoy, was sunk by U-boat *U-454* off Kola with the loss of 198 crew members. *s of Jesse & Alice.* PLYMOUTH NAVAL MEMORIAL. [G/GOC]
(See also Ned Broadbent who died in this action.)

**MORTON William,** Sgt. 1073134 R.A.F. (V.R.) 221 Sqdn. 18 April 1943. Aged 23. This Coastal Command aircraft crashed into the sea. All members of the crew were killed and have no known graves. *s of Wilfred & Selena.* MALTA MEMORIAL. [L/LAS/LGS/LTC]

**MOSS Colin,** Sgt.(Flt. Engr.) 2205500 R.A.F. 432 Sqdn. 15 October 1944 Age 20. His Halifax bomber was lost during a raid on Wilhelmshaven. All seven members of the crew (which included four Canadians) perished and are buried together in Sage War Cemetery. *s of Robert & Margaret, Pemberton .* SAGE WAR CEMETERY, GERMANY. [HIY/PC]

**MOSS Frank,** Lieut. 224755 Royal Engineers. Died of wounds in Tunisia 11 May 1943. Aged 22. *s of George & Lily.* MEDJEZ-EL-BAB WAR CEMETERY, TUNISIA. [X]

**MOXEY Frederick William,** Steward LT/LX27668 R.N. Patrol Service. H.M. Trawler *Orpheus.* 20 April 1942. Aged 21. *s of Frederick William & Amelia, Lowestoft; h of Violet May, Leigh.* LOWESTOFT (KIRKLEY) CEMETERY. [X]

**MULLEN Thomas,** Gnr. 3527013 7 Bty., 5 H.A.A. Regiment, Royal Artillery. Killed in action 19 December 1941 during the invasion of Hong Kong. Aged 25. He has no known grave. *s of Elizabeth & Thomas.* SAI WAN BAY MEMORIAL, HONG KONG. [W]

**MULROONEY Herbert,** Fus. 3710312 2nd Bn. The Lancashire Fusiliers. Died 27 November 1944 in Italy after an accident resulting in gunshot wounds. Aged 29. BARI WAR CEMETERY, ITALY. [X]

**MURISON James,** Cpl. 2694671 Corps of Military Police Died 10 August 1941. Aged 29. *h of Ivy May.* LEIGH CEMETERY. [X]

**MURPHY James,** L.A.C. 1006794 R.A.F. (V.R.) 1 August 1942 in the Middle East. Aged 30. *s of James & Elizabeth.* HELIOPOLIS WAR CEMETERY, EGYPT. [W]

**MURPHY Lawrence,** Pte. 3861004 2nd Bn. The King's Regiment (Liverpool). Killed in Italy 20 July 1944. Aged 29. *s of Peter & Florence, Pemberton; h of Olive, Higher Ince.* AREZZO WAR CEMETERY, ITALY. [W]
(According to CWGC records, Pte. Murphy is incorrectly shown on the Wigan memorial as serving in the Loyal Regiment at the time of his death.)

**MURRAY Harry,** Gnr. 1767899 281 Bty., 88 H.A.A. Regiment, Royal Artillery. Died of pneumonia in Italy 17 December 1943. Aged 26. *s of William & Sarah, Hindley.* SANGRO RIVER WAR CEMETERY, ITALY. [HC]

**MURRAY Jacob (Jaques),** Capt. 313633 General List. Killed 25 June 1945 in a motor accident whilst serving with the Allied Military Government of Occupation. Aged 41. BECKLINGEN WAR CEMETERY, GERMANY. [L]

**MYERS Francis,** Sgt. (Flt. Eng.) 2209603 R.A.F. (V.R.) 90 Sqdn. 13 August 1944. Aged 26. His Lancaster bomber took-off from Tuddenham on a raid on Braunschweig but was lost over Germany with all members of the crew. *s of George & Frances, Astley.* BECKLINGEN WAR CEMETERY, GERMANY. [X]
(Almost certainly the brother of James who also died in action with the R.A.F.)

**MYERS Herbert Richard,** Gnr. 983466 22nd Field Regiment, Royal Artillery. Died of wounds in Italy 24 June 1944. Aged 24. *s of George & Margaret.* BOLSENA WAR CEMETERY, ITALY. [SSC/W/WSB]

**MYERS James,** Flt. Sgt. (Air Gnr.) 1015522 R.A.F. (V.R.) 156 Sqdn. 29 August 1942. Aged 28. The Wellington III bomber crashed near Brussels while engaged on a raid on Nuremburg. There were no survivors from the crew of five. *s of George & Frances, Astley.* HEVERLEE WAR CEMETERY, BELGIUM. [X]
(Almost certainly the brother of Francis who also died in action with the R.A.F.)

**MYERS Leonard,** Sgt. 1533554 R.A.F. (V.R.) 12 Sqdn. 18 August 1943. Aged 29. His Lancaster III bomber on a raid on Pennemunde was believed to have been shot down and crashed off the coast of Denmark. No bodies were found. *s of George & Emma.* RUNNYMEDE MEMORIAL. [W]

**NAYLOR Gerald,** Marine PLY/X109574 Royal Marines. Killed in action on D-Day, 6 June 1944, when his landing-craft was hit by an enemy shore battery. Aged 20. *s of Peter & Edith.* BAYEAUX WAR CEMETERY, NORMANDY. [ABC/AGS]

**NEARY Wilfred,** Pte. 3856327 2nd Bn. The Loyal Regiment (North Lancashire) Killed in action during the fall of Singapore 23 January 1942. Aged 29. He has no known grave. *s of Thomas & Honorah, Leigh.* SINGAPORE MEMORIAL. [L/LTA]

**NEEDHAM Eric,** Flt. Sgt. (Flt. Eng.) 1685783 R.A.F. (V.R.) Killed 4 January 1946 when the Coastal Command Liberator in which he was flying was forced down in fog. All eight crew members were killed. Aged 22. *s of Robert & Hannah, Hindley Green.* STAVANGER CHURCHYARD, NORWAY. [HGC]
(See also Warrant Officer Frank Brindle from Leigh who was the pilot of the aircraft.)

**NEEDHAM George,** Pte. 3780156 13th Bn. The King's Regiment (Liverpool) Died of wounds 12 May 1943 while serving with the Chindits in Burma. He has no known grave. Aged 32. *s of George & Alice; h of Alice.* RANGOON MEMORIAL. [L/LTC]

**NEEDLE Harold,** Sgt. 983086 R.A.F. (V.R.) 90 Sqdn. 16 August 1941. Aged 21. The Fortress I bomber was on a raid on Brest but it was shot-up by fighters. Three crew members including Sgt Needle were killed but the aircraft managed to crash-land near Plymouth. *s of G & H.* GOLBORNE (ST THOMAS) CHURCHYARD. [AGS/G/GOC]

**NEILD Robert,** Sto. 1st Class. D/KX114408 R.N. H.M.S. *Londonderry* 3 February 1943. Aged 22. *s of Thomas & Mary, Kitt Green, Wigan.* PLYMOUTH NAVAL MEMORIAL. [PC]

**NELSON Edward Bullough,** Cook. D/MX101192 R.N. H.M.S. *Kite.* 21 August 1944. Off Norway, the sloop was sunk by the German U-boat *U-344.* PLYMOUTH NAVAL MEMORIAL. [L/LMC/WMC]
(See: Thomas Aldred; Albert Grundy and Thomas Payne who also died when H.M.S. *Kite* was sunk.)

**NELSON Leonard,** A.B. P/JX162048 R.N. H.M.S. *Sultan* 16 February 1942. Aged 18. H.M.S. *Sultan* was the Naval Base at Singapore and it is assumed that he lost his life during the battle which resulted in the fall of the colony. He has no known grave. PORTSMOUTH NAVAL MEMORIAL. [UP/UPC]

**NEVILLE John,** Flt. Lt. 131567 R.A.F. (V.R.) 635 Sqdn. 30 August 1944. Aged 31. His Lancaster III bomber took off from Downham Market on an operation to bomb Stettin. It was lost without trace. *s of William & Elizabeth.* RUNNYMEDE MEMORIAL. [B]

**NEWALL Albert Stephenson,** 2932563 2nd Bn. The Queen's Own Cameron Highlanders. Died 3 November 1941 in the Middle East. HALFAYA SOLLUM WAR CEMETERY, EGYPT. [X]

**NEWELL Edward,** Gnr. 1780880 197 Bty., 61 Lt. A.A. Regiment, Royal Artillery. Killed 14 November 1942 in the Middle East. Aged 22. He has no known grave. *s of James & Jane, Platt Bridge.* ALAMEIN MEMORIAL. [PBC]

**NICHOLLS Harold,** Pte. 3523903 The Manchester Regiment attd. Auxiliary Military Pioneer Corps. Killed in France 17 June 1940 when a troop train was bombed by German aircraft at Rennes. Aged 36. RENNES EASTERN COMMUNAL CEMETERY, FRANCE. [JC/W]

**NICHOLLS Leonard Raymonds,** Cpl. 3709749 2nd Bn. The King's Own Royal Regiment (Lancaster). Killed in the Middle East 21 November 1941. *s of Edward & Mary Elizabeth.* KNIGHTSBRIDGE WAR CEMETERY, LIBYA. [BNC]

**NICHOLLS Stanley,** Sgt. (W.Op.) 973969 R.A.F. (V.R.) 502 Sqdn. Killed in a flying accident 5 November 1940. Aged 21. *s of Robert & Annie, Wigan.* PRESTON (NEW HALL LANE) CEMETERY. [SSC/W]

**NICHOLLS William Henry,** Pte. 3529402 The Manchester Regiment. Died 12 June 1947. GOOSE GREEN (ST PAUL) CHURCHYARD. [JC]

**NICHOLSON Edmund,** Pte. 5674834 7th Bn. The Oxfordshire & Buckinghamshire Light Infantry. Killed in Italy 20 January 1944. Aged 34. He has no known grave. *s of Edmund & Mary; h of Elsie, Tyldesley.* CASSINO MEMORIAL. [A/HAC]
(His brother John was killed in the Middle East while serving with the Royal Tank Regiment)

**NICHOLSON Harry Alec,** Pilot Offr. (Pilot) 106229 R.A.F. (V.R.) Killed 4 November 1941. Aged 25. *s of Samuel Gordon & Amy Elizabeth. P.O. Nicholson was the P.E. Instructor at Wigan Grammar School from 1938 until the outbreak of war.* EALING & OLD BRENTFORD CEMETERY, EALING. [WGS]

**NICHOLSON John,** Tpr. 3535836 1st Royal Tank Regiment, R.A.C. Killed 6 November 1942 in the Middle East. Aged 26. *s of Edmund & Mary; h of Minnie, Atherton.* EL ALAMEIN WAR CEMETERY, EGYPT. [A/HAC]
(His brother Edmund was killed in 1944 while serving with the Oxfordshire & Buckinghamshire Light Infantry in Italy)

**NICHOLSON John Thomas,** Pte. 14209599 2nd Bn. The Monmouthshire Regiment. Killed in France 15 August 1944. Aged 22. *s of Ernest & Nellie, Billinge.* BANNEVILLE-LA-CAMPAGNE CEMETERY, FRANCE. [BC]

**NICHOLSON William,** Pte. 3134802 7th Bn. The Argyll & Sutherland Highlanders. Killed 23 March 1945. Aged 29. *s of William & Lilian; h of Margaret, Bamfurlong.* REICHSWALD FOREST WAR CEMETERY, GERMANY. [AIM/BMC]

**NIGHTINGALE Leonard,** Pte. 3524397 The King's Shropshire Light Infantry, D.E.M.S. Personnel. Drowned at sea on active service 28 April 1941. Aged 28. He has no known grave. *s of Thomas & Sarah; h of Edna May.* PLYMOUTH NAVAL MEMORIAL. [L/LTC]

**NOLAN Charles,** Pte. 3715938 1ˢᵗ Bn. The King's Own Royal Regiment (Lancaster). Died at sea 23 July 1941. Aged 26. *s of Charles & Catherine; h of Ruth, Tyldesley.* BROOKWOOD MEMORIAL, SURREY. [T]

**NORBURN James,** A.B. D/JX366864 R.N. H.M.S. *Warwick.* 20 February 1944. Aged 21. Off Trevose Head, this destroyer was sunk by the German U-boat *U-413. s of Peter & Elizabeth, Wigan.* PLYMOUTH NAVAL MEMORIAL. [SGC/W]

**NORCROSS Horace Pilling,** Sgt. 1120097 R.A.F. (V.R.) 115 Sqdn. Killed 29 October 1942. Aged 28. His Wellington bomber took-off from Mildenhall to bomb Essen. It was presumed lost in the sea off the Dutch coast. *s of Herbert P. & Emma.* RUNNYMEDE MEMORIAL [AGS]

**NORRIS Alick Clem,** Sgt. (Air Gnr.) 1589308 R.A.F. (V.R.) 619 Sqdn. 6 November 1944. Aged 19. His Lancaster bomber was tasked to attack the Dortmund-Ems and Mitteland canal system near Gravenhorst.. Three members of the crew were killed and four became PoWs. *s of Joshua & Winifred.* REICHSWALD FOREST WAR CEMETERY, GERMANY. [L]

**NORRIS Ellis,** Seaman LT/JX203675 R.N. Patrol Service. H.M. Trawler *Northern Princess.* 7 March 1942. Aged 24. *s of James & M.A.; h of Edith.* LOWESTOFT MEMORIAL. [L/LTC]

**NORRIS Eric,** L.Cpl. 3866211 1ˢᵗ Bn. The Loyal Regiment (North Lancashire). Killed in Italy 20 August 1944. Aged 24. *s of John & Mary, Wigan.* FLORENCE WAR CEMETERY, ITALY. [BHC/W]

**NORTON Michael,** Lieut. 288376 Royal Corps of Signals. Died of sickness in India 4 December 1944. Aged 28. *s of Hugh & Jennie; h of Lilian.* KIRKEE WAR CEMETERY, INDIA. [X]

**NUTTER Fred,** Air Mech. 1ˢᵗ Class. L/FX108428 R.N. H.M.S. *Grebe.* Died from multiple injuries in Royal Naval Hospital Alexandria, 24 August 1945. Aged 36. *s of Richard & Annie; h of May.* ALEXANDRIA (HADRA) CEMETERY, EGYPT. [HAC/T/TC]

**OAKES Arnold,** Flying Offr. (Nav.) 152084 R.A.F. 39 Sqdn. Killed in Sardinia 17 June 1944. Aged 23. PHALERON WAR CEMETERY. [L/LGS/T/TC]

**O'BRIEN Joseph,** A.B. D/SSX15568 R.N. H.M.S. *Barham.* 25 November 1941. Aged 28. In the eastern Mediterranean, this battleship was torpedoed by German U-boat *U-331* and blew-up with the loss of 862 crew. *s of Michael & Cecily.* PORSMOUTH NAVAL MEMORIAL. [L]
(See also J.H. Gerrard; J.T. Mills and John Robinson who were lost in this action.)

**O'BRIEN Robert,** Seaman LT/JX199078 R.N. Patrol Service, H.M. Drifter *Reed* He died 7 November 1940. Aged 17. This drifter was sunk by a mine in the Thames Estuary. *s of James & Edith.*. WARRINGTON CEMETERY. [X] (The brother of Thomas who was killed in action in France.)

**O'BRIEN Thomas,** Pte. 3651215 1st Bn. The South Lancashire Regiment (The Prince of Wales's Volunteers) Killed in action in France 24 June 1944. Aged 30. *s of James & Edith; h of Elizabeth, Ashton-in-Makerfield.* LA DELIVERANDE WAR CEMETERY, NORMANDY. [X] (His brother Robert also died on service.)

**O'DONNELL Joseph,** L.Cpl. 2716792 1st Bn. Irish Guards. Killed in Italy 30 January 1944. Aged 42. *s of John & Annie; h of Annie, Atherton.* ANZIO WAR CEMETERY, ITALY. [A/HBC]

**O'GARA Dominic,** Pte. 14613406 1st Bn. The Queen's Royal Regiment (West Surrey). Killed in France 3 August 1944. Aged 19. He has no known grave. *s of Dominic & Ellen, Ashton-in-Makerfield.* BAYEAUX MEMORIAL. [X]

**OLDBURY Victor Howard Edgar,** L.A.C. 1409487 R.A.F. (V.R.) 245 Sqdn. Died 6 February 1946. Aged 24. *s of Howard & Dorothy; h of Phyllis Eileen, Wigan.* WIMBORNE MINSTER CEMETERY. [X]

**O'LEARY Thomas,** Pte. 4206436 2/5th Bn. The Royal Leicestershire Regiment. Killed 14 September 1943. Aged 19. He has no known grave. *s of Edward & Agnes, Wigan.* CASSINO MEMORIAL. [W]

**OLIVER Frederick,** Sgt. (Air Gnr.) 1006958 R.A.F. (V.R.) 622 Sqdn. 24 June 1944. Aged 22. His Lancaster I bomber took-off from Mildenhall to destroy a flying-bomb site. It crashed near Bergues. *s of John & Agnes; h of Kathleen, Beech Hill, Wigan.* SOCX CHURCHYARD, FRANCE. [W]

**OLLERTON John,** Ordnance Mech. D/MX90823 R.N. H.M.S. *Asphodel.* 9 March 1944. Aged 33. Off Cape Finisterre, the corvette was sunk by the German U-boat *U-575*. *s of Walter & Elizabeth; h of Lilian.* PLYMOUTH NAVAL MEMORIAL. [BL/BCC]

**OLSSON Richard,** L.Cpl. 3523990 1st Bn. The Manchester Regiment. Killed 14 February 1942 during the battle for Singapore. Aged 28. He has no known grave. SINGAPORE MEMORIAL. [W]

**ORMISHER Harry,** Pte. 3654442 1st Bn. The South Lancashire Regiment (Prince of Wales's Volunteers.) Killed 31 May 1940 during the withdrawal to Dunkirk. Aged 27. *s of William & Gertrude, Appley Bridge.* DE PANNE COMMUNAL CEMETERY, BELGIUM. [AP/APC]

**ORRELL John,** Sgt. 1232301 R.A.F. (V.R.) 25 October 1942. Aged 19. Lost his life while flying from a Canadian base. He has no known grave. *s of Thomas & Mary, Up Holland.* OTTAWA MEMORIAL. [UPC/UPH]

**OSBORNE Jack,** Sgt (Flt. Eng.) 1539830 R.A.F. (V.R.) 101 Sqdn. 23 June 1943. Aged 21. His Lancaster III bomber from Ludford Magna was shot down and crashed near Nijmegen, Holland. *s of Robert & Edith, Hindley.* UDEN WAR CEMETERY, HOLLAND. [HC]

**O'TOOLE John Gerrard,** Spr. 14221795 238 Field Coy., Royal Engineers. Killed in North Africa 29 April 1943. Aged 34. *h of Dorothy Elsie, Haigh.* MASSICAULT WAR CEMETERY, TUNISIA. [X]

**OWEN Edward,** Fus. 3446190 2nd Bn. The Lancashire Fusiliers. Killed 26 May 1940 during the withdrawal to Dunkirk. Aged 25. He has no known grave. *s of Albert & Lily.* DUNKIRK MEMORIAL. [W]

**OWEN Herbert,** Sjt. 3527077 6th Bn. The Royal Inniskilling Fusiliers. Killed in North Africa 7 April 1943. Aged 28. *s of Mr & Mrs. John; h of Catherine.* OUED ZARGA WAR CEMETERY, TUNISIA. [W]

**OWEN Jack,** Seaman. LT/JX377537 R.N. Patrol Service. H.M. Minesweeping Trawler *Avanturine.* 1 December 1943. Aged 20. This vessel was sunk by a German E-boat off Beachy Head. *s of William & Louisa, Atherton.* LOWESTOFT MEMORIAL. [A]

**OWEN Richard Cecil,** A.C.1. 1483664 R.A.F. (V.R.) 911 Balloon Sqdn. Killed in a motor accident 22 December 1942. Aged 31. *s of John & Mary; h of Ellen.* LEIGH CEMETERY. [L/LAS/LTC]

**OXBURY Arthur,** Gnr. 1703230 103 H.A.A. Regiment, Royal Artillery. Killed in anti-aircraft action in England, 28 November 1940. Aged 28. *h of Lily May, Golborne.* GOLBORNE (ST THOMAS) CHURCHYARD. [AIM/G/GOC]

**PAGE Roy,** Flt. Sgt. (Flt. Eng.) 996520 R.A.F. (V.R.) 355 Sqdn. Died 6 October 1944 whilst being held as a PoW of the Japanese. Aged 24. KANCHANABURI WAR CEMETERY, THAILAND. [L/LTC]

**PAINTER Thomas,** Cpl. 14206699 4th Bn. The Somerset Light Infantry. Killed 22 September 1944 in Holland. Aged 21. GROESBEEK CANADIAN WAR CEMETERY, HOLLAND. [AIM/AMS]

**PALMER Joseph,** Fus. 3859637 9th Bn. The Royal Fusiliers (City of London Regiment) Killed in action in Italy 30 October 1943. Aged 25. *s of John & Jane.* NAPLES WAR CEMETERY. [L]

**PARKER William,** A.C.1. 1083870 R.A.F. (V.R.) Died 27 October 1944 while a PoW of the Japanese. Aged 36. *s of William & Mary; h of Nancy of Swinley, Wigan.* AMBON WAR CEMETERY, INDONESIA. [W]

**PARKINSON Ernest,** Gnr. 14347151 114 Field Regiment, Royal Artillery Died in Burma 23 March 1944. Aged 32. He has no known grave. *s of Thomas & Elizabeth, Newtown, Wigan.* RANGOON MEMORIAL. [NC/W]

**PARKINSON Harry,** L.A.C. (Obs. U/T) 1251725 R.A.F. (V.R.) Killed in a flying accident in the U.K. 16 January 1941. Aged 27. *s of Walter & Ann, Lamberhead Green.* PEMBERTON CEMETERY. [AGS/PC]

**PARKINSON Jack,** L.Bdr. 3527034 434 Coast Bty., Royal Artillery. Died in Egypt 23 February 1943. Aged 27. HELIOPOLIS WAR CEMETERY. [W]

**PARKINSON James,** Pte. Q145441 A.C.M.F. 36 Bn. Australian Infantry. Killed 25 December 1942 while serving in New Guinea with Australian Imperial Forces. Aged 35. *s of Thomas & Mary Parkinson, Garswood, Ashton. He emigrated to Australia in 1926.* PORT MORESBY (BOMANA) WAR CEMETERY, PAPUA NEW GUINEA. [AC/NAV]

**PARKINSON Joseph,** Gnr. 5260084 136 Field Regiment, Royal Artillery. Killed in action in India 24 July 1943. Aged 32. *s of Joseph & Alice, Hindley.* RANCHI WAR CEMETERY, INDIA. [X]

**PARKINSON Norman James,** Pte. 13076347 240 Coy., The Pioneer Corps. Died 24 January 1944. Aged 34. *s of Ann.* BIRCHLEY (ST MARY) R.C. CHURCHYARD, BILLINGE & WINSTANLEY. [X]

**PARKINSON Ronald,** Pte. 1156747 7th Bn. The Somerset Light Infantry. Died in Germany 24 May 1945. Aged 22. *s of Walter & Mary Alice, Orrell.* HAMBURG WAR CEMETERY. [OC]

**PARKINSON William,** Dvr. T/10662437 Royal Army Service Corps. Died 16 April 1946. Aged 25. *s of Paul & Frances, Wigan.* CELLE WAR CEMETERY, GERMANY. [X]

**PARKINSON William Ronald,** Sgt. (Air Gnr.) 2204260 R.A.F. (V.R.) 57 Sqdn. 22 June 1944. Aged 19. The Lancaster III bomber took-off from East Kirby on a raid on Wesseling but was intercepted by a night-fighter and crashed near Julich. *s of Mr. & Mrs. William, Lower Ince.* RHEINBERG WAR CEMETERY, GERMANY. [IN]

**PARR Samuel,** Eng. Officer. Merchant Navy. m.v. *Dolius* 5 May 1943. Aged 29. This cargo liner, which was part of a United Kingdom to U.S.A. convoy, was sunk by the U-boat *U-628* south of Cape Farewell. *s of Reuben & Helen.* TOWER HILL MEMORIAL. [LGS]

**PARR William Henry,** Marine PO/X112668 1 Bty., 1 H.A.A. Regiment, Royal Marines. Died 19 February 1947. Aged 31. *h of Beatrice.* STANDISH (ST WILFRED) CHURCHYARD. [SMC]

**PARRY John Richard,** Fus. 3780995 6th Bn. The Royal Inniskilling Fusiliers. Died of wounds in North Africa 19 January 1943. Aged 32. *s of Edward & Anne; h of May.* MEDJEZ-EL-BAB WAR CEMETERY, TUNISIA. [L/LPC]

**PARRY John William,** Sick Berth P.O. P/X6490 R.N. H.M.S. *Prosperine.* Killed 17 November 1943. Aged 41. TYLDESLEY CEMETERY. [T/TC]

**PARRY Robert Thomas,** Sto. D/KX572298 R.N. H.M.S. *Hartland Point.* Died 27 December 1945. Aged 20. *s of John & Alice; h of Mildred, Wigan.* COLOMBO CEMETERY, CEYLON. [ACC/AMS]

**PARSONS James,** Ord. Artificer D/MX59418 R.N. H.M.S. *Illustrious.* 10 January 1941. Aged 25. West of Malta, some Ju-87 dive-bombers attacked this aircraft-carrier which was badly damaged but reached Malta still on fire. *s of James & Alice. His mother lost her first husband in the First World War and two sons in the Second World War. His brother William also died in service with the Royal Navy.* PLYMOUTH NAVAL MEMORIAL. [G/GOC]
(See also Reginald James Taylor who also died in this action.)

**PARSONS William,** E.R.A. 4$^{th}$ Class. D/MX60248 R.N. H.M. Submarine *Tetrarch.* 22 November 1941 Aged 25. The submarine was homeward-bound from Alexandria but was lost by an unknown cause between Malta and Gibraltar. *s of James & Alice. His mother lost her first husband in the First World War and two sons in the Second World War. His brother Thomas also died in service with the Royal Navy.* PLYMOUTH NAVAL MEMORIAL. [G/GOC]

**PARTINGTON Granville,** Fus. 3606979 2/5$^{th}$ Bn. The Lancashire Fusiliers. Died of wounds received during the invasion of France. 8 July 1944. Aged 21. *s of Fred & Hannah, Leigh.* LA DELIVERANDE WAR CEMETERY, FRANCE. [X]

**PARTINGTON Ian,** Flying Offr. (Nav.) 156772 R.A.F.(V.R.) 514 Sqdn. 20 September 1944. Aged 23. His Lancaster I bomber took off from Waterbeach to raid targets near Calais and crashed into the sea. *s of George & Beatrice; h of Kathleen, Westhoughton.* CALAIS CANADIAN WAR CEMETERY. [HGS]

**PASSANT Fred Vincent,** Sgt. 1480175 R.A.F. (V.R.) 77 Sqdn. 20 December 1942. Aged 23. His Halifax II bomber was on a training flight when it crashed near York. All the crew died. *s of G.W. & Fanny, Leigh.* LEIGH CEMETERY [L/LTC]

**PATMORE Arthur,** Gnr. 14583879 72 Anti-Tank Regiment, Royal Artillery. Died of wounds in Italy 3 August 1944. Aged 32. *h of Ellen.* AREZZO WAR CEMETERY, ITALY. [W]

**PATRICK John Buckley,** L.A.C. 1081463 R.A.F. (V.R.) Died 28 January 1943. Aged 29. *h of Florence, Appley Bridge.* WORSLEY CHURCHYARD. [X]

**PAXTON James,** L.Cpl. 3859191 18$^{th}$ (5$^{th}$ Bn. The Loyal Regiment [North Lancashire]) Regiment, Reconnaissance Corps. Died as a PoW of the Japanese 25 November 1943. Aged 24. *s of Thomas & Alice.* THANBYUZAYAT WAR CEMETERY, BURMA. [JC]

**PAYNE Thomas,** Sto. 1$^{st}$ Class. D/KX106398 R.N. H.M.S. *Kite.* 21 August 1944. Aged 26. Off north Norway, the sloop was sunk by the German U-boat *U-344.* PLYMOUTH NAVAL MEMORIAL. [L/LTC]
(See also Thomas Aldred; Albert Grundy and Edward Nelson who also died when this vessel was sunk.)

**PEAKE John,** Pte. 14290214 2nd Bn. The Border Regiment. Killed in Burma 3 February 1945. Aged 23. *s of Issac & Mary Jane, Leigh.* TAUKKAYAN WAR CEMETERY, BURMA. [L/LMC]

**PEEL Robert,** Sto. 1st. Class P/KX128138 R.N. H.M.S. *Andelle.* Died in a naval base hospital 18 November 1943. *s of Abel & Jane.* HODSACK (LANGOLD) CEMETERY, NOTTINGHAMSHIRE. [X]

**PEET Peter,** Gnr. 1560561 7/4 Maritime Regiment, Royal Artillery. Killed at sea while serving as a gunner in the Merchant Service. 11 September 1941. Aged 21. PLYMOUTH NAVAL MEMORIAL. [HIC/MZC/W]

**PENDLEBURY Herbert,** Sjt. 3531412 111th (5th Bn. The Manchester Regiment), R.A.C. Died in a road accident 29 June 1943. Aged 23. He was a survivor of the Dunkirk evacuation. *s of Wilfred & Doris.* LEIGH CEMETERY [L/LMC]

**PENDLEBURY Kenneth,** Cpl. 7906832 'B' Squadron, 13/18th Royal Hussars, R.A.C. Killed in Normandy 22 July 1944. Aged 24. *s of Ernest & Maggie; h of Margaret.* RANVILLE WAR CEMETERY. [L/LTC]

**PENDLEBURY Michael Kenny,** 2nd. Lieut. 331902 The East Lancashire Regiment. Killed 16 April 1945 in Germany. Aged 19. *s of Brig. James William, D.S.O., M.C. & Dorothy.* BECKLINGEN WAR CEMETERY. [X]

**PENDLEBURY Samuel,** Gnr. 1803544 137 Lt. A.A. Regiment, Royal Artillery. Died 28 May 1942. Aged 30. *h of Bertha.* ATHERTON CEMETERY. [X]

**PENNINGTON Arnold,** L.Cpl. 7611187 Royal Army Ordnance Corps. Killed 22 December 1941 during the defence of Hong Kong. Aged 22. He has no known grave. *s of William & Jennie, Goose Green, Wigan.* SAI WAN BAY MEMORIAL, HONG KONG. [GGC/W]

**PENNINGTON Edward,** Pte. 3856207 2nd Bn. The Loyal Regiment (North Lancashire). Killed 23 January 1942 during the fierce actions which preceded the fall of Singapore. Aged 25. He has no known grave. *Foster s of Mr. & Mrs. D.* SINGAPORE MEMORIAL [X]

**PENNINGTON Harold Hammond,** Capt. 1340871 The Hampshire Regiment & No. 4 Commando. Killed during the St. Nazaire raid, 28 March 1942. Aged 23. *s of Walter & Ada, Ashton-in-Makerfield; h of Edna Elizabeth, Ashton-in-Makerfield.* ESCOUBLAC-LA-BAULE WAR CEMETERY. [ACC]

**PENNINGTON Henry,** Pte. 3528612 The Manchester Regiment. Died 12 August 1946. Aged 47. *s of William & Mary; h of Sarah Alice, Ince.* INCE-IN-MAKERFIELD CEMETERY. [ISM]

**PENNINGTON Jack,** Sgt. (W.Op./Air Gnr.) 1040748 R.A.F. (V.R.) Died 16 December 1943. Aged 23. *s of William & Margaret, Billinge; h of Lilian, Billinge.* ORRELL (ST LUKE) CHURCHYARD. [OC]

**PERRY Andrew,** Pte. 3866214 1$^{st}$ Bn. The Loyal Regiment (North Lancashire) Killed in action 26 May 1944 at the Anzio landing. Aged 36. *s of Samuel & Alice; h of Elizabeth, Wigan.* BEACH HEAD WAR CEMETERY, ANZIO, ITALY. [W]

**PETERKIN James Smith,** Pilot Offr. 135517 R.A.F. (V.R.) Died 13 May 1943 in Canada. Aged 25. *s of James Roger & Annie.* VICTORIA (ROYAL OAK) BURIAL PARK, CANADA. [W]

**PETTET Alexander Henry,** Pilot Offr. 85011 R.A.F. (V.R.) 248 Sqdn. Killed 13 December 1940 on a Coastal Command anti-shipping operation in a Blenheim aircraft. Aged 28. He has no known grave. *s of Alexander Charles & Ada Lewis.* RUNNYMEDE MEMORIAL. [W/WGS/WPC]

**PHILLIPS Edward,** Pte. 3781088 7$^{th}$ Bn. The Oxfordshire & Buckinghamshire Light Infantry. Killed 4 September 1944 in Italy. Aged 34. CORIANO RIDGE WAR CEMETERY. [T]

**PHILLIPS Frederick James,** Sto. 1$^{st}$ Class. D/KX88550 R.N. H.M. Submarine *Rainbow.* 19 October 1940. Aged 24. The submarine was sunk off Calabria with the loss of all 56 members of the crew. *s of Fred & Letitia, Wigan.* PLYMOUTH NAVAL MEMORIAL. [W]

**PICKERING Mathew,** Pte. 3456737 1$^{st}$ Bn. The Essex Regiment. Killed 8 April 1944 in Burma. Aged 30. He has no known grave. RANGOON MEMORIAL. [A]

**PICKERING Ralph,** A.B. D/JX285362 R.N. H.M.S. *Itchen.* 23 September 1943. Aged 23. South-east of Cape Farewell, this frigate was sunk by the German U-boat *U-260. s of Thomas & Alice; h of Nellie Pickering, Leigh.* PLYMOUTH NAVAL MEMORIAL. [L]
(See also Albert Fairhurst and Gwilym Evans who died in the same action.)

**PICKERING Thomas William,** Major 88267 144$^{th}$ (8$^{th}$ Bn. The East Lancashire Regiment) Regt; R.A.C. Killed 16 July 1944. Age 32. *s of Thomas & Gertrude; h of Peggie, Tutshill, Monmouthshire.* ST MANVIEU WAR CEMETERY, FRANCE. [HGS]

**PICKERVANCE Joseph,** Gnr. 1714349 26 Lt. A.A. Regiment, Royal Artillery. Died 15 February 1946 in Germany. Aged 32. *s of John & AlicePickervance; h of Sarah Ellen Pickervance, Ashton-in-Makerfield.* MUNSTER HEATH WAR CEMETERY, GERMANY. [AIM]

**PICKTON Arthur,** Pte. 3657987 4$^{th}$ Bn. The Border Regiment. Killed in India 27 July 1944. Aged 28. *s of Henry & stepson of Hilda May, Hindley Green.* IMPHAL WAR CEMETERY, INDIA. [HGC]
(Some sources give the spelling as *Picton*)

**PIERCE Ernest,** Fus. 14628761 2$^{nd}$ Bn. The North Staffordshire Regiment (The Prince of Wales's) Killed in Italy 13 March 1944. Aged 28. *s of Charles E. & Ada; h of Annie, Leigh.* BEACH HEAD WAR CEMETERY, ANZIO, ITALY. [L/LMC]

**PILKINGTON Thomas,** Gnr. 1082683 71 Field Regiment, Royal Artillery. Killed in North Africa 22 February 1943. Aged 27. ENFIDAVILLE WAR CEMETERY. [HDC/AS/ASC]

**PILKINGTON William,** Sjt. 2019853 853 Heavy Bridging Coy., Royal Engineers. Died of typhus in India 1 January 1945. Aged 28. *s of William & Ann; h of Hilda, Wigan.* IMPHAL WAR CEMETERY, INDIA. [W/WPC]

**PILLING Douglas,** Ord. Seaman D/JX188539 R.N. H.M.S. *Neptune* 19 December 1941. Aged 17. This cruiser ran on to a minefield while hunting an Italian convoy and sank with the loss of all but one of her entire crew. *s of Arthur & Martha.* PLYMOUTH NAVAL MEMORIAL. [W]
(See also Colin F. Coppock; John Hughes and Joseph Simm who died in this action.)

**PILLING Harold,** Cpl. 2762173 1st Bn. The Black Watch (Royal Highland Regiment) Killed 20 July 1943 in action during the invasion of Sicily. Aged 26. *s of James Harry & Sarah Jane; h of Nellie, Ashton-in-Makerfield.* CATANIA WAR CEMETERY, ITALY. [ACC/AIM/AMS]

**PIMBLETT Eric,** Cpl. 572595 R.A.F. Captured in 1942 and died in a Japanese PoW camp, 1 July 1945. Aged 24. He has no known grave. *s of Stanley & Nora Edith.* SINGAPORE MEMORIAL. [L]

**PIMBLETT Frank,** Sto. 1st Class. D/KX179502 R.N. H.M.S. *Whitaker.* 1 November 1944. Aged 20. Off Londonderry, this frigate was seriously damaged by a torpedo from the U-boat *U-483* and was towed to Belfast - a total loss. *s of Harold & Elsie, Astley.* PLYMOUTH NAVAL MEMORIAL. [T]
(See Thomas Mercer who also died in this action.)

**PIMBLETT Herbert,** Pte. 3859523 1st Bn. The Gordon Highlanders. Died of wounds in the Middle East 17 April 1943. HELIOPOLIS WAR CEMETERY, EGYPT. [GGC/HIY/W]

**PIMBLETT Peter,** Pilot Offr.(Observer) 104568 R.A.F. 139 Sqdn. Killed in the Far East 23 April 1942. Aged 31. *He had family connections with Leigh.* CHITTAGONG WAR CEMETERY, INDIA. [X]

**PLACE Arthur Austin,** Pte. 3654799 1st Bn. The South Lancashire Regiment (The Prince of Wales's Volunteers) Killed 18 June 1940 in the aftermath of the Dunkirk evacuation. Aged 21. He has no known grave. *s of John William & Nellie, Up Holland.* DUNKIRK MEMORIAL. [UPC/UPH]

**PLATT Archie Craig,** Pte. 3530988 5th Bn. The Manchester Regiment. Killed 29 May 1940 during the Dunkirk evacuation. Aged 20. He has no known grave. *s of Harry H. & Isobel.* DUNKIRK MEMORIAL. [W]

**PLATT Fred,** Sgmn. 2340800 Royal Corps of Signals. Died 3 July 1943 whilst a PoW of the Japanese. Aged 27. *s of Thomas Yates & Mary, Westhoughton.* THANBYUZAYAT WAR CEMETERY, BURMA. [HGS]

**PLATT Henry,** Sjt. 3856866 1st Bn. The Loyal Regiment (North Lancashire) Killed in Italy 20 February 1944. Aged 26. *s of John & Jane; h of Ella, Orrell.* ANZIO WAR CEMETERY, ITALY. [OC]

**PLATT Thomas,** Sgt. (Air Gnr.) 3011828 R.A.F. (V.R.) 1651 C.U. 4 March 1945. His Lancaster III bomber was shot down by a German intruder during a training flight and crashed near Cottesmore airfield in Rutland. Aged 19. GOLBORNE (ST THOMAS) CHURCHYARD. [G/GOC]

**POMFRET Fred,** A.B. D/JX212917 R.N. H.M.S. *Copra.* 17 June 1944. Aged 20. *s of Fred & Ethel.* BIGUGLIA CEMETERY, FRANCE. [A]

**POPPLESTON George,** Sgt. 1005744 R.A.F. 70 Sqdn. Killed 7 May 1943 in the Middle East. Aged 28. *s of Peter & Susanna; h of Pauline.* TRIPOLI WAR CEMETERY, LIBYA. [W/WGS/WPC]

**PORTER Vincent,** Lieut. 132353 *M.C.* The Lancashire Fusiliers attd. The Gold Coast Regiment. Killed 14 January 1942. Aged 27. *s of William & Miriam.* CHRISTIANSBORG WAR CEMETERY, ACCRA. [BDC/L]

**POSTLEWAITE Arthur,** Pte. 14202919 2nd Bn. The North Staffordshire Regiment (The Prince of Wales's) Killed in action in Italy 12 February 1944. Aged 20. *s of Eliza, Haigh.* ANZIO WAR CEMETERY, ITALY. [AS/HDC]

**POTTER Frederick,** Bdr. 884462 5 Regiment, Royal Horse Artillery. Killed in North Africa 22 April 1943. Aged 24. *s of Joseph & Margaret Ann; h of Mabel Ann, Lowton St Marys.* ENFIDAVILLE WAR CEMETERY, TUNISIA. [G/GOC]

**POTTER Henry Johnson,** Dvr. 192166 Royal Electrical & Mechanical Engineers Killed 9 September 1943 in Italy. Aged 28. *s of Robert & Mezzesley; h of Alice, Bryn.* SALERNO WAR CEMETERY, ITALY. [AMS]

**POWER James,** Pte. S/157986 R.A.S.C. He died 12 May 1945 whilst being held as a PoW of the Germans and awaiting repatriation. Aged 26. BERLIN 1939-45 WAR CEMETERY [AGS]

**POWER John,** Gnr. 3660113 3 H.A.A. Regiment, Royal Artillery. He was taken prisoner at the fall of Singapore and died 21 September 1944 following the sinking of a Japanese transport ship conveying PoWs from Thailand to Japan. Aged 31. *s of Michael & Mary; h of Hilda.* SINGAPORE MEMORIAL. [A]

**POWER Peter,** L.Bdr. 798836 52 Field Regiment, Royal Artillery. He was killed in action in Italy, 4 December 1943. Aged 31. SANGRO RIVER WAR CEMETERY, ITALY [W]

**POWER Patrick Joseph,** Cpl. T/3855334 Royal Army Service Corps. Died 23 December 1942 whilst a PoW of the Japanese and working on the Burma-Siam railway. Aged 26. *s of Michael & Mary Bridget, Atherton.* KANCHANABURI WAR CEMETERY, THAILAND. [A]

**POWNALL John,** Dvr. T/14514962 *Mentioned in Despatches.* Royal Army Service Corps. Killed in Holland 25 November 1944. Aged 20. *s of Paul & Elizabeth, Ashton-in-Makerfield.* MAARHEEZE CEMETERY, HOLLAND. [AMS]

**PRESCOTT Albert E.** Cpl. 1530983 R.A.F. (V.R.) 40 Air Stores Park. Died after a short illness in hospital in Italy 22 September 1945. Aged 24. *s of James Arthur & Phoebe.* ROME WAR CEMETERY, ITALY. [L]

**PRESCOTT James,** Pte. 3653331 8<sup>th</sup> Bn. The Durham Light Infantry. Killed in action in Sicily 17 July 1943. Aged 23. *s of Elizabeth, Golborne.* CATANIA WAR CEMETERY, ITALY. [G/GOC]

**PRESCOTT Marcus Richard,** Sto. P.O. P/KX76674 R.N. H.M.S. *Hood.* 24 May 1941. Aged 36. The battle-cruiser H.M.S. *Hood* was hit and blown-up in an action in the North Atlantic against the German battleship *Bismark* and the cruiser *Prinz Eugen.* There were only three survivors from *Hood's* crew of 1419. *s of Albert & Barbara; h of Annie.* PORTSMOUTH NAVAL MEMORIAL. [L/LMC]

**PRESHO Harold,** Gnr. 114865 72 Anti-Tank Regiment, Royal Artillery. Killed in the Middle East 10 December 1943. Aged 36. MEDJEZ-EL-BAB WAR CEMETERY. [B]

**PRESTON George,** Pte. 4922014 2<sup>nd</sup> Bn. The South Staffordshire Regiment. Died of pneumonia 6 June 1941. *h of Beatrice Eileen Preston, Astley.* TYLDESLEY CEMETERY. [X]

**PRESTON Stephen,** Sgt. 1541030 R.A.F. (V.R.) 207 Sqdn. 28 August 1943. Aged 21. His Lancaster III bomber took-off from Langar on an operation to bomb Nuremburg. The aircraft crashed in Germany and all seven members of the crew were killed. They all rest in Durnbach. *s of Stephen & Ellen.* DURNBACH WAR CEMETERY, GERMANY. [T]

**PRICE Albert Edward,** Pte. 3858840 2<sup>nd</sup> Bn. The Loyal Regiment (North Lancashire) Killed 23 January 1942 during the battle which culminated in the fall of Singapore. Aged 22. He has no known grave. *s of Albert Edward & Mary, Beech Hill, Wigan.* SINGAPORE MEMORIAL. [BHC/W]

**PRICE Aubrey Clarence,** Fus. 14779946 7<sup>th</sup> Bn. The Royal Welch Fusiliers. Killed in Holland 7 March 1945. Aged 19. *s of John Harry & Mercy.* GROESBEEK CANADIAN WAR CEMETERY, HOLLAND. [X]

**PRICE George James,** Fus. 4206545 70<sup>th</sup> Bn. The Royal Welch Fusiliers. Died in Bracebridge Military Hospital 12 May 1942. Aged 19. *s of Ada & stepson of William Mason.* LEIGH CEMETERY. [X]

**PRICE Jack,** Pte. 3527695 2<sup>nd</sup> Bn. The Loyal Regiment (North Lancashire) Died 27 January 1943 while a PoW of the Japanese and working on the Burma-Siam railway. Aged 26. *h of Mrs. J.* KANCHANABURI WAR CEMETERY, THAILAND. [L/LMC]

**PRICE John,** Pte. 3453114 1/4th Bn. The King's Own Yorkshire Light Infantry. Killed in France 29 June 1944. Aged 26. *s of Henry & Edith.* RYES WAR CEMETERY, FRANCE. [AIM]

**PRICE Robert,** L.Sgt. 3453446 2/5th Bn. The Lancashire Fusiliers. Killed in action in Normandy 8 July 1944. *h of Jane, Poolstock* CAMBES-EN-PLAINE WAR CEMETERY, FRANCE. [JC/W]

**PRIESTLEY Sidney,** Fus. 14662090 7th Bn. The Royal Welch Fusiliers. Killed in Germany 16 February 1945. Aged 30. *s of Herbert & Jane, Wigan.* REICHSWALD FOREST WAR CEMETERY, GERMANY. [SSC/W/WSB]

**PRIOR Thomas,** Sjt. 3854144 18th(5th Bn. The Loyal Regiment [North Lancashire]) Reconnaissance Corps. Died of cholera 31 May 1943 while a PoW of the Japanese. Aged 30. *h of Margaret.* THANBYUZAYAT WAR CEMETERY, BURMA. [X]

**PRITCHARD Henry,** Cpl. 3777091 1st Bn. The Royal Irish Fusiliers (Princess Victoria's) Killed in Italy 28 October 1943. Aged 33. *s of Henry & Margaret; h of Mary Elizabeth, Orrell.* SANGRO RIVER WAR CEMETERY, ITALY. [X]

**PRITCHARD William,** Pte. 3855095 1st Bn. The Loyal Regiment (North Lancashire). Killed in North Africa 23 April 1943. Aged 27. He has no known grave. *s of John & Mary Elizabeth, Wigan; h of Margaret.* MEDJEZ-EL-BAB MEMORIAL, TUNISIA. [W]

**PRUDEN Cecil Peter,** Pte. 3530202 1st Bn. The Manchester Regiment. Died 3 October 1943 while a PoW of the Japanese and working on the Burma-Siam railway. Aged 31. *s of Thomas & Marion, Beech Hill, Wigan.* THANBYUZAYAT WAR CEMETERY, BURMA. [W]

**PURVIS William Robert,** Pte. 5783457 2/6th Bn. The Queen's Royal Regiment (West Surrey) Killed in Italy 9 September 1943. Aged 21. *s of James & stepson of Gertrude, Orrell.* SALERNO WAR CEMETERY, ITALY. [X]

**PYE Henry,** Pte. 2379617 2/4th Bn. The King's Own Yorkshire Light Infantry. Killed in North Africa 21 April 1943. Aged 21. *s of James & Elizabeth, Pemberton.* MEDJEZ-EL-BAB WAR CEMETERY, TUNISIA. [PC/W/WGS]

**PYKE Thomas,** Fus. 3461411 2nd Bn. The Lancashire Fusiliers. Killed in North Africa 27 April 1943. Aged 22. *s of Joseph & Anne, Whelley.* MEDJEZ-EL-BAB WAR CEMETERY, TUNISIA. [W]

**QUALEY Peter,** A.B. D/JX306074 R.N. H.M.S. *Loyalty* 22 August 1944. Off the Normandy coast, the minesweeper was sunk by U-boat *U-480.* PLYMOUTH NAVAL MEMORIAL. [W]

**QUIRK John Clifford,** L.Cpl. 3451811 1st Bn. The Lancashire Fusiliers. Accidentally drowned in India 30 September 1943. Aged 24. *s of Alfred A. & Elizabeth.* KIRKEE WAR CEMETERY, INDIA. [X]

**RABBITT Peter,** Marine PLY/X105258 Royal Marines H.M.L.C.G. *9* Died in this landing craft off the Normandy coast 25 June 1944. He was buried at sea. Aged 22. *s of Peter & Nancy.* PLYMOUTH NAVAL MEMORIAL. [L]

**RAINFORD Thomas Ralph,** Ord. Sig. P/JX196494 R.N. H.M.S. *Cossack* 23 October 1941. This destroyer was on convoy duty when it was torpedoed by *U-563* in the North Atlantic. *s of William & Catherine, New Springs, Wigan.* PORTSMOUTH NAVAL MEMORIAL. [AS/NSC]
(See also John Atherton and John Hargreaves who died in this action.)

**RALPH William Henry,** L.Sjt 3445996 9th Queen's Royal Lancers, R.A.C. Killed in Italy 27 December 1944. Aged 31. *s of Rose; h of Ellen, New Springs.* ANCONA WAR CEMETERY, ITALY. [AS/NSC/W]
(Some local sources give the surname spelling as *Ralphs.*)

**RALPHSON Robert,** Ldg. Sto. P/KX76360 R.N. H.M.S. *Wivern.* Died of wounds 15 May 1940. Aged 33. *s of John Snape & Mary Ann; h of Alice.* SHORNCLIFFE MILITARY CEMETERY, KENT. [L]

**RANDALL John Victor,** Sgt. 974663 R.A.F. 61 Sqdn. 7 December 1941. This Manchester I bomber from Woolfax Lodge exploded and crashed into the sea off Boulogne. All members of the crew perished. RUNNYMEDE MEMORIAL. [AP/APC/S]

**RATCLIFFE Albert,** Cpl. T/182507 Royal Army Service Corps. Died in a Middle East hospital 28 May 1941. Aged 24. *s of Peter Wright & Margaret, Leigh.* ISMAILIA WAR MEMORIAL CEMETERY. [L]

**RATCLIFFE Jack (Jacky),** Sgt.(Air Gnr.) 2209639 R.A.F. (V.R.) 57 Sqdn. 22 June 1944. Aged 19. This Lancaster III bomber from East Kirby on a raid on Wesseling crashed near Vlijmen, Holland. Only one member of the seven-man crew survived. *s of James & May, Billinge.* BERGEN-OP-ZOOM WAR CEMETERY, HOLLAND. [BC]

**RATCLIFFE John,** Pte. 4865673 2nd Bn. The Seaforth Highlanders (Ross-Shire Buffs, The Duke of Albany's). Killed in action in Holland 10 February 1945. Aged 25. MOOK WAR CEMETERY, HOLLAND. [T]

**RATCLIFFE Walter,** Pte. 286132 Royal Army Ordnance Corps. Died 8 June 1946. Aged 44. *h of Lucy Amelia.* LEIGH CEMETERY. [L]

**RAWSON John,** Sick Bay P.O. D/MX47444 R.N. H.M.S. *Maori* 12 February 1942. Aged 34. This destroyer was sunk in Dockyard Creek, Malta in one of ten air-raids on the island that day. *s of John & Alice; h of Jessie.* PLYMOUTH NAVAL MEMORIAL. [IN]

**READ James,** Gnr. 1809011 242 Bty., 48 Lt. A.A. Regiment, Royal Artillery. Died 2 July 1945 in North Borneo while a PoW of the Japanese. Aged 24. He has no known grave. *s of James & Mary, Wigan.* SINGAPORE MEMORIAL. [X]

**READ Thomas**, A.B. D/JX303497 R.N. H.M.S. *Tynedale*. Died 5 February 1947. Aged 24. WIGAN CEMETERY. [X]

**REDFERN Edwin**, Pte. NX 51511 A.I.F. 2/19th Bn. Australian Infantry. Died 25 May 1944 while a PoW of the Japanese and working on the Burma-Siam railway. Aged 37. *s of Edwin & Emily, Pemberton.* THANBYUZAYAT WAR CEMETERY, BURMA. [HIC/W]
(It is believed that Pte Redfern emigrated to Australia in the mid-1930's. His brother John Thomas also died on active service in the Far East.)

**REDFERN John Thomas**, Spr. 2143924 604 Railway Construction Coy., Royal Engineers. Killed in the Far East 15 July 1943. Aged 34. *s of Edwin & Emily; Pemberton; h of Eleanor, Pemberton.* MAYNAMATI CEMETERY, PAKISTAN. [HIC/W]
(His brother Edwin died in service with the Australian Infantry.)

**REDFORD John**, Pte. 14735816 1/5th Bn. The Queen's Royal Regiment (West Surrey) Killed in Holland 29 January 1945. Aged 19. NEDERWEERT WAR CEMETERY, HOLLAND. [ABC]

**REDMOND Alexander**, Pte. 14206700 7th Bn. The Duke of Wellington's Regiment (West Riding). Died of wounds in France 19 June 1944. Aged 21. *s of John & Margaret, Pemberton.* BAYEAUX WAR CEMETERY, FRANCE. [W]

**REED George Nuttall**, Pte. 14373013 2nd Bn. The South Lancashire Regiment (The Prince of Wales's Volunteers). Killed 11 June 1944 in Burma. Aged 35. *s of Murray & Louisa, Up Holland; h of Jane Catherine, Up Holland.* KOHIMA WAR CEMETERY. [UPC/UPH]

**REED William Henry**, Pte. 3654899 2/4th Bn. The South Lancashire Regiment (The Prince of Wales's Volunteers) Died 6 September 1941. Aged 21. *s of Charlton & Cicely.* BRANDON & BYSHOTTLES (MEADOWFIELD) CEMETERY, DURHAM. [X]

**RENFREY James**, Dvr. 4208433 Royal Corps of Signals, Special W/T Section. Died of wounds in Italy 4 June 1944. Aged 22. *h of Elizabeth, Hindley.* CASSINO WAR CEMETERY, ITALY. [X]

**RHODEN Kenneth**, Flt. Sgt. 1623310 R.A.F. (V.R.) 169 Sqdn. Killed 6 May 1945. The Mosquito XIX in which he was navigator crashed near Hove while on a training exercise. Flt. Sgt. Williams (the pilot) and Flt. Sgt. Rhoden were the last deaths sustained by Bomber Command prior to the official surrender which ended the war in Europe. Aged 21. *s of Frank & Edith.* ATHERTON CEMETERY. [A/HBC]

**RICHARDS John**, Cpl. 13009048 13 Salvage Unit, Auxiliary Military Pioneer Corps. Killed 28/29 May 1940 during the retreat from France. He died aboard the steamer *Abukir* which was sunk by an E-boat north of Dunkirk while carrying over 200 troops and refugees from Ostend to Dover. He has no known grave. He was aged 42 and had served in the First World War. DUNKIRK MEMORIAL. [X]

**RICHARDS Walter,** Pte. 3859411 1<sup>st</sup> Bn. The Loyal Regiment (North Lancashire) Killed in action in North Africa 30 April 1943. Aged 26. *s of James & Margaret.* MASSICAULT WAR CEMETERY, TUNISIA. [T/TMC]

**RICHARDSON Sydney,** Lieut. 302230 Royal Engineers. Killed by machine-gun fire on Walcheren Island during the battle for the Scheldt Estuary 1 November 1944. Aged 23. He took part in the D-Day landings. *s of James Eric & May.* BERGEN-OP-ZOOM WAR CEMETERY, HOLLAND. [T/TC]

**RIDING Richard Norman,** Spr. 14237517 952 Railway Operating Coy., Royal Engineers. Killed in Holland on VE Day, 8 May 1945. Aged 38. *s of Richard & Jane.* TILBURG GENERAL CEMETERY, HOLLAND. [W]

**RIDLEY Eric,** Ordnance Artificer P/MX98438 R.N. H.M.S. *Kongoni* Accidentally drowned in South Africa 21 March 1943. Aged 31. *s of Arthur & Elizabeth Annie.* DURBAN (STELLAWOOD) CEMETERY, SOUTH AFRICA. [PC/W/WGS]

**RIDYARD Wilfred,** Fus. 3461438 2<sup>nd</sup> Bn. The Lancashire Fusiliers. Killed in North Africa 26 November 1942. Aged 26. *s of Robert & Ethel; h of Lily.* MEDJEZ-EL-BAB WAR CEMETERY, TUNISIA. [L/LTA]

**RIGBY Cyril,** Eng. Offr. Merchant Navy m.v. *Abosso.* 29 October 1942. Aged 29. About 700 miles north of the Azores this passenger-cargo liner, en route from Cape Town to Liverpool, was sunk by the German U-boat *U-575.* There were only 30 survivors from 282 passengers and crew. *s of Lancet Archibald & Elizabeth Ann; h of Marjorie, Wigan.* TOWER HILL MEMORIAL. [AIM]

**RIGBY Edward Henry,** Tpr. 3453429 40<sup>th</sup> (The King's Regiment [Liverpool] ) Royal Tank Regiment, R.A.C. Killed in Italy 27 September 1943. Aged 25. *s of James Edward & Jane, Orrell.* SALERNO WAR CEMETERY, ITALY. [OC]

**RIGBY Eric,** L.Cpl. 3656371 1<sup>st</sup> Bn. The East Lancashire Regiment. Killed in action in Germany 26 April 1945. Aged 25. BECKLINGEN WAR CEMETERY, GERMANY. [UPC/UPH]

**RIGBY Henry,** Lieut. 303774 Royal Army Service Corps. While travelling home on leave from Ceylon he was killed by a British anti-aircraft shell in London 18 June 1944. Aged 35. *s of Boyd & Mary Elizabeth, Golborne; h of Ethel.* LEEMING (ST JOHN THE BAPTIST) CHURCHYARD, EXELBY, YORKSHIRE. [AGS]

**RIGBY James,** Bdr. 3860516 97 Anti-Tank Regiment, Royal Artillery. Killed in Holland 31 October 1944. Aged 29. *h of Jane, Hindley.* MIERLO WAR CEMETERY, HOLLAND. [HGC]

**RIGBY John Edward,** Flying Offr. (Pilot) 127881 R.A.F. 51 Sqdn. 24 May 1943. Aged 21. He was the pilot of a Lancaster bomber which took-off from Snaith to bomb Dortmund, but was shot down over the Leiden area of Holland when returning from the successful raid. *s of William Albert & Ethel.* OEGSTGEEST PROTESTANT CHURCHYARD, HOLLAND. [AP/APC/UPH/S/WGS]

**RIGBY Joseph,** Flying Offr. (Nav.) 156774 R.A.F. (V.R.) 635 Sqdn. 25 April 1944. Aged 23. This Lancaster III bomber from Downham Market was attempting to attack Karlsruhe but crashed at Loon-op-Sand in Holland. Six members of the crew died. *s of Richard & Margaret.* BERGEN-OP-ZOOM WAR CEMETERY, HOLLAND. [L/LTA]

**RIGBY Richard,** Pte. 4698378 1$^{st}$ Bn. The King's Own Yorkshire Light Infantry. Died in Italy 5 February 1944. Aged 21. *His parents lived in Higher Ince.* CASERTA WAR CEMETERY, [X]

**RIGBY Richard Williamson,** Flt. Sgt. (Pilot) 1218437 R.A.F. 20 November 1943. Aged 22. *s of Mr. & Mrs. J.H.* WRIGHTINGTON (ST JOSEPH) R.C. CHURCHYARD. [W]

**RIGBY Vernon,** Fus. 3451512 1/8$^{th}$ Bn. The Lancashire Fusiliers. He died 16 April 1944 in captivity whilst being held as a PoW of the Germans. He was captured at the fall of France. Aged 25. *s of Fred & Lily, Hindley.* POZNAN OLD GARRISON CEMETERY, POLAND. [X]

**RIGBY William Henry (Harry),** Sto. P.O. D/KX81754 R.N. H.M.S. *Penylan* 3 December 1942. Off Start Point, this destroyer was sunk by German E-boats. *s of Moses & Ella Jane; h of Eunice, Platt Bridge.* PLYMOUTH NAVAL MEMORIAL. [PBC]

**RILEY Henry,** Pte. 5193316 1/4$^{th}$ Bn. The Essex Regiment. Killed in North Africa 20 April 1943. Aged 20. He has no known grave. *s of Henry & Hannah Rebecca, Higher Ince.* MEDJEZ-EL-BAB MEMORIAL, TUNISIA. [X]

**RILEY Patrick,** Pte. 3853898 1$^{st}$ Bn. The Loyal Regiment (North Lancashire). Killed in France 1 June 1940 during the evacuation of Dunkirk. Aged 27. TOUFFLERS COMMUNAL CEMETERY, FRANCE. [W]

**RILEY Thomas,** Sgt. (W.Op./Air Gnr.) 1032154 R.A.F. (V.R.) 408 (R.C.A.F.) Sqdn. 4 July 1943. Aged 22. This Halifax II bomber from Leeming crashed at Bonnelean, France while engaged on an operation to Cologne. One member of the crew became a PoW; the rest perished. *s of Mrs. E., Wallgate, Wigan.* POIX-DE-LA-SOMME CHURCHYARD. [W]

**RING Arthur,** Gnr. 14512648 97 Anti-Tank Regiment, Royal Artillery. Died of wounds in France 27 June 1944. Aged 20. BAYEAUX WAR CEMETERY. [A]

**ROACH Wilfred,** Gnr. 835952 5 Regiment, Royal Horse Artillery. Killed in action in Holland 11 March 1945. Aged 30. NEDERWEERT WAR CEMETERY, HOLLAND. [X]

**ROBERTS Arthur Fred Noel,** W.O. (Pilot) 590902 R.A.F. 613 Sqdn. Killed 25 December 1944 whilst on night-intruder duties in a Mosquito. Aged 27. *s of Arthur Fred & Ruth; h of Ruby Irene, UpHolland.* CAMBRAI COMMUNAL CEMETERY, FRANCE. [X]

**ROBERTS David Douglas,** Cadet. Merchant Navy s.s. *Observer.* 16 December 1942. Aged 17. The cargo liner, en route from Turkey to U.S.A., was sunk by the German ‚U-boat *U-176* off Brazil. *s of George J. & Alice M.* TOWER HILL MEMORIAL. [OC]

**ROBERTS James,** Fus. 14562303 7th Bn. The Royal Welch Fusiliers. Died of wounds in Belgium 5 January 1945. Aged 19. *s of Fred & Gertrude, Atherton.* HOTTON WAR CEMETERY, BELGIUM. [A]

**ROBERTS James,** Gnr. 1697661 Royal Artillery. Died 6 March 1941. Aged 30. *h of Nellie, Leigh.* LEIGH CEMETERY. [L/LGS]

**ROBERTS Raymond Parry,** Gdsmn. 2724366 3rd Bn. The Irish Guards. Killed in Germany 8 April 1945. Aged 19. *s of Robert & Rose, Wigan.* SAGE WAR CEMETERY, GERMANY. [W/WPC]

**ROBERTS Thomas,** Pte. 5382999 7th Bn. The Oxfordshire & Buckinghamshire Light Infantry. Killed in Italy 19 January 1944. Aged 26. *s of David & Elizabeth, Pemberton.* MINTURNO WAR CEMETERY, ITALY. [PC/W]

**ROBERTS William,** Gnr. 1108478 90 H.A.A. Regiment, Royal Artillery. Killed in France 8 August 1944. Aged 35. *h of Agnes.* TILLY-SUR-SEULLES WAR CEMETERY. [JC/W]

**ROBINSON John,** Flying Offr. (Pilot) 186338 R.A.F. (V.R.) Killed in a flying accident in the Middle East 19 April 1945. Aged 25. *s of John & Ellen, Wigan.* SUEZ WAR MEMORIAL CEMETERY. [W/WPC]

**ROBINSON John,** Gnr. 872357 8 Coast Regiment, Royal Artillery. Lost in the s.s. *Lisbon Maru* 2 October 1942. Aged 22. He has no known grave. *s of John & Elizabeth, Ashton-in-Makerfield.* SAI WAN BAY MEMORIAL, HONG KONG. [AIM/AMS]

**ROBINSON John,** Sto. P.O. D/KX81885 R.N. H.M.S. *Barham* 25 November 1941. Aged 31. In the eastern Mediterranean, this battleship was torpedoed by the U-boat *U-331* and blew-up with the loss of 862 crew members. *s of John & Margaret; h of Lily, Wigan.* PLYMOUTH NAVAL MEMORIAL. [W]
(See also James Henry Gerrard; John Thomas Mills and Joseph O'Brien who died in the sinking of this ship.)

**ROBINSON Nathan,** Pte. 3858601 2nd Bn. The Loyal Regiment (North Lancashire) Captured at the fall of Singapore and died 9 April 1945 whilst being held as a PoW of the Japanese Aged 25. *h of G. Robinson, Standish.* YOKOHAMA BRITISH COMMONWEALTH WAR CEMETERY, JAPAN. [AS/HDC/STC]

**ROBINSON William Swann,** Sgt. (Pilot) 971021 R.A.F. (V.R.) 500 Sqdn. Killed 7 August 1941 during a Coastal Command anti-shipping operation in a Blenheim bomber. Aged 30. He has no known grave. *s of William Swann & Edith, Leigh.* RUNNYMEDE MEMORIAL [L/LMC]

**ROBY Frank,** Fus. 3453710 2<sup>nd</sup> Bn. The Lancashire Fusiliers. Killed in North Africa 26 November 1942. Aged 23. *s of Adam & Mary, Whelley, Wigan.* MEDJEZ-EL-BAB WAR CEMETERY, TUNISIA. [SCC/W/WSB]

**ROBY George Leslie,** Fus. 3858876 1<sup>st</sup> Bn. The Royal Irish Fusiliers. Killed in Sicily 14 August 1943. CATANIA WAR CEMETERY, ITALY. [OC]

**ROBY Thomas Arthur,** Sgt. 1764138 R.A.F. (V.R.) 576 Sqdn. 25 June 1944. Aged 20. His Lancaster III bomber took-off from Elsham Woods to attack a flying-bomb site but was lost without trace. *s of Thomas & Emily, Orrell.* RUNNYMEDE MEMORIAL. [OC]

**RODAN William Percy,** Pte. 3528718 1<sup>st</sup> Bn. The Manchester Regiment. Died 29 May 1943 while a PoW of the Japanese and working on the Burma-Siam railway. Aged 32. *s of Thomas & Lily, Standish.* THANBYUZAYAT WAR CEMETERY, BURMA. [X]

**RODEN Stanley,** Pte. 3865857 13<sup>th</sup> Bn. The King's Regiment (Liverpool). Killed in Burma 9 May 1943 while operating behind Japanese lines with General Wingate's Chindits. Aged 23. He has no known grave. *s of Stanley & Amelia, Wrightington.* RANGOON MEMORIAL. [AP/APC]

**RODEN Thomas Sidney,** Pte. 14344706 General Service Corps Died 25 April 1943. Aged 31. *h of Gladys, Worsley Mesnes.* WIGAN CEMETERY. [WPC]

**ROE William,** Pte. S/109917 Royal Army Service Corps. Died of pneumonia in a Cardiff hospital 22 October 1940 after being evacuated from Le Harve during the retreat from France. Aged 25. LEIGH CEMETERY. [L/LMC]

**ROGERS Alan Roy,** Sgmn. 14256416 Royal Corps of Signals. Died in a Worcester hospital 20 March 1945. Aged 21. *s of E. & Gladys, Abram.* ABRAM (ST JOHN) CHURCHYARD. [AB/ABC]

**ROGERS Jack,** Cpl. 3451745 1/8<sup>th</sup> Bn. The Lancashire Fusiliers. Killed in action in Burma 4 May 1944. Aged 25. He has no known grave. *s of Samuel & Lily, Hindley Green.* RANGOON MEMORIAL. [HGC]

**ROGERSON John Joseph,** Sailor. Merchant Navy. Killed 7 September 1940 when his ship s.s. *Bennevis* was bombed in the Port of London. Aged 32. This cargo liner was repaired and re-entered the Merchant Service and was captured in December 1941 by the Japanese off Hong Kong and renamed *Gyokuro Maru*. It was sunk by the U.S. Navy in November 1944. *s of Mr. & Mrs. Patrick.* CITY OF LONDON CEMETERY. [W/WGS]

**ROLLINS Harold,** Sgt.(Bomb Aimer) 1588200 R.A.F. (V.R.) 463 (R.A.A.F.) Sqdn. Killed 11 March 1945. His Lancaster bomber collided with a Hurricane while participating in a fighter affiliation training flight and it crashed near Sleaford in Lincolnshire. All seven crew members and the Hurricane pilot were killed. Aged 31. LEIGH CEMETERY. [L]

**ROLLINS John,** Fus. 3654437 1st Bn. The Lancashire Fusiliers. Killed in Burma 1 May 1944. Aged 25. TAUKKYAN WAR CEMETERY. [NC/W]

**ROSCOE Alfred,** Tpr. 3853346 18th (5th Bn. The Loyal Regiment [North Lancashire]) Regiment., Reconnaissance Corps., R.A.C. Died in Hong Kong 29 November 1944 whilst being held as a PoW of the Japanese. Aged 37. *s of Harry & Mary; h of Annie, Leigh.* SAI WAN BAY WAR CEMETERY, HONG KONG. [L] (Some local sources give the spelling of his surname as *Ruscoe*)

**ROSCOE Fred,** L.A.C. 1018427 R.A.F. (V.R.) Killed in a flying accident 4 April 1945. Aged 31. *s of Thomas & Emily; h of Freda.* CHESTER (BLACON) CEMETERY. [AMS]

**ROSE Charles Gordon,** Ord. Smn. P/JX291696 R.N. H.M.S. *Arbutus* 5 February 1942. Aged 33. In the North Atlantic, this corvette was on convoy duty when it was torpedoed and sunk by the German U-boat *U-136. s of Arthur George & Elizabeth, Wigan; h of Myra May.* PORTSMOUTH NAVAL MEMORIAL. [W/WGS]

**ROSTRON Thomas Hayes,** Pte. 3531013 2nd Bn. The Manchester Regiment. Killed 26/27 May 1940 during the evacuation of Dunkirk. Aged 30. He has no known grave. *s of James & Emily; h of Catherine.* DUNKIRK MEMORIAL. [IN]

**ROTCHFORD Thomas,** Gdsmn. 2722987 3rd Bn. The Irish Guards. Died 9 April 1945 in a London military hospital of wounds which he received in Germany. Aged 29. LEIGH CEMETERY. [L]

**ROTHERHAM Robert,** Pte. 3453420 2/5th Bn. The Royal Leicestershire Regiment. Killed in Italy 30 August 1944. Aged 28. *s of William & Elizabeth, Platt Bridge.* MONTECCHIO WAR CEMETERY, ITALY. [PBC]

**ROTHWELL Edward,** Sto. P.O. D/KX80573 R.N. H.M.S. *Dragonfly.* Killed 14 February 1942. Aged 35. Japanese aircraft sunk this river gunboat off Singapore. P.O. Rothwell had been in the Royal Navy for sixteen years. *s of Noah & Emma, Atherton; h of Elsie May.* PLYMOUTH NAVAL MEMORIAL. [A/HBC]

**ROTHWELL Harold,** Sgt.(Air Gnr.) 2206323 R.A.F. (V.R.) 166 Sqdn. 13 June 1944. Aged 28. This Lancaster III bomber took-off from Kirmington to attack Gelsenkirchen but was brought down by a night-fighter near Tongeren. All the crew died. EPE GENERAL CEMETERY, HOLLAND. [W]

**ROTHWELL John,** Pilot Offr. (Pilot) 413990 R.N.Z.A.F. Killed 7 November 1943 in a flying accident while serving with Bomber Command. Aged 24. His home was in Hikurangi, New Zealand having left Leigh with his parents when he was seven years old. *s of Thomas & Agnes (formerly of Mere Street, Leigh); h of Nancy Ethel, New Zealand.* CHESTER (BLACON) CEMETERY. [X]

**ROTHWELL Joseph Walter,** L.Cpl. 3195135 1st Bn. The Cameronians (Scottish Rifles). Died of malaria in India 20 May 1944. Aged 28. *h of Ida, Pemberton.* GAUHATI WAR CEMETERY, INDIA. [W]

**ROTHWELL Thomas,** Pte. 3531922 9th Bn. The Border Regiment. Killed in Burma 7 June 1944. Aged 35. He has no known grave. *s of Thomas & Elizabeth Rothwell, Worsley Mesnes; h of Catherine Rothwell, Worsley Mesnes.* RANGOON MEMORIAL. [JC/W]

**ROTHWELL Walter,** Sgt. 974231 R.A.F. (V.R.) Died 16 February 1946 in Scotland as the result of motor accident a week earlier. PITSLIGO PARISH CHURCHYARD, SCOTLAND. [HGC]

**ROUGHLEY Ernest,** Sjt. 3859396 9th Bn. The Manchester Regiment. Killed in Italy 10 September 1944. Aged 27. *s of Richard & Margarette; h of Esther, Up Holland.* CORIANO RIDGE WAR CEMETERY, ITALY. [UPC/UPH]

**ROUGHLEY William,** Pte. 4132219 2nd Bn. The Cheshire Regiment. Killed in action in Normandy 19 June 1944. Aged 29. *s of Harry & Mary; h of Doris.* BAYEAUX WAR CEMETERY, FRANCE. [A]

**ROWBOTTOM William,** Pte. 14629191 2nd Bn. The North Staffordshire Regiment (The Prince of Wales's) Killed in Italy 12 February 1944. Aged 19. *s of John & Maggie Rowbottom, Platt Bridge, Wigan* BEACH HEAD WAR CEMETERY, ANZIO, ITALY. [PBC]

**ROWSON James Rogers,** Pte. 3858922 1st Bn. The Loyal Regiment (North Lancashire) Killed in North Africa 29 April 1943. Aged 25. *s of Frank & Annie.* MASSICAULT WAR CEMETERY, TUNISIA. [T]

**ROWSON John Joseph,** Fus. 3451825 1st Bn. The Lancashire Fusiliers. Killed in Burma 23 June 1944. Aged 25. *s of James & Margaret, Leigh.* TAUKKYAN WAR CEMETERY, BURMA. [L/LTA]

**ROYLE Richard Edward,** Gnr. 1111053 'H/I' Bty., 2 Regiment, Royal Artillery. Killed in North Africa 31 May 1942. Aged 32. He has no known grave. *s of Richard; h of Rose.* ALAMEIN MEMORIAL. [L]

**RUDD Albert William,** Pte. 3530394 1st Bn. The Manchester Regiment. Died 8 August 1943 in the Far East. Aged 31. THANBYUZAYAT WAR CEMETERY, BURMA. [IN]

**RUDD Alexander,** A.B. P/JX 334136 R.N. H.M.S. *Ferniceness Range.* He was one of twelve naval ratings killed 27 April 1943 when a training aircraft crashed into the bus in which they were travelling. Aged 20. *s of Alexander & Hannah, Frizington, Cumberland. His connection with Atherton and the Chapel arose because he lived for some time in the town with his sister (Mrs Miller) and her family.* FRIZINGTON (ST PAUL) CHURCHYARD, CUMBERLAND. [ABL]

**RUDD Alfred,** Sailor. Merchant Navy. s.s. *Otterpool.* 20 June 1940. Aged 34. In the South-west Approaches, the steamer Otterpool, en route from Bona to Tees with iron-ore, was sunk by the U-boat *U-30.* Twenty-four crew members perished. TOWER HILL MEMORIAL. [W]

**RUDDICK John Grindrod,** Lieut. 182869 The South Lancashire Regiment, attd. 8th Bn. The Parachute Regiment, Army Air Corps. Shot by a sniper at Dozule, Normandy 20 August 1944. Aged 29. *s of James & Lucy; h of Dorothy Jean.* RANVILLE WAR CEMETERY. [AGS/S/STC/W]

**RUSSELL Charles,** Flt. Sgt. 620538 R.A.F. 297 Sqdn. Killed in a flying accident 21 December 1943. Aged 28. ATHERTON CEMETERY. [A]

**RUSSELL Harold,** Pte. 4804858 1st Bn. The West Yorkshire Regiment (The Prince of Wales's Own.) Killed in Burma 24 May 1944. Aged 26. He has no known grave. *s of Mr. & Mrs. John; h of S.C., Wigan.* RANGOON MEMORIAL. [X]

**RUSSELL John,** Sgt. (Obs. U/T) 1069582 R.A.F.(V.R.) Killed in an accident while engaged on flying training at Wigtown, Scotland 15 June 1942. Aged 26. *s of John & E.L Russell, Newton-le-Willows.* NEWTON-LE-WILLOWS CEMETERY. [AGS]

**RUTTER Jack,** Gnr. 1828503 21 Lt. A.A. Regiment, Royal Artillery. Died 12 August 1945. Aged 40. *s of Levi & Sarah, Blackrod.* DJAKARTA WAR CEMETERY, INDONESIA. [BL/BCC]

**RYAN Joseph Henry,** Fus. 3451826 2nd Bn. The Lancashire Fusiliers. Killed sometime between 22 and 23 May 1940 during the retreat to Dunkirk. Aged 21. WAARMAARDE CHURCHYARD, BELGIUM. [L]

**RYAN Thomas,** Pte. 6093595 2nd Bn. The Queen's Own Royal West Kent Regiment. Killed in Malta 27 March 1942. Aged 24. PEMBROKE MILITARY CEMETERY, MALTA. [W]

**RYDER Robert,** L.Sgt. 3597027 49th Regiment Reconnaissance Corps, R.A.C. Killed in Holland 15 March 1945. Aged 29. *s of John & Jane Ryder, Ashton-in-Makerfield; h of Ida Ryder.* JONKERBOS WAR CEMETERY, NIJMEGEN, HOLLAND. [AC/NAV]

**RYDER Wilfred Geoffrey,** Cpl. 2333657 Royal Corps of Signals, 14th Army Signals. Killed in India 26 April 1944. Aged 24. *s of Thomas & Margaret, Abram; h of Patricia Margaret.* MAYNAMATI CEMETERY, PAKISTAN. [ABC]

**RYDER William,** Sgt. 16001040 Royal Electrical & Mechanical Engineers Died 9 September 1943. Aged 31. *h of Joyce Ryder.* ASPULL (ST ELIZABETH) CHURCHYARD. [X]

**RYNN Gordon John,** L.A.C. 1459936 R.A.F. (V.R.) Lost his life during pilot training in Canada 12 October 1943. Aged 19. *s of John Robert & Edith Doris.* CALGARY (BURNSLAND) CEMETERY, CANADA. [WGS]

**SALTS Reginald John,** Cpl. 575325 R.A.F. Died 23 July 1943 while a PoW of the Japanese. Aged 20. *s of Reginald Thomas & Ellen, Whelley, Wigan.* AMBON WAR CEMETERY, INDONESIA. [SSC/WGS]

**SAUNDERSON Joseph,** Cpl. 7253448 Corps of Military Police. Died 29 January 1942. Aged 44. He served in the R.A.M.C. in the First World War. *s of Joseph & Margaret; h of Mary.* LEIGH CEMETERY. [L]

**SCHOFIELD Jack,** Tpr. 7910674 10th Royal Hussars (Prince of Wales's Own), R.A.C. Killed in action in the Middle East 28 May 1942. Aged 26. He has no known grave. *s of William & Maud Schofield, Wigan; h of Olive Schofield, Wigan.* ALAMEIN MEMORIAL. [W/WGS]

**SCHOFIELD Leslie,** Spr. 11001272 193 Railway Operating Coy., Royal Engineers. Died 28 June 1946. Aged 25. *s of Thomas & Clara, Beech Hill, Wigan.* KHAYAT BEACH WAR CEMETERY, ISRAEL. [W]

**SCHOFIELD Thomas,** W.O. II (C.S.M.) 3851687 18th(5th Bn. The Loyal Regiment [North Lancashire] ) Regiment., Reconnaissance Corps. Died of wounds in Singapore Civil Hospital 15 February 1942. Aged 38. *h of Deborah.* SINGAPORE CIVIL HOSPITAL GRAVE MEMORIAL. [A]

**SCOTT Harold,** L.Cpl. 3709751 2nd Bn. The King's Own Royal Regiment (Lancaster). Died in the Middle East 30 December 1939. Aged 25. *s of John & Mary, Abram.* RAMLEH CEMETERY, ISRAEL. [ABC]

**SEDDON Arnold,** Pte. S/212875 Royal Army Service Corps. Died 3 January 1943. Aged 28. *h of Ethel.* BLACKROD CEMETERY. [X]

**SEDDON Edward,** Ord. Smn. P/JX416186 R.N. H.M.S. *Abdiel* Accidentally drowned 10 October 1943. Aged 21. *s of James & Elizabeth.* PORTSMOUTH NAVAL MEMORIAL. [BCC/BL]

**SEDDON Edward,** Pte. 14206703 7th Bn. The Duke of Wellington's Regiment (West Riding). Accidentally killed in Scotland 2 January 1944. Aged 20. *s of Robert & Ellen.* WIGAN CEMETERY. [SGC/W]

**SEDDON Frederick,** Sjt. 3515308 111th (5th Bn. The Manchester Regiment) Regt.; R.A.C. Accidentally killed 7 September 1943. WIGAN CEMETERY. [W]

**SEDDON Hugh,** Spr. 1913483 Royal Engineers. Killed at sea 31 May 1940 during the evacuation of Dunkirk. Aged 24. DOVER (ST JAMES) CEMETERY. [A/BDC/L]

**SEDDON James,** Sgt. (Air Gnr.) 2203354 R.A.F. (V.R.) 207 Sqdn. 28 August 1943. Aged 19. A member of the crew of a Lancaster III bomber which took off from Langar on a bombing mission to Nuremburg. All seven members of the crew (which included four Australians) were killed. *s of Percy & Elizabeth, Worthington.* DURNBACH WAR CEMETERY, GERMANY. [BCC/BL]

**SEDDON Joseph,** Pte. 5682747 The Pioneer Corps. Killed 12 February 1945 in Belgium. Aged 22. *s of Thomas & Elizabeth, Aspull.* SCHOONSELHOF CEMETERY, ANTWERP. [AS/HDC]

**SEDDON Kenneth,** Sgt. 987848 R.A.F. (V.R.) 227 Sqdn. Killed in the Middle East 27 August 1942. Aged 22. *s of Andrew & Nellie, Standish.* ALAMEIN MEMORIAL. [ST/STC/W/WGS]

**SEDDON Leslie,** A.B. P/JX563423 R.N. H.M. Trawler *Lord Wakefield.* 29 July 1944. Age 19. Off the Normandy beaches, this anti-submarine trawler was sunk by German aircraft. *s of Edward & Margaret, New Springs.* PORTSMOUTH NAVAL MEMORIAL. [AS/NSC]

**SEDDON Thomas,** A.B. P/JX282621 R.N. H.M.S. *Trinidad* 14 May 1942. Aged 29. This cruiser was damaged by one of her own torpedoes and then, near Murmansk, was attacked and set on fire by a German Ju-88 bomber. *s of Thomas & Margaret; h of May.* PORTSMOUTH NAVAL MEMORIAL. [HGC/L/LTC]

**SEDDON Walter,** L.Cpl. 3451842 2nd Bn. The Essex Regiment. Killed in Belgium 26 October 1944. Aged 25. *s of Edward & Jane Elizabeth.* GEEL WAR CEMETERY, BELGIUM. [W/WPC]

**SELL William,** Pte. 14347526 Royal Army Medical Corps. Died 28 November 1945. PEMBERTON (ST JOHN) CHURCHYARD. [X]

**SENIOR Peter,** Pte. 13088069 The Pioneer Corps. Died 3 November 1944. WIGAN CEMETERY. [X]

**SERGEANT Joseph,** Pte. 3858869 1st Bn. The Gordon Highlanders Died of wounds received whilst serving in France 19 June 1944. Aged 24. *s of William & Mary Elizabeth Sergeant, Ince; h of Edith Sergeant.* HERMANVILLE WAR CEMETERY, FRANCE. [IN]

**SETTLE William,** L.A.C. 1359340 R.A.F. (V.R.), 2769 Sqdn. R.A.F. Regiment. Died 14 May 1944 in Prestonhall Hospital, Kent. Aged 31. *s of Joseph & Mary Ann, New Springs.* HAIGH (ST DAVID) CHURCHYARD. [AS/NSC]

**SHACKLETON Harry Douglas,** Gnr. 1493368 *M.M.* 1 Bty., 1 Searchlight Regiment, Royal Artillery. Died 24 May 1945. Aged 26. *s of Robinson & Margaret Shackleton, Westhoughton.* HAGGATE BAPTIST CHAPELYARD, BRIERFIELD, LANCASHIRE. [HGS]

**SHANNON Edward,** Gnr. 3912974 14 Lt. A.A. Regiment, Royal Artillery. Died 21 December 1944. Aged 31. *s of James & Margaret Shannon, Wigan.* WIGAN CEMETERY. [X]

**SHARP Walter,** Spr. 2126376 21 Field Park Squadron, Royal Engineers. Killed in action in the Middle East 24 October 1942. Aged 28. He has no known grave. *h of Renee, Leigh.* ALAMEIN MEMORIAL. [L]

**SHARPLES Frank,** Cpl. 3389404 1st Bn. The Duke of Wellington's Regiment (West Riding) Killed in action in Italy 20 August 1944. Aged 24. *s of Andrew & Amy.* FLORENCE WAR CEMETERY. [HAC/T]

**SHARPLES George,** Bdr. 3763471 13 Bty., 7 H.A.A. Regiment, Royal Artillery. Killed in Malta 1 November 1941. Aged 38. *He had family connections with Ince.* IMTARFA MILITARY CEMETERY, MALTA. [X]

**SHARPLES Victor Hugo,** Dvr. 106293 Royal Army Service Corps. Died sometime between 28 May 1940 and 23 June 1940 during the retreat to (and subsequent evacuation of) Dunkirk. Aged 26. *s of Mr. & Mrs. C.A.; h of Mary, Wigan.* ST AUBIN-SUR-MER CHURCHYARD, FRANCE. [W]

**SHARROCK Harry,** A.C.2. 1064357 R.A.F. (V.R.) Captured at the fall of Singapore and died as a Japanese PoW in Fuknoka Camp 29 November 1942. Aged 31. *s of J. & Jane, Standish.* YOKOHAMA CREMATION MEMORIAL, JAPAN. [ST/STC]
(His brother Thomas also died in the Far East while a PoW of the Japanese.)

**SHARROCK John,** Dvr. T/286105 15 Field Bakery, Royal Army Service Corps. Died 6 July 1943 in the Middle East. Aged 42. *s of Joe & Elizabeth; h of Sarah.* SUEZ WAR MEMORIAL CEMETERY, EGYPT. [W]

**SHARROCK Thomas,** A.C.1. 1032510 R.A.F. (V.R.) Died 16 August 1945 while a PoW of the Japanese. s of J. & Jane, Standish. DJAKARTA WAR CEMETERY, INDONESIA. [ST/STC]
(His brother Harry also died while being held as a PoW of the Japanese.)

**SHAW Benjamin,** Pte. 3866039 2nd Bn. The Hampshire Regiment. Killed in Italy 25 September 1943. Aged 21. *s of Benjamin & Maggie, Platt Bridge.* SALERNO WAR CEMETERY, ITALY. [PBC]

**SHAW Edward,** L.Cpl. 14337398 5/7th Bn. The Gordon Highlanders. Died of wounds 13 July 1944 in Normandy. Aged 20. *s of William Henry & Jesse, Poolstock.* RANVILLE WAR CEMETERY, FRANCE. [JC/W]

**SHAW Harry,** C.S.M. 3453645 The Lancashire Fusiliers and No. 3 Commando. Killed during the invasion of France on D-Day, 6 June 1944. Aged 24. C.S.M. Shaw was a very experienced soldier and had seen service in Norway, Dieppe, Sicily, Crete , St Nazaire and North Africa. *s of E. & F.; h of Amelia.* HERMANVILLE WAR CEMETERY, NORMANDY. [A/WMC]

**SHAW James,** Pte. 3859525 2nd Bn. The Loyal Regiment (North Lancashire) Killed 13 February 1942 during the battle for Singapore. Aged 24. He has no known grave. SINGAPORE MEMORIAL. [AIM]

**SHAW James,** Pte. 7645845 3 Ordnance Field Park, Royal Army Ordnance Corps. Killed in Durban, South Africa 30 March 1941. Aged 24. *s of Mr. & Mrs. James.* DURBAN (STELLAWOOD) CEMETERY, SOUTH AFRICA. [SCC/W/WSB]

**SHAW John,** Pte. 3858915 2nd Bn. The Loyal Regiment (North Lancashire) Died 9 November 1943 while a PoW of the Japanese and working on the Burma-Siam railway. Aged 23. THANBYUZAYAT WAR CEMETERY. [X]

**SHAW Richard,** Gnr. 940280 110 Field Regiment, Royal Artillery. Died of wounds in Holland 4 December 1944. Aged 25. *s of Thomas & Margaret, Platt Bridge.* NEDERWEERT WAR CEMETERY, HOLLAND. [PBC]

**SHAW Ronald John,** Flying. Offr. 138298 R.A.F. (V.R.) 104 Sqdn. Killed 5 May 1944. BUDAPEST WAR CEMETERY, HUNGARY. [HBC]

**SHAW William,** E.R.A. 4th. Class. D/MX79545 R.N. H.M.S. *Samphire.* 30 January 1943. Aged 20. Off Bougie, this corvette was sunk by the Italian submarine *Platino. s of George & Matilda, Ashton-in-Makerfield.* PLYMOUTH NAVAL MEMORIAL. [AIM]

**SHEPHERD Horace,** Sgt. 553812 R.A.F. (V.R.) 209 Sqdn. Killed 8 September 1942 during a patrol over the Indian Ocean. Aged 20. He has no known grave. *s of John & Harriet.* ALAMEIN MEMORIAL. [AIM/AMS]

**SHERRIFF Bernard Henry,** Lieut. 281194 The Lancashire Fusiliers attd. The Gold Coast Regiment. Killed in West Africa 5 February 1944. Aged 23. *s of William & Gertrude, Wigan.* TAMALE EUROPEAN CEMETERY, GHANA. [W/WGS]

**SHERRIFF Claude William,** Lieut. 2$^{nd}$ Bn. The 1$^{st}$ Punjab Regiment. Killed in Burma 18 February 1943. Aged 31. *s of Davidson & Charlotte, Worthington.; h of Joyce.* TAUKKYAN WAR CEMETERY, BURMA. [AS/HDC]

**SHERRINGTON Norman Cecil,** Tpr. 7934973 4$^{th}$ County of London Yeomanry (Sharpshooters), R.A.C. Killed in the Middle East 31 August 1942. Aged 27. *s of Ralph & Martha Alice; h of Beatrice Elizabeth, Whelley, Wigan.* EL ALAMEIN WAR CEMETERY, EGYPT. [SSC/W/WSB]

**SHONE Samuel,** Pte. 3527242 The Manchester Regiment. Died 7 May 1945. Aged 31. *h of Bessie.* ATHERTON CEMETERY. [A]

**SHORROCKS William James C.,** Pte. 2086114 7$^{th}$ Bn. The Duke of Wellington's Regiment (West Riding). Died of wounds in France 10 August 1944. Aged 23. *h of Elizabeth Alice, Standish.* RANVILLE WAR CEMETERY, NORMANDY. [ST/STC]

**SHORT Harry,** Marine PO/X104094 Royal Marines R.M. Group, M.N.B.D.O. (1) Accidentally killed in Alexandria 22 August 1942. Aged 20. *s of Herbert & Mary, Leigh.* ALEXANDRIA (HADRA) CEMETERY, EGYPT. [L/LAS/LTC]

**SHORT Robert,** Sgt. 63991 R.A.F. 467 (R.A.A.F.) Sqdn. 3 October 1943. Aged 22. His Lancaster III bomber ran out of petrol and came down in the sea off Beachy Head. One member of the crew was rescued; the other six perished. *s of John & Anne, Up Holland.* RUNNYMEDE MEMORIAL [UPC/UPH]

**SHOVELTON Wright,** W.O.II. 835788 97 Anti-Tank Regiment, Royal Artillery. Killed in France 11 July 1944. Aged 29. *s of Thomas & Hannah; h of Edna Frances.* BROUAY WAR CEMETERY, FRANCE. [BDC/L]

**SIDLOW Frederick Arthur,** Pte. 3524363 1st Bn. The Manchester Regiment. Captured at the capitulation of Singapore and died whilst being held as a PoW of the Japanese 27 May 1943. Aged 30. *s of Frederick & Emily, Westleigh.* THANBYUZAYAT WAR CEMETERY, BURMA. [L]

**SIDLOW Thomas William,** C.S.M. 3451839 1/8th Bn. The Lancashire Fusiliers. Died of wounds in Burma 19 March 1945. Aged 26. TAUKKYAN WAR CEMETERY, BURMA. [CUC]

**SILCOCK William,** Cpl. 10590092 Royal Electrical & Mechanical Engineers. Killed in action 8 June 1944 in Normandy. Aged 22. He has no known grave. *s of Richard & Ann, Orrell.* BAYEAUX MEMORIAL. [OC/OCY]

**SIMM John,** Gnr. 1826605 21 Lt. A.A. Regiment, Royal Artillery. Died 22 April 1944 in Borneo while a PoW of the Japanese. Aged 30. *s of Peter & Annie.* LABUAN WAR CEMETERY, NORTH BORNEO. [L]

**SIMM John,** L.Cpl. 14389392 1st Bn. The Tyneside Scottish, The Black Watch (Royal Highland Regiment) Killed in Normandy 17 July 1944. Aged 23. *s of James & Elizabeth, Pemberton.* TILLY-SUR-SEULLES WAR CEMETERY, FRANCE. [NC/PC/W]

**SIMM Joseph,** Ord. Smn. P/JX257714 R.N. H.M.S. *Neptune.* 19 December 1941. Aged 21. This cruiser ran on to a minefield while hunting an Italian convoy and sank with the loss of all but one of her entire crew. *s of Henry & Elizabeth, New Springs.* PORTSMOUTH NAVAL MEMORIAL. [AS/NSC]
(See Colin F. Coppock, John Hughes and Douglas Pilling who also died in this action.)

**SIMMS Henry (Harry),** Pte. 3456034 16th Bn. The Durham Light Infantry. Died in North Africa 9 June 1943. Aged 27. *s of Robert & Catherine.* MEDJEZ-EL-BAB WAR CEMETERY, TUNISIA. [T]

**SIMPSON Bernard,** Pte. 6093600 1st Bn. The Queen's Own Royal West Kent Regiment. Killed in North Africa 27 April 1943. Aged 25. *s of A Simpson, Poolstock, Wigan.* MASSICAULT WAR CEMETERY, TUNISIA. [W]

**SIMPSON Leslie Harry.** Pte. 1714295 Royal Army Ordnance Corps. Died 26 June 1947. Aged 36. *s of George Jaques & Mary Ann; h of Edna May, Wigan.* WIGAN CEMETERY, [X]

**SINGLETON Charles Philip,** Cook. P/MX122585 R.N. H.M.S. *Bickerton* 22 August 1944. Aged 19. This frigate was torpedoed by German U-boat *U-354* off the coast of Norway. *s of Clarence & Elsie Singleton.* PORTSMOUTH NAVAL MEMORIAL. [BCC/BL]

**SINGLETON Harry,** L.Cpl. 2613752 505 Independent Mobile Provost Coy., Corps of Military Police. Died 10 February 1944 in Italy. Aged 30. *s of Edmund & Margaret Singleton, Bryn; h of Phyllis Singleton.* NAPLES WAR CEMETERY, ITALY. [BNC]

**SINGLETON Richard,** Sto. 1st Class. C/KX100964 R.N. H.M.S. *Harvester* 11 March 1943. Aged 25. In mid-Atlantic this destroyer was on convoy escort when it was sunk by the U-boat *U-432. s of Jack & Jane; h of Elsie, Atherton.* CHATHAM NAVAL MEMORIAL. [X]

**SLATER Jeffrey,** Ldg. Sto. D/KX139149 R.N. H.M. *M.T.B. 494* 7 April 1945. Aged 24. *s of Ernest & Laura Ann, Leigh; h of Doris.* PLYMOUTH NAVAL MEMORIAL. [L]

**SLATER John Aspinal,** Tpr. 7911624 H.Q. Squadron, 12th Royal Lancers, R.A.C. Killed in action 28 April 1945 in Italy. Aged 32. *s of John & Annie; h of Jane.* PADUA WAR CEMETERY, ITALY. [WGS]

**SLEEMAN Lewis John,** Sig. D/SSX25405 R.N. H.M.S. *Eclipse* 24 October 1943. Aged 23. This destroyer was sunk by a mine east of Kalymnos. *s of Lewis & Maria, Astley.* PLYMOUTH NAVAL MEMORIAL. [X]

**SLEGG Cyril,** L.A.C. 1007464 R.A.F. (V.R.) Died 31 August 1946 in South Africa. Aged 35. *s of William & Eunice; h of Edna, Golborne.* JOHANNESBURG (WEST PARK) CEMETERY, SOUTH AFRICA. [G/GOC]

**SMALL Jack,** Tpr. 3855291 18th (5th Bn. The Loyal Regiment [North Lancashire]) Regiment., Recconaissance Corps. Died 20 July 1943 whilst being held as a PoW of the Japanese and working on the Burma-Siam railway. Aged 27. *s of Ben & Emily, Tyldesley; h of Minden Rose, Tyldesley.* THANBYUZAYAT WAR CEMETERY, BURMA. [X]

**SMALL Robert,** Pte. 2182817 Auxiliary Military Pioneer Corps. Killed in the Liverpool blitz 2 May 1941. Aged 26. *h of Marion.* ATHERTON CEMETERY. [A]

**SMALLEY Joseph,** Pte. 7932136 5th Bn. The Northamptonshire Regiment Killed in Italy 23 November 1943. Aged 23. SANGRO RIVER WAR CEMETERY. [W]

**SMALLEY Richmond,** E.R.A. D/MX75813 R.N. H.M.S. *Charybdis.* 23 October 1943. Aged 30. This cruiser was sunk by German torpedo boats off Northern France. *h of Mary, Wigan.* DINARD CEMETERY, FRANCE. [X]
(In addition see: William Butler; William Clayton; Robert Finney, and Kenneth Gibson who were also killed in this action.)

**SMALLMAN Alan,** Pte. 3660432 9th Bn. The Durham Light Infantry. Killed in the Middle East 5 September 1942. Aged 27. *His mother lived in Tyldesley; h of Hilda.* EL ALAMEIN WAR CEMETERY, [T]

**SMALLSHAW Leslie,** Sgmn. 14070046 Royal Corps of Signals, 28th Div. Signals. Died in Austria 23 August 1946. Aged 19. *s of George & Margaret Jane, Pemberton.* KLAGENFURT WAR CEMETERY, AUSTRIA. [X]

**SMITH Alexander,** Sgt. (Obs.) 1050686 R.A.F. (V.R.) 600 Sqdn. Killed 22 August 1941. Aged 28. He has no known grave. RUNNYMEDE MEMORIAL. [A]

**SMITH Alfred,** Pte. 3859526 1st Bn. The Loyal Regiment (North Lancashire). Died of wounds in North Africa, 1 May 1943. Aged 26. *s of Fred & Eliza Ellen, Wigan; h of May, Pemberton.* OUED ZARGA WAR CEMETERY, TUNISIA. [UPC/UPH]

**SMITH Arthur Stanley,** Pte. 14395833 8th Bn. The Royal Scots (The Royal Regiment) Died of wounds in Holland 22 December 1944. Aged 20. *s of William & Ada, Standish.* NEDERWEERT WAR CEMETERY, HOLLAND. [ST/STC]

**SMITH Donald,** L.A.C. 972275 R.A.F. Died whilst a PoW of the Japanese 29 November 1943. Aged 25. SINGAPORE MEMORIAL. [A/HBC]

**SMITH Frank,** Flt. Sgt. (W.Op./Air Gnr.) 1025977 R.A.F. (V.R.) 9 Sqdn. 2 December 1943. Aged 23. His Lancaster I bomber from Bardney on a Berlin raid crashed near Brusendorf. There were no survivors from the crew. *s of John & Elizabeth.* BERLIN 1935-45 WAR CEMETERY, GERMANY. [L/LPC]

**SMITH Francis (Frank) Austin,** Pte. 13075884 242 Coy., The Pioneer Corps. Died of wounds in Italy 12 April 1944. Aged 36. *s of Ben & Agnes.* BEACH HEAD WAR CEMETERY, ANZIO, ITALY. [G/GOC]

**SMITH Francis (Frank),** Fus. 1791306 1st Bn. The Royal Fusiliers (City of London Regiment) Died of wounds in Italy 27 August 1944. Aged 23. *s of Fred & Alice, Wigan; h of Gladys, Pemberton.* FLORENCE WAR CEMETERY, ITALY. [NC/W]

**SMITH Frederick,** L.Sjt. 2616695 1st Bn. The Grenadier Guards. Killed in France 3 August 1944. Aged 24. *s of Frederick Thomas & Agnes; h of Dorothy.* ST CHARLES DE PERCY WAR CEMETERY, FRANCE. [X]

**SMITH Frank James,** Pte. 3865663 2nd Bn. The Border Regiment. Killed in action in Burma 24 May 1944. Aged 23. He has no known grave. *s of Arthur & Mary, Wrightington.* RANGOON MEMORIAL. [X]

**SMITH George,** Dvr. T/16255614 Royal Army Service Corps. Killed in Holland 6 April 1945. Aged 30. He has no known grave. *s of Elizabeth, Ince.* GROESBEEK MEMORIAL. [IN/ISM]

**SMITH Gordon Alan,** Sgt.(W.Op.) 974757 R.A.F. (V.R.) 101 Sqdn. 2 August 1941. Aged 22. His Wellington bomber on a Hamburg raid was shot-down and crashed in the Ijsselmeer, Holland. Four of the six members of the crew have no known graves. *s of Thomas & Eliza.* RUNNYMEDE MEMORIAL. [LGS/T/TC]

**SMITH Herbert,** Gnr. 1105424 65 Field Regiment, Royal Artillery. Killed 31 August 1942 in the Middle East. Aged 31. *s of John & Emily; h of Ann.* EL ALAMEIN WAR CEMETERY, EGYPT. [PBC]

**SMITH James,** L.Cpl. 3531730 H.Q. 247 Provost Coy., Corps of Military Police. Died 5 January 1946. Aged 25. *s of Harry & Annie; h of Edith.* BRUSSELS TOWN CEMETERY, BELGIUM. [L/LTC]

**SMITH John,** Bdr. 835273 1 Regiment, Royal Horse Artillery. Killed in action 14 April 1941 in the Middle East. Aged 27. TOBRUK WAR CEMETERY. [AIM]

**SMITH John Francis,** Sgt. (Nav.) 1491254 R.A.F. (V.R.) 16 O.T.U. 25 January 1944. Aged 21. His Wellington III bomber from Upper Heyford was to bomb Granville but it crashed into the sea off the Cherbourg peninsula. He has no known grave. *s of James & Mary Ellen.* RUNNYMEDE MEMORIAL. [L]

**SMITH Joseph Kenneth,** Flt. Sgt. 1578244 R.A.F. (V.R.) 177 Sqdn. Killed 24 November 1944 in the Far East while on operations in a Beaufighter aircraft. He has no known grave. SINGAPORE MEMORIAL. [PC]

**SMITH Norman Henry,** L.Cpl. 3530205 1st Bn. The East Lancashire Regiment. Killed in Belgium 7 January 1945. Aged 24. *s of Richard & Rose.* HOTTON WAR CEMETERY, BELGIUM. [A]

**SMITH Richard,** Pte. D/15004 6th (HD) Bn. The East Lancashire Regiment. Died 10 May 1944. THORNTON GARDEN OF REST, CROSBY. [W]
(According to CWGC records, he is shown incorrectly on the Wigan Cenotaph as serving in the Lancashire Fusiliers at the time of his death.)

**SMITH Stanley Waring,** Sgt.(Flt. Eng.) 1592691 R.A.F. (V.R.) 158 Sqdn. 18 July 1944. Aged 31. This Halifax III bomber from Lissett was tasked to bomb fortified positions near Caen. It crashed near St-Pierre-du-Jonquet. BANNEVILLE-LA-CAMPAGNE CEMETERY, FRANCE. [W]

**SMITH Thomas,** Sgt. 996850 R.A.F. (V.R.) 47 Sqdn. Killed 14 April 1942 during an anti-submarine operation off the North African coast. Aged 23. *s of Joseph & Emma, Tyldesley; h of Nora.* ALAMEIN MEMORIAL. [T/HBC]

**SMITH Thomas,** Pte. 3595436 1st Bn. The Border Regiment. Killed 21 May 1940 during the retreat to Dunkirk. Aged 34. He has no known grave. *s of Fred & Elizabeth, Wigan; h of Mary* Ann. DUNKIRK MEMORIAL. [W]

**SMITH Thomas Haig,** Sgt. (W.Op/Air Gnr.) 993817 R.A.F. (V.R.) 431 (R.C.A.F.) Sqdn. Killed 13 May 1943. Aged 26. His Wellington X bomber on a Duisburg raid crashed at Huppel on the Holland-German border. *s of Thomas & Lily, Atherton.* WINTERSWIJK GENERAL CEMETERY, HOLLAND. [CUC/LGS]

**SMITH Walter Ramsdale,** Fus. 3452663 The Lancashire Fusiliers. Died 7 May 1940 Aged 32. *h of May.* WIGAN CEMETERY. [X]

**SMITH William Brimelow,** Sgt. 1113712 R.A.F. (V.R.) 13 O.T.U. Killed 18 June 1942. Aged 21. He has no known grave. *s of Harry & Rachel, Boothstown.* RUNNYMEDE MEMORIAL [LGS]

**SMITH William Everard,** Sgt. (Pilot) 1112639 R.A.F. (V.R.) Died 6 February 1942. *s of Mr. & Mrs. T.I., Wigan.* CHORLEY (ST GREGORY) R.C. CHURCHYARD. [W]

**SNAPE Ernest Lawrence,** Gdsmn. 2618468 6<sup>th</sup> Bn. The Grenadier Guards. Killed in action in Italy 5 December 1943. Aged 27. *s of William Lawrence & Sarah Ellen, Shevington; h of Elizabeth.* MINTURNO WAR CEMETERY, ITALY. [S/STC]

**SNAPE Joseph,** Cpl. 3780785 *M.M.* 4<sup>th</sup>/7<sup>th</sup> Royal Dragoon Guards, R.A.C. Killed in action in Germany 18 April 1945. Aged 33. *His parents lived in Lower Ince.* BECKLINGEN WAR CEMETERY, GERMANY. [ISM]

**SOUTHERN Albert,** Cpl. 631521 R.A.F. 37 Sqdn. Killed in the Middle East 12 March 1942. Aged 23. *s of Walter & Edith, Aspull.* SUEZ WAR MEMORIAL CEMETERY. [AS/ASC]

**SOUTHWORTH Charles Henry,** Sgt. (Flt. Eng.) 2209114 R.A.F. (V.R.) 106 Sqdn. 28 June 1944. Aged 20. His Lancaster I bomber from Metheringham was on an operation to attack rail targets at Vitry-le-Francois. It was shot-down by a night fighter and crashed at Thibie. *s of Issac & Mary, Wigan.* DIEPPE CANADIAN WAR CEMETERY. [W]

**SOUTHWORTH Herbert,** Pte. 4460224 8<sup>th</sup> Bn. The Durham Light Infantry. Killed in action in France 10 June 1944 having arrived in Normandy on D-Day four days earlier. Aged 24. *s of Thomas & Anne, Wigan.* BAYEAUX WAR CEMETERY, NORMANDY. [KMC/W]

**SPEAKMAN George,** Gnr. 1782383 2/1 Maritime Regiment, Royal Artillery. Killed in action at sea 15 February 1942. Aged 21. PORTSMOUTH NAVAL MEMORIAL. [L]

**SPEAKMAN Harry,** Pte. 14439126 1<sup>st</sup> Bn. The Gordon Highlanders. Killed in France 23 August 1944. Aged 18. *s of John T. & Helen Amelia, Standish.* ST DESIR WAR CEMETERY. [ST/STC]

**SPEAKMAN James Ronald,** A.B. D/JX396029 R.N. H.M.S. *Mahratta.* 25 February 1944. Aged 19. On convoy escort duty in the Barentz Sea, this destroyer was sunk by the German U-boat *U-956. s of Harry & Elsie, Astley.* PLYMOUTH NAVAL MEMORIAL. [T]
(See also William Barnes; James Clare; Owen Dootson and Alfred Henry Urmston who died in this action.)

**SPEAKMAN Richard,** L.Sjt. 3522572 4<sup>th</sup> Bn. The Border Regiment. Died in a Middle East hospital 17 June 1941. Aged 37. *s of William & Emma Speakman, Goose Green; h of Lilian Speakman, Pemberton, Wigan.* HALFAYA SOLLUM CEMETERY, EGYPT. [MZC/W]

**SPEAKMAN Richard,** Seaman. LT/JX379847 R.N. Patrol Service. H.M.S. *Nadine.* Accidentally shot by a messmate. 22 December 1943. Aged 19. *s of Ethel Kinane & stepson of Michael.* WIGAN CEMETERY. [HIC/W]

**SPEAKMAN Thomas,** Engineman. LT/KX131732 R.N. Patrol Service. H.M.S. *Sunspot.* 9 December 1946. Aged 43. *h of Esther.* WIGAN CEMETERY. [X]

**SPEAKMAN William,** Sgt. 1080677 R.A.F. (V.R.) 103 Sqdn. 28 January 1944. Aged 23. This Lancaster III bomber from Elsham Wolds was lost on an operation to bomb Berlin. *s of Thomas & Hannah, Atherton.* RUNNYMEDE MEMORIAL [X]

**SPENCER Albert,** Sto. 1st. Class. D/KX133120 R.N. H.M. Submarine *Untamed.* 30 May 1943. Aged 32. The submarine failed to surface during an exercise off Cambeltown, Scotland. Thirty-four bodies were recovered when the vessel was salvaged, and it was later refitted and renamed *Vitality*. *h of Marrie Spencer, Atherton.* DUNOON CEMETERY. [A]

**SPENCER Allan,** Cpl. 4203339 7th Bn. The Royal Welch Fusiliers Killed in France 17 July 1944. BAYEAUX WAR CEMETERY, NORMANDY. [BBC/BL]

**SPENCER Henry (Harry),** Pte. 3709055 1st Bn. The Loyal Regiment (North Lancashire). Killed in Italy 30 May 1944. Aged 35. *s of Edwin & Bertha, Leigh; h of Catherine, Leigh.* BEACH HEAD WAR CEMETERY, ANZIO, ITALY. [L/LTA]

**SPENCER Leslie,** L.Cpl. 2622359 6th Bn. The Grenadier Guards. Killed in action in Italy 7 November 1943. Aged 22. *s of Geoffrey & Emily; h of Elsie, Tyldesley.* CASSINO WAR CEMETERY, ITALY. [T]

**STABELER John,** Sgmn. 2335147 Royal Corps of Signals, XIII Corps Signals. Died in hospital in Iraq 10 October 1941. Aged 22. *s of George & Agnes, Ashton-in-Makerfield.* BAGHDAD (NORTH GATE) WAR CEMETERY. [AGS]

**STANLEY Douglas,** Pte. 14605230 1st Bn. The Loyal Regiment (North Lancashire) Killed 18 February 1944. Aged 20. BEACH HEAD WAR CEMETERY, ANZIO, ITALY. [G/GOC]

**STANTON William,** Gnr. 1709671 5 Searchlight Regiment, Royal Artillery. Died 14 July 1943 while a PoW of the Japanese. Aged 28. *His family connections were in Higher Ince.* KANCHANABURI WAR CEMETERY [X]

**STARKEY James,** Pte. 7365897 Royal Army Medical Corps attd. 12th (10th Bn. The Green Howards [Yorkshire Regiment] ) Bn., The Parachute Regiment, A.A.C. Killed in action in Belgium 5 January 1945. Aged 25. *s of Eva, Leigh.* HOTTON WAR CEMETERY, BELGIUM. [L/WMC]

**STARKIE Benjamin Thomas,** Ldg. Cook. D/MX53864 R.N. H.M.S. *Glorious.* 9 June 1940. Aged 23. This aircraft-carrier was sunk by the German battlecruisers *Gneisenau* and *Scharnhorst* 300 miles west of Narvik. There were only 43 survivors. *s of Benjamin Thomas & Harriet.* PLYMOUTH NAVAL MEMORIAL. [HC]
(See also the following who died in this action: Samuel Alker; Walter L. Duckworth; John F. Gorton; John Jameson; Edward Knight; Peter McNicholas; Frederick Swann.)

**STARR Donald,** Capt. 111791 Royal Army Medical Corps. Died on active service in the Middle East 11 May 1941. Aged 39. *s of James & Annie, Wigan; h of Elizabeth Mary Starr, Victoria, Australia. He was formerly a doctor at Manchester Infirmary.* CAIRO WAR MEMORIAL CEMETERY, EGYPT. [W/WGS]

**STATHAM Geoffrey,** Pte. 14202890 1st Bn. The York & Lancaster Regiment. Killed in action in Italy 10 October 1943. Aged 20. *s of Hannah, Leigh.* SANGRO RIVER WAR CEMETERY, ITALY. [L/LMC/LTC]

**STEELE Leslie,** Fus. 1640739 7th Bn. The Royal Welch Fusiliers. Killed in action in Germany 14 April 1945. Aged 25. BECKLINGEN WAR CEMETERY, GERMANY. [W]

**STEELE Thomas,** Fus. 3860530 1st Bn. The Royal Irish Fusiliers. Killed in Sicily 5 August 1943. CATANIA WAR CEMETERY, ITALY. [AIM]

**STEPHEN William,** Sto. C/KX132925 R.N. H.M.S. *Sussex.* Died 7 December 1942. Aged 33. WIGAN CEMETERY. [X]

**STEPHENSON Albert,** Pte. 3861876 1/7th Bn. The Royal Warwickshire Regiment. Killed in action 30 July 1944. Aged 34. *s of Albert & Mary; h of Lilian, Poolstock.* FONTENAY-LE-PESNEL WAR CEMETERY. [JC/W]

**STEVENS Harold,** L.Bdr. 1087209 68 Medium Regiment, Royal Artillery. Died of wounds in Belgium 21 October 1944. Aged 32. *He had family connections in Orrell.* GEEL WAR CEMETERY, BELGIUM. [PC]

**STEVENS Joseph,** Flt. Lt. (Nav.) 125607 R.A.F. (V.R.) 75 Sqdn. Killed when his Lancaster I bomber from Mepal on an operation to Hamburg crashed near Veghel in Holland 21 July 1944. Aged 32. *s of Joseph & Hilda, Newton-le-Willows.* UDEN WAR CEMETERY, HOLLAND. [AGS]

**STEWART Fred James,** Cpl. 2000711 59 Field Coy., Royal Engineers. Killed in Italy 29 October 1944. Aged 26. *s of Percy & Florence; h of Barbara Ruby, Wigan.* CESENA WAR CEMETERY. [X]

**STEWART Jack,** Bdr. 1552599 51 Bty., 69 Field Regiment, Royal Artillery. Died of wounds in India 31 July 1944. Aged 30. *s of William & Alice, Atherton; h of Esther, Atherton.* DELHI WAR CEMETERY, INDIA. [A]

**STIRRUP Arthur,** Flt. Sgt.(W.Op./Air Gnr.) 908245 R.A.F. (V.R.) 108 Sqdn. Killed 24 February 1941 in the Middle East. Aged 21. *s of Harold & Elizabeth, Haydock.* KNIGHTSBRIDGE WAR CEMETERY, LIBYA. [AGS]

**STOPFORTH Eric John,** L.Cpl. 14345374 603 Railway Construction Coy., Royal Engineers. Killed in Belgium 19 January 1945. Aged 33. *s of Albert & Rose, Kitt Green.* SCHOONSELHOF WAR CEMETERY, ANTWERP. [PC]

**STONES Frank,** Sgt.(W.Op/Air Gnr.) 975763 R.A.F. (V.R.) 40 Sqdn. 12 March 1941. Aged 21. This Wellington bomber was on a Boulogne raid but crashed near the target area with the loss of all the crew. The two pilots and the observer were aged just nineteen, and Sgt. Stones was the oldest member of the very young crew which was on its first operational sortie. *s of William & Emma, Tyldesley.* WIMILLE COMMUNAL CEMETERY, FRANCE. [LGS/T/TC]

**STOPPFORTH Walter,** Pte. 3857295 2<sup>nd</sup> Bn. The Loyal Regiment (North Lancashire) Died 13 February 1942 while a PoW of the Japanese having been captured at the fall of Singapore. Aged 20. He has no known grave. *s of Mr. & Mrs. A.* SINGAPORE MEMORIAL. [A]
(In local sources his name is spelt variously as *Stopforth* and *Stopford.*)

**STOTT William,** A.B. D/JX266042 R.N. H.M.S. *President III* Died 9 February 1943. Aged 30. *s of John Thomas & Charlotte; h of Ann, Lower Ince.* PLYMOUTH NAVAL MEMORIAL. [IN/ISM]

**STOTTON James Edward,** Cpl. 25<sup>th</sup> County of Lancaster (Leigh) Bn., Home Guard. Died 29 March 1946. Aged 47. *s of Thomas & Kate; h of Doris Eveline, Leigh.* LEIGH CEMETERY. [X]

**STOWELL James,** Cpl. 554054 7<sup>th</sup> Bn. The Queen's Own Hussars, R.A.C. Captured at Benghazi and died at sea 14 November 1942 whilst being held as a PoW and being transferred from North Africa to Italy. The ship in which he was being transported (s.s. *Scillia*) was sunk by a British submarine. Aged 27. *s of Mr. & Mrs. J.J.* ALAMEIN MEMORIAL. [L/LMC]

**STRETCH John,** Tpr. 3856747 18<sup>th</sup> (5<sup>th</sup> Bn. The Loyal Regiment [North Lancashire]) Regiment., Reconnaissance Corps. Died 12 October 1943 while a PoW of the Japanese and working on the Burma-Siam railway. *s of Samuel & Bertha.* KANCHANABURI WAR CEMETERY. [HC]

**STRINGER John Richard,** Fus. 5961609 9<sup>th</sup> Bn. The Royal Fusiliers (City of London Regiment). Died of wounds in Italy 14 January 1944. Aged 21. *s of John & Lena, Poolstock, Wigan.* NAPLES WAR CEMETERY. [JC]

**STRINGFELLOW Herbert,** Spr. 28463 8 Field Coy., New Zealand Engineers. Killed 23 September 1944 in Italy. Aged 28. *s of Peter & Lois, Wigan, and having connections with Platt Bridge. He emigrated to New Zealand when he was six years old.* RAVENNA WAR CEMETERY, ITALY. [X]

**STRINGFELLOW William,** L.Cpl. 3855662 L.Cpl. 351 Field Security Section, Intelligence Corps. Died 29 November 1943 while a PoW of the Japanese. He has no known grave. Aged 30. *s of William &Margaret, Hindley.* SINGAPORE MEMORIAL. [X]

**STRONG William James,** Cabin Boy. Merchant Navy s.s.*Darcoila.* The cargo ship was sunk by U-boat *U-32* south of Iceland 28 September 1940. Weeks later a vague note from him was found in a bottle which was washed ashore on the Cumberland coast. It requested that it be taken to his grandmother with whom he lived in Leigh. TOWER HILL MEMORIAL. [L]
(See also Douglas Arthur Kay)

**STUART Henry C.,** Pte. 3519375 1<sup>st</sup> Bn. The King's Shropshire Light Infantry. Killed in Italy 16 May 1944. Aged 41. *s of John & Ellen, Wigan; h of Elizabeth, Goose Green.* BEACH HEAD WAR CEMETERY, ANZIO, ITALY. [GGC/W]

**SULLIVAN Frederick,** Flt. Sgt. (Pilot) 1087865 R.A.F. (V.R.) 357 Sqdn. Killed flying a Liberator in the Far East 6 April 1944. Aged 23. *s of Philip & Catherine, Platt Bridge.* SAI WAN BAY WAR CEMETERY, HONG KONG. [X]

**SULLIVAN Thomas,** L.Cpl. 3964353 1/5th Bn. The Welch Regiment. Killed 20 September 1944 in Belgium. Aged 25. *s of Thomas & Bertha, Newtown, Wigan.* ADEGEM CANADIAN WAR CEMETERY, BELGIUM. [W]

**SUMMERS Herbert,** Dvr. 2366991 Royal Corps of Signals Killed 18 December 1944. Aged 39. *s of James & Margaret Jane; h of Lily, Billinge.* PHALERON WAR CEMETERY, ATHENS. [OC]

**SUTCH Robert Henry,** Pte. 3964295 1/5th Bn. The Welch Regiment. Killed in action in France 12 August 1944. Aged 25. *s of John & Mabel; h of Doris, Aspull.* BANNEVILLE-LA-CAMPAGNE WAR CEMETERY. [AS/ASC]

**SUTTON Harry,** A.B. D/JX272499 R.N. H.M.S. *Stanley.* 19 December 1941. Aged 24. While on convoy escort duty, this destroyer was sunk by U-boat *U-574* in the Mediterranean. *s of Henry & Sarah Elizabeth.* PLYMOUTH NAVAL MEMORIAL. [W/WSB]

**SUTTON William,** Pte. 3658315 7th Bn. The Green Howards (Yorkshire Regiment). Killed in France on D-Day, 6 June 1944. Aged 28. *s of Thomas & Maria, Blackrod.* BAYEAUX WAR CEMETERY, NORMANDY. [BCC/BL]

**SWAIN Arnold,** L.Bdr. 1578401 544 Coast Regiment, Royal Artillery. Died 22 July 1943. Aged 27. *s of Edmund & Sarah Jane.* WIGAN CEMETERY. [W]

**SWALWELL Anthony,** L.A.C. 978160 R.A.F. Died 9 July 1940. Aged 20. *s of Harold & Mabel Mary.* WIGAN CEMETERY. [W/WSB]

**SWANN Frederick,** Sto. 1st Class. D/KX91834 R.N. H.M.S. *Glorious.* 6 June 1940. Aged 25. This aircraft-carrier was sunk by the German battlecruisers *Gneisenau* and *Scharnhorst* 300 miles west of Narvik. There were only 43 survivors. *s of Thomas & Margaret.* PLYMOUTH NAVAL MEMORIAL. [W]
(See also: Samuel Alker; Walter L. Duckworth; John F. Gorton; John Jameson; Edward Knight; Peter McNicholas and Benjamin Starkie who perished in this action.)

**SWEENEY James,** Dvr. T/10705229 349 Army Troops Coy., Royal Army Service Corps. Died in hospital in the Middle East 22 December 1942. Aged 20. *s of James & Margaret, Wallgate, Wigan.* LE PETIT LAC CEMETERY, ALGERIA. [W]

**SWIFT Harry,** Sjt. 3710959 Royal Army Ordnance Corps. Killed in Crete 16 May 1941. Aged 24. *s of William & Margaret.* ATHENS MEMORIAL. [HGC]

**SWIFT Richard,** Gnr. 1640308 409 Bty., 79(The Hertfordshire Yeomanry) H.A.A. Regiment, Royal Artillery. Died 30 March 1941 in Leicester Infirmary as a result of an accident. Aged 20. *s of James Ralph & Elizabeth, Bamfurlong., h of Cecilia.* WIGAN CEMETERY. [W]

**SWIFT Walter,** Tpr. 3391661 1st Royal Tank Regiment, R.A.C. Killed in action in Italy 2 October 1943. Aged 22. *s of Harry & Lily, Ince.* NAPLES WAR CEMETERY. [IN]

**SWINDELL William,** Pte. 3530295 2nd Bn. The Manchester Regiment. Died in France 26 May 1940 during the withdrawal to Dunkirk. Aged 20. He has no known grave. *h of Gladys, Leigh.* DUNKIRK MEMORIAL. [A]

**SWITHENBY James,** Pte. 3780871 13th Bn. The King's Regiment (Liverpool.) Missing and presumed killed in action behind Japanese lines while serving with Wingate's Chindits, 2 April 1943. Aged 33. He has no known grave. *s of Nehemiah & Lily Swithenby, Leigh; h of Edith Hannah Swithenby.* RANGOON MEMORIAL. [L/LMC]

**TABERNER George,** Pte. 3861196 1st Bn. The East Lancashire Regiment. Killed in action in Germany 7 April 1945. Aged 32. REICHSWALD FOREST WAR CEMETERY, GERMANY. [L]

**TALBOT Gerard Joseph,** Sgt. 970360 R.A.F. (V.R.) 99 Sqdn. 9 May 1941. Aged 22. His Wellington II bomber took-off from Waterbeach to bomb Berlin and was last heard on radio calling for help. The aircraft and all the crew were lost without trace. *s of Joseph & Elizabeth; h of Belinda.* RUNNYMEDE MEMORIAL. [SSC/W]

**TAPLIN Harry,** Tpr. 191860 Royal Armoured Corps, H.Q. Sqdn., 11th Armoured Div. Killed in France 3 September 1944. Aged 29. *s of Mrs. E. Taplin, Wigan.* HIGHWOOD LONGUEVNE CEMETERY. [GGC/JC/W]

**TATUM Abell,** Spr. 2135970 24 Mechanical Equipment Section, Royal Engineers. Killed in action in France 11 August 1944. Aged 29. *s of Edward & Mary, Leigh.* RANVILLE WAR CEMETERY, NORMANDY. [L]

**TAYLOR Charles Leslie,** Cpl. 2391241 1st Bn. The South Lancashire Regiment (The Prince of Wales's Volunteers.) Killed in action in Germany 16 April 1945. Aged 21. BECKLINGEN WAR CEMETERY, GERMANY. [BHC/W/WGS]

**TAYLOR Frank,** Tpr. 14380875 15th Regiment, Reconnaissance Corps, R.A.C. Killed 24 October 1944 in Holland. Aged 20. *s of Tom & Ellen, Wrightington.* VALKENSWAARD WAR CEMETERY, HOLLAND.

**TAYLOR Herbert Edwin,** Pilot Offr. 1086462 R.A.F. (V.R.). Died 19 February 1943. Aged 33. *s of Edwin & Mary Ellen; h of Dorothy. In spite of every effort, it has not been possible to discover why he is buried in Redbourn.* REDBOURN (ST MARY) CHURCHYARD, REDBOURN, HERTS. [HGS]

**TAYLOR James,** L.Cpl. 3527543 1st Bn. The Manchester Regiment. Died 28 December 1943 whilst being held as a PoW of the Japanese and working on the Burma-Siam railway. Aged 29. *s of Frederick & Elizabeth Ann, Standish.* KANCHANABURI WAR CEMETERY, THAILAND. [STC]

**TAYLOR James Reginald B.,** Air Mechanic 1st Class. FAA/FX76801 R.N. H.M.S. *Illustrious* 10 January 1941. Aged 21. West of Malta, Ju-87 dive-bombers attacked this aircraft-carrier and it was badly damaged but managed to reach Malta although still on fire. *s of Ernest & Lily.* LEE-ON-SOLENT MEMORIAL. [L/LPC]
(See also James Parsons who died while serving in H.M.S. *Illustrious.*)

**TAYLOR John,** Gnr. 1062477 6 A.A. Regiment, Royal Artillery. Killed 12 January 1940. Aged 30. *s of Thomas & Mary Taylor; h of Eva.* BEUVRY COMMUNAL CEMETERY EXTENSION, FRANCE. [G]

**TAYLOR John Daniel,** Dvr. T/191974 Royal Army Service Corps Killed in action in the Middle East 29 May 1942. Aged 26. *s of Thomas & Ann; h of Evelyn, Wigan.* KNIGHTSBRIDGE WAR CEMETERY, ACROMA, LIBYA. [BHC/BNC/W]

**TAYLOR John Sharrock,** Sgt. (Pilot) 1024292 R.A.F. (V.R.) Killed 10 February 1942. Aged 28. *h of Harriet Taylor, Whelley, Wigan.* HAIGH (ST DAVID) CHURCHYARD. [SCC/SSC/W/WGS]

**TAYLOR John Tildesley,** Flt. Sgt. (Nav.) 1621012 R.A.F. (V.R.) 140 Sqdn. Killed 2 October 1944 whilst flying in an operation in a Mosquito aircraft. Aged 23. *s of Jack & Hilda, Leigh; h of Veronica.* BRUSSELS TOWN CEMETERY. [L/LGS/LPC]

**TAYLOR Robert,** Pte. 3854830 2nd Bn The Loyal Regiment (North Lancashire) Died 9 June 1942 as a PoW of the Japanese. Aged 22. *His mother lived in Wigan.* KRANJI WAR CEMETERY, SINGAPORE. [X]

**TAYLOR Robert,** Pte. 14973733 Royal Army Medical Corps. Died 5 July 1945. Aged 19. *s of Thomas & Elizabeth, Wigan.* HIGHFIELD (ST MATTHEW) CHURCHYARD. [W]

**TAYLOR Samuel,** Pte. 3527536 1st Bn. The Manchester Regiment. Died 3 June 1943 in the Far East as a PoW of the Japanese. Aged 34. *s of Thomas & Jane Ann.* KANCHANABURI WAR CEMETERY. [G/GOC]

**TAYLOR Thomas,** Pte. 3779082 2nd Bn. The King's Own Royal Regiment (Lancaster) Killed in action in Burma 25 May 1944. Aged 32. He has no known grave. *h of Evelyn, Bryn.* RANGOON MEMORIAL. [BNC/W]

**TAYLOR William,** Pte. 14782284 4th Bn. The Welch Regiment. Killed in action in Germany 7 March 1945. Aged 18. REICHSWALD FOREST WAR CEMETERY. [SCC/W]

**TAYLOR William,** Pte. 3531910 6th Bn. The Manchester Regiment. Died 7 February 1940. Aged 39. WIGAN CEMETERY. [W]

**TAYLOR William Ernest,** Gnr. 1643937 2/1 Maritime Regiment, Royal Artillery. Lost at sea while serving as a gunner on a merchant ship, 23 February 1942. *s of Mrs. E., Bryn.* PORTSMOUTH NAVAL MEMORIAL. [X]

**TELFORD George,** Pte. 14583536 7<sup>th</sup> Bn. The Royal Norfolk Regiment. Killed in action in France 7 August 1944. Aged 18. *s of William & Elizabeth, Beech Hill, Wigan.* BAYEAUX WAR CEMETERY, NORMANDY. [BHC/W]

**TELFORD James Sidney,** Dvr. T/63178 18 Div. Transport Coy., Royal Army Service Corps. Died of cholera 22 July 1943 while a PoW of the Japanese and working on the Burma-Siam railway. Aged 32. *s of Mr. & Mrs. James, Wigan.* THANBYUZAYAT WAR CEMETERY, BURMA. [AP/APC/W]

**THOMAS Frank,** Ord. Smn. LT/JX409875 R.N. Patrol Service. H.M. Trawler *Wallasea.* Died 6 January 1944. Aged 19. This naval trawler was sunk off the Lizard by German E-boats. *s of Richard Owen & Mary, Wigan.* PENZANCE CEMETERY, CORNWALL. [SSC]

**THOMAS Howell,** Sto. C/KX79228 R.N. H.M.S. *Medway.* Died 23 November 1942. Aged 34. *s of John & Mary Maud.* ATHERTON CEMETERY. [X]

**THOMAS Roland,** L.A.C. 1455060 R.A.F. (V.R.) Died 9 December 1944. Aged 21. *s of Robert & Harriet, Wigan.* WIGAN CEMETERY. [X]

**THOMAS William,** Pte 851137 1<sup>st</sup> Bn. The Manchester Regiment. Died 2 June 1943 while a PoW of the Japanese and working on the Burma-Siam railway. Aged 25. THANBYUZAYAT WAR CEMETERY, BURMA. [W]

**THOMASON Albert,** Pte. 4981510 5<sup>th</sup> Bn. Sherwood Foresters (Nottinghamshire & Derbyshire Regiment). Killed 23 September 1944 in Italy. Aged 28. *s of Joseph & Emma Thomason, Lowton St. Marys.* CORIANO RIDGE WAR CEMETERY, ITALY. [X]

**THOMASON Francis L.,** C. Sjt. 3852549 9<sup>th</sup> Bn. The Border Regiment. Killed in Burma 21 May 1944. Aged 34. He has no known grave. *s of William & Martha; h of Violet, Lowton St. Marys.* RANGOON MEMORIAL. [A]

**THOMASON Peter,** Sjt. 13002487 Auxiliary Military Pioneer Corps. He was much older than was usual for a serving soldier but he had served in the First World War. Lost in the sinking of s.s. *Lancastria* 17 June 1940. Aged 44.. *h of Emma, Tyldesley.* CHATEAU-D'OLONNE CHURCHYARD. [A]
(Twelve other local men perished when this ship was sunk. See the **Herbert Cunliffe** entry for names and details of the sinking.)

**THOMPSON Robert James,** Fus. 3455013 6<sup>th</sup> Bn. The Royal Scots Fusiliers. Died of wounds 10 November 1944 in Holland. Aged 28. *s of John Thomas & Alice Thompson; h of Eliza Thompson.* MIERLO WAR CEMETERY, HOLLAND. [IN/SCC/W]

**THOMPSON Sydney,** Fus. 3457846 2<sup>nd</sup> Bn. The Lancashire Fusiliers. Killed in action 26 November 1942 in North Africa. Aged 29. *s of Albert & Alice Thompson; h of Ann. Ashton-in-Makerfield.* MEDJEZ-EL-BAB WAR CEMETERY, TUNISIA. [AIM/AMS/SIM]

**THOMPSON Thomas William,** Sgt. (Flt. Eng.) 966222 R.A.F. (V.R.) 50 Sqdn. 24 July 1944. Aged 27. His Lancaster III bomber took-off from Skellingthorpe on a raid on Stuttgart but crashed near Nogent-le-Rotrou. *s of Peter & Polly, Atherton.* NOGENT-LE-ROTROU CEMETERY, FRANCE. [A/HBC]

**THORPE Albert,** Dvr. T/157214 Royal Army Service Corps attd. 48 Lt. A.A. Regiment, Royal Artillery. Died 29 November 1943 whilst being held as a PoW of the Japanese. He was lost in the sinking of a Japanese transport ship which was transferring prisoners to Java. Aged 25. *s of Elizabeth Thorpe, Atherton.* SINGAPORE MEMORIAL. [A]

**THORPE Arthur,** Gnr. 1120589 60 (5<sup>th</sup> Bn. The Royal Welch Fusiliers) Anti-Tank Regiment, Royal Artillery. Killed in action in Italy 13 September 1944. Aged 39. *s of William & Florence, Wigan; h of Sarah Ann, Pemberton.* GRADARA WAR CEMETERY, ITALY. [NSC/SSC/W]

**THORPE James Matthew,** Sjt. 7939719 1<sup>st</sup> Bn. The Manchester Regiment. Killed in Normandy 11 July 1944. Aged 24. *s of Matthew & Mary, Leigh.* BROUAY WAR CEMETERY, FRANCE. [L/LGS/LTA]

**THORPE Joseph,** Tpr. 3854145 18<sup>th</sup>(5<sup>th</sup> Bn. The Loyal Regiment [North Lancashire]) Regiment, Reconnaissance Corps. Died 17 August 1943 of cholera while a PoW of the Japanese. Aged 31. *h of Evelyn, Higher Ince.* THANBYUZAYAT WAR CEMETERY, BURMA. [X]

**THORPE Robert,** A.C.1. 1082098 R.A.F. (V.R.) Died in hospital in Malta 15 September 1943. Aged 22. *s of Mr & Mrs. Richard Thorpe, Wigan.* MALTA (CAPUCCINI) NAVAL CEMETERY. [W/WPC]

**TICE Alan,** Sgt. (Flt. Eng.) 1138805 R.A.F. (V.R.) 158 Sqdn. 18 August 1943. Aged 20. His Halifax II bomber (which was on a Peenemunde raid) crashed near Griefswald. Two of the crew members became PoWs; the rest lie in Berlin War Cemetery. *s of Frederick & Ann, Standish.* BERLIN 1939-45 WAR CEMETERY. [ST/STC]

**TICKLE Frank G.,** Asst. Cook. Merchant Navy. s.s. *Empire Tower.* Died 5 March 1943. Aged 17. Off Cape Finisterre, this cargo ship en route from Gibraltar to U.K., was sunk by the U-boat *U-130. s of Brian & Lucy.* TOWER HILL MEMORIAL. [HG/L]

**TICKLE Joseph,** Fireman & Trimmer. Merchant Navy. s.s. *Ocean Courage.* 15 January 1943. Aged 26. South of Cape Verde Islands, this cargo ship was sunk by U-boat *U-182. s of Mr. & Mrs. Peter, New Springs.* TOWER HILL MEMORIAL. [AS/NSC]
(See Edward Fazackerley who was also a member of the crew of this ship.)

**TIERNEY Albert,** Pte. 3780874 1<sup>st</sup> Bn. The Gordon Highlanders Killed in the Middle East 23 October 1942. Aged 32. EL ALAMEIN WAR CEMETERY. [AS/ASC]

**TIMPSON James,** Fus. 3451854 1/8<sup>th</sup> Bn. The Lancashire Fusiliers. Killed in France sometime between 24 May 1940 and 2 June 1940 during the withdrawal to Dunkirk. Aged 21. LONGUENESSE (ST OMER) CEMETERY. [L/LMC]

**TITHER Matthew,** Cpl. 3778251 4<sup>th</sup> Bn. The Dorsetshire Regiment. Killed 1 December 1944 in Holland. Aged 31. *s of Matthew & Elizabeth; h of Lily, Orrell.* BRUNSSUM WAR CEMETERY, HOLLAND. [OC/OCY]

**TODD Lancelot Beaumont,** Capt. 188093 General List.. Died 14 November 1942. Aged 58. *s of John & Letitia; h of Ann Blaylock.* WIGAN CEMETERY. [X]

**TOPPING Elias,** Pte. D/16032 9<sup>th</sup> (H.D.) Bn. The East Surrey Regiment. Died 17 September 1940. Aged 55. *h of Bridget.* WIGAN CEMETERY. [X]

**TOPPING George,** L.Cpl. 13086952 9<sup>th</sup> Bn. The Border Regiment. Died of wounds in the Far East 15 April 1945. Aged 34. *s of Thomas & Mary; h of Mary Ellen.* MAYNAMATI WAR CEMETERY, PAKISTAN. [L/TC]

**TOPPING William,** Pte. 3453426 Corps of Military Police. Killed in a motor-cycle accident 6 August 1941. *s of Mr. & Mrs. R.* WIGAN CEMETERY. [W]

**TOWELL William Hamilton,** Sto. 1<sup>st</sup> Class. P/KX227727 R.N. H.M.S. *Vortigern.* 15 March 1942. Aged 21. This destroyer was sunk by an German E-boat off Cromer. *s of George & Christina, Orrell.* PORTSMOUTH NAVAL MEMORIAL. [X]

**TOWLER Esmond Frank,** Capt. 98891 129 Field Regiment, Royal Artillery. Killed in India 11 November 1943. Aged 26. *s of Frank & Elizabeth; h of Kathleen.* GAUHTI WAR CEMETERY, INDIA. [L/LGS/LMC]

**TOZE Harold James,** Sgt. (Nav.) 1218772 R.A.F. (V.R.) 101 Sqdn. 26 June 1943. His Lancaster I bomber took-off from Ludford Magna but was shot-down off the Dutch coast. All seven members of the crew baled out but only one survived. AMSTERDAM NEW EASTERN CEMETERY. [A]

**TUNNEY Walter,** L.A.C. 1531020 R.A.F. (V.R.) Died 28 May 1943. Aged 21. *s of James & Mary Ann.* REYKJAVIK CEMETERY, ICELAND. [W]

**TUNSTALL Walter,** L.Sgt. 3531472 Royal Engineers. Accidentally killed at the Royal Military College 3 November 1942. Aged 28. LEIGH CEMETERY. [A]

**TURNER James Arthur,** Tpr. 3857270 18<sup>th</sup> (5<sup>th</sup> Bn. The Loyal Regiment [North Lancashire]) Regiment., The Reconnaissance Corps, R.A.C. Taken prisoner in 1942 and died 18 January 1944 while a PoW of the Japanese. Aged 24. SAI WAN BAY WAR CEMETERY, HONG KONG. [HGC]

**TURNER Jack,** A.B. D/SSX15771 R.N. H.M.S. Stanley. 19 December 1941. Aged 22. While on convoy escort duty, this destroyer was sunk by the German U-boat *U-574* in the Mediterranean. *s of Henry & Annie; h of Vera.* PLYMOUTH NAVAL MEMORIAL. [L]

**TURNER Joseph,** Fus. 3527984 1st Bn. The Lancashire Fusiliers. Killed in action in Burma 27 March 1944. Aged 25. He has no known grave. *s of James & Ellen.* RANGOON MEMORIAL. [W]

**TURNER William Henry,** Pte. 3858750 2nd Bn. The Wiltshire Regiment. Killed in Italy 22 January 1944. Aged 25. *s of James & M.E. Turner, Poolstock, Wigan.* MINTURNO WAR CEMETERY, ITALY. [JC/W]

**TURTON George,** Pte. 1120108 Army Catering Corps attd. 192 Bty., 57 Anti-Tank Regiment, Royal Artillery. Killed in Italy 9 February 1944. Aged 33. *s of Fred & Lily, Leigh; h of Edith.* ANZIO WAR CEMETERY, ITALY. [L]

**TWEEDALE Robert,** Pte. 4922766 2nd (Airborne) Bn., The South Staffordshire Regiment. Killed 9 July 1943 in Italy. Aged 28. He has no known grave. *s of Mr. & Mrs. William., Wigan.* CASSINO MEMORIAL. [W]

**TYRER Ernest,** Sjt. 828192 18th (5th Bn. The Loyal Regiment [North Lancashire] ) Regiment, Reconnaissance Corps. Killed in Singapore sometime between 5 February and 15 February 1942. Aged 28. He has no known grave. *s of Thomas & Eliza; h of Edith Maud, Hindley.* SINGAPORE MEMORIAL. [HC]

**TYRER Joseph,** Fus. 3460325 10th Bn. The Lancashire Fusiliers. Died in India 30 November 1942. Aged 32. He has no known grave. *h of Rosa Ann, Atherton.* RANGOON MEMORIAL. [A]

**UNSWORTH Frederick,** Pte. 13002426 50 Coy. Auxiliary Military Pioneer Corps. Lost in the sinking of s.s. *Lancastria* 17 June 1940. Aged 30. *h of Mary Ann.* DUNKIRK MEMORIAL. [T/TC]
(Twelve other local men perished when this ship was sunk. See the **Herbert Cunliffe** entry for names and details of the sinking.)

**UNSWORTH James,** Cpl. CH/X3886 Royal Marines, No. 47 R.M. Commando. Killed in action in Holland 2 November 1944. Aged 21. BERGEN-OP-ZOOM WAR CEMETERY. [PBC]

**UNSWORTH John,** Capt. 114955 Pioneer Corps Died 2 January 1941 ORRELL (ST JAMES) R.C. CHURCHYARD.

**UNSWORTH Walter,** Sjt. 1902520 633 Artisan Works Coy., Royal Engineers. Lost in the sinking of s.s. *Lancastria.* 17 June 1940. Aged 45. *h of Alice, Orrell.* LA BERNERIE-EN-RETZ CEMETERY, FRANCE. [OC]
(Twelve other local men perished when this ship was sunk. See the **Herbert Cunliffe** entry for names and details of the sinking.)

**URMSTON Alfred Henry,** A.B. D/SSX21935 R.N. H.M.S. *Mahratta.* 25 February 1944. Aged 28. This destroyer on convoy escort duty was sunk by the German U-boat *U-956* in the Barentz Sea. *s of Thomas & Louisa.* PLYMOUTH NAVAL MEMORIAL. [L]    (See also: William Barnes, James Clare, Owen Dootson and James R. Speakman who died in this action.)

**URMSTON John Joseph,** L.Cpl. 3858908 2nd Bn. The Loyal Regiment (North Lancashire) He had been a PoW of the Japanese from February 1942, but died 22 June 1945 in a base hospital soon after gaining his freedom. Aged 27. *s of William & Teresa; h of Gladys.* KRANJI WAR CEMETERY, SINGAPORE. [L]

**VALENTINE James,** Tpr. 14296710 The Nottinghamshire Yeomanry, Royal Armoured Corps. Killed in Germany 10 February 1945. *He had family connections with Wigan.* REICHSWALD FOREST WAR CEMETERY. [X]

**VAREY David,** Gnr. 1824328 89 Bty., 35 Lt. A.A. Regiment, Royal Artillery. Died while a PoW of the Japanese 25 November 1942. Aged 39. *h of Doris.* YOKOHAMA CREMATION MEMORIAL, JAPAN. [W]

**VINCENT Henry Peter,** Cpl. 3855692 2nd Bn. The Loyal Regiment (North Lancashire). Died of malnutrition while a PoW of the Japanese and working on the Burma-Siam railway 13 February 1944. Aged 25. *s of William & Elizabeth, Leigh.* CHUNGKAI WAR CEMETERY, THAILAND. [L]

**WAGGETT Clifford,** Pte. 3457997 5th Bn. The Northamptonshire Regiment. Died of wounds in Italy 25 June 1944. Aged 30. *s of William & Ellen; h of Alice, Leigh.* ORVIETO WAR CEMETERY, ITALY. [L]

**WAGSTAFF Samuel,** Spr. 1894862 994 Docks Operating Coy., Royal Engineers. Lost at sea on board s.s. *Yoma* 17 June 1943. Aged 34. Near Derna, this passenger-cargo liner serving as a troopship and heading for Egypt was sunk by a submarine. 450 servicemen were lost. *s of David & Hannah.* BROOKWOOD MEMORIAL, SURREY. [T/TC]

**WAINWRIGHT Harry,** Dvr. T/100785 54 Infantry Brigade Group Coy., Royal Army Service Corps. Died 18 December 1943 whilst being held as a PoW of the Japanese and working on the Burma-Siam railway. Aged 25. *s of William & Sarah, UpHolland; h of Nellie.* KANCHANABURI WAR CEMETERY, THAILAND. [UPC/UPH]

**WALDRON Percival,** Elec. Artificer. D/MX45339 R.N. H.M.S. *Courageous.* 17 September 1939. Aged 37. West of Ireland, this aircraft carrier was torpedoed and sunk by the U-boat *U-29.* 519 of her crew were lost. *His mother lived in Wigan; h of Ruth.* PLYMOUTH NAVAL MEMORIAL. [W]
(See also Horace Barker and Harold B. Hocken.)

**WALKER Francis Hunt,** A.B. D/SSX24011 R.N. H.M.S. *Diamond.* 27 April 1941. Aged 27. This ship was engaged in the evacuation of Greece and was lost with all hands and evacuated soldiers. *s of Francis Henry & Jennie, Newton-le-Willows.* PLYMOUTH NAVAL MEMORIAL. [AGS]

**WALKER Horace James,** Pte. 3859564 2nd Bn. The Loyal Regiment (North Lancashire) Captured at the fall of Singapore and died whilst being held as a PoW of the Japanese 5 June 1943. Aged 26. *s of Reginald Arthur & Stella, Orrell.* KANCHANABURI WAR CEMETERY, THAILAND. [OC/OCY]

**WALKER Margaret,** Pte. W/170587 Auxiliary Territorial Service. Died 5 October 1945. Aged 33. *d of Arthur & Elizabeth.* HINDLEY CEMETERY. [HC]

**WALKER Robert,** Pte. 3521361 1st Bn. The King's Own Royal Regiment (Lancaster) Died 28 August 1942 in a Middle East hospital. Aged 36. *s of William & Jane, Leigh; h of Agnes.* BENGHAZI WAR CEMETERY, LIBYA. [X]

**WALKER Roland Vivian Warren,** Sgt. 1052257 R.A.F. (V.R.) 18 Sqdn. Killed 19 November 1941. Aged 21. He has no known grave. *s of Beatrice Walker & stepson of G.R. Endley, Wigan.* MALTA MEMORIAL. [X]

**WALKER Ronald Arthur,** Flt. Lt. 149550 *D.F.C., Mentioned in Dispatches.* R.A.F. (V.R.) 83 Sqdn. Killed in action 9 July 1944. Aged 21. *s of Horace Thomas & Ethel Walker, Wigan.* RUNNYMEDE MEMORIAL. [BHC/W]
(His name is not on the memorial plaque in the church. In his memory, two collecting plates were presented to the church by his family.)

**WALKER Thomas.** Spr. 1869996 Royal Engineers. Killed in France 17 June 1940 when the troop train in which he was travelling was bombed. Aged 29. *His mother and his wife lived in Wigan.* RENNES EASTERN COMMUNAL CEMETERY. [W]

**WALKER Thomas Ellwood,** Sgt.(Nav.) 1623780 R.A.F. (V.R.) 49 Sqdn. Killed 8 January 1945. His Lancaster from Fulbeck was shot down over France while on an operation to Munich. Aged 27. *s of Mr. & Mrs. Thomas, Pemberton.* VILLENEUVE-ST GEORGES OLD COMMUNAL CEMETERY, FRANCE. [W]

**WALLS William,** Gnr. 3524444 230 Bty., 4(M) H.A.A. 'Z' Regiment., Royal Artillery. Died in hospital in Winchester 10 June 1943. Aged 29. *h of Winifred, Wigan.* WIGAN CEMETERY. [W]

**WALLWORK Bernard,** Sgt.(Obs.) 1100036 R.A.F. (V.R.) 8 November 1941. Aged 26. His Stirling I bomber was shot down and crashed in Rotterdam. There were no survivors from the crew. *s of Peter & Clara; h of Phyllis Mary.* ROTTERDAM CEMETERY. [LGS/T/TC/TMC]

**WALMESLEY Peter,** Fus. 3453785 1/8th Bn. The Lancashire Fusiliers. Died of wounds in India 5 May 1944. Aged 26. *s of Joseph & Mary Elizabeth, Platt Bridge.* KOHIMA CEMETERY, INDIA. [PBC]

**WALMSLEY William,** Sgt. (W.Op/Air Gnr.) 1458471 R.A.F. (V.R.) 433 (R.C.A.F.) Sqdn. 25 March 1944. Aged 21. This Halifax III bomber took-off from Skipton-on-Swale, Yorkshire on a Berlin raid but it crashed near Legden. Four of the crew became PoW; the others lie in Reichswald Forest Cemetery. *s of James & Ellen Walmsley, New Springs.* REICHSWALD FOREST WAR CEMETERY, GERMANY. [AS/NSC]

**WALSH Charles,** Pte. 2989315 7th Bn. The Argyll & Sutherland Highlanders. Killed in France 4 July 1944. Aged 30. *s of William & Jane, Blackrod.* RANVILLE WAR CEMETERY, NORMANDY. [BL/BCC]

**WALSH David,** Pte. 3530376 1ˢᵗ Bn. The Manchester Regiment. Died in the Far East 1 June 1943. *s of David & Minnie, Wigan.* THANBYUZAYAT WAR CEMETERY, BURMA. [X]

**WALSH David Latham,** Lieut. (A) R.N.V.R. Lost his life flying in a Swordfish aircraft from the escort carrier H.M.S. *Vindex* 28 October 1944. Aged 30. He has no known grave. *s of Mr & Mrs John.* LEE-ON-SOLENT FLEET AIR ARM MEMORIAL. [WGS]

**WALSH Edgar,** Sjt. 2007666 17 Movement Control Group, Royal Engineers. Killed in Normandy 5 August 1944.. Aged 27. *s of James & Ellen; h of Marguirete Edna.* BAYEAUX WAR CEMETERY. [A]

**WALSH Harry,** Pte. 3858640 10ᵗʰ Bn. The Loyal Regiment (North Lancashire) Died in a military hospital 19 May 1941 after being accidentally shot. Aged 23. *s of William & Margaret, Wigan.* WIGAN CEMETERY. [W/WPC]

**WALSH John,** Sgt. 645117 R.A.F. 233 Sqdn. Killed 31 October 1941 while on a patrol over the English Channel in a Blenheim aircraft. He has no known grave. *s of Andrew & Ann, Appley Bridge.* RUNNYMEDE MEMORIAL. [X]

**WALSH John,** Cook D/MX65174 R.N. H.M. Boom Defence Vessel *Ben Rossal.* Died 28 November 1942. Aged 27. *s of Alfred & Martha.* LYNESS ROYAL NAVAL CEMETERY. [L]

**WALSH William H.** Pte. 3461146 Royal Pioneer Corps. Died 22 November 1946. Aged 39. *h of Maud, Pemberton.* HIGHFIELD (ST MATTHEW) CHURCHYARD, WIGAN. [W]

**WANE John,** Fus. 5682523 8ᵗʰ Bn. The Royal Fusiliers (City of London Regiment.) Killed in North Africa 5 October 1943. Aged 21. *s of Martha, Orrell.* BONE WAR CEMETERY, ALGERIA. [OC]

**WANE Sydney,** L.Bdr. 1774076 168 Bty., 56 Lt. A.A. Regiment, Royal Artillery. Died of wounds in Cairo 6 January 1943. Aged 35. *s of John & Jane, Orrell; h of Evelyn, Kitt Green.* HELIOPOLIS WAR CEMETERY, EGYPT. [OC/OUC]

**WARBURTON Edwin,** Gnr. 1744862 338 Bty., 102 Lt. A.A. Regiment, Royal Artillery. Killed in action in Belgium, 24 October 1944. Aged 36. *h of Doris, Tyldesley.* LEOPOLDSBURG WAR CEMETERY, BELGIUM. [T]

**WARBURTON John,** Gnr. 1492565 12 Coast Regiment, Royal Artillery. Lost in the s.s. *Lisbon Maru.* 2 October 1942. Aged 23. *s of John & Lily.* SAIWAN BAY MEMORIAL, HONG KONG. [CUC]

**WARD John Hesketh,** Pte. 3655696 2ⁿᵈ Bn. The South Lancashire Regiment (Prince of Wales's Volunteers). Killed in Burma 4 March 1945. Aged 26. He has no known grave. *s of Thomas & Ada Ward, Wigan.* RANGOON MEMORIAL. [SSC/W/WSB]

**WARD Joseph,** Pte. 1533768 2/4<sup>th</sup> Bn. The King's Own Yorkshire Light Infantry. Killed in Italy 12 September 1944. Aged 29. *h of Margaret, New Springs; parents Hallgate, Wigan.* CORIANO RIDGE WAR CEMETERY, ITALY. [AS/NSC/W] (It is probable that he is the Joseph Ward who is incorrectly shown on the Wigan Cenotaph as serving in the Royal Artillery at the time of his death. His service number does indicate however that he was originally in the R.A. )

**WARD William,** Spr. 1873920 22 Fortress Coy., Royal Engineers. Killed in Hong Kong 18 December 1941. Aged 26. He has no known grave. *s of Mr. & Mrs. William, Lower Ince.* SAIWAN BAY MEMORIAL, HONG KONG. [ISM]

**WARDLE William,** Pte. 3529736 1<sup>st</sup> Bn. The East Lancashire Regiment. Killed in action 20 May 1940 in the withdrawal to Dunkirk. Aged 21. *s of James & Margaret, Goose Green.* WARHEM COMMUNAL CEMETERY. [GGC/W]

**WARNER Thomas,** Fus. 3456746 1/8<sup>th</sup> Bn. The Lancashire Fusiliers. Killed in Burma 9 June 1944. Aged 30. He has no known grave. *s of Fred & Mary, Higher Ince.* RANGOON MEMORIAL. [IN]

**WATERWORTH George,** Dvr. T/151164 Royal Army Service Corps. Died in a military hospital 18 May 1941. Aged 27. *h of Jessie Waterworth.* LEIGH CEMETERY, [L]

**WATKINS Albert Edward,** Dvr. T/124841 5 Res. M.T. Coy., Royal Army Service Corps. Killed 29 June 1942 in the Middle East. Aged 23. He has no known grave. ALAMEIN MEMORIAL. [A/HBC]

**WATKINSON Reginald,** L.A.C. 1009915 R.A.F. (V.R.) Killed 14 February 1942 at the fall of Singapore. Aged 25. *s of Walter & Florence.* SINGAPORE MEMORIAL. [W]

**WATKINSON Thomas,** Dvr. T/1730107 321 Troop Carrying Coy., Royal Army Service Corps. Died of wounds in Belgium 30 December 1944. Aged 32. LEOPOLDSBURG WAR CEMETERY, BELGIUM. [L]

**WATSON Cyril,** L.Cpl. 2319022 Royal Corps of Signals. Died 30 May 1940 from injuries which he received during the evacuation of Dunkirk.. Aged 30. *He was a former member of Wigan Borough Police Force.* DOVER (ST JAMES) CEMETERY. [PHW/W]

**WATSON Ernest,** Cpl. 3451972 6<sup>th</sup> Bn. Royal Scots Fusiliers. Died of wounds in Holland 5 November 1944. Aged 27. *s of William & Sarah, Hindley; h of Edna, Hindley.* MIERLO WAR CEMETERY, HOLLAND. [HGC]

**WEAVER Stanley,** A.B. D/JX313621 R.N. H.M.S. *President* but lost in s.s. *Clan MacTavish* 8 October 1942. Aged 29. Off the Cape of Good Hope this cargo liner, en route from South Africa to the United Kingdom, was sunk by the U-boat *U-159. s of Richard John & Martha; h of Edith, Hindsford.* PLYMOUTH NAVAL MEMORIAL. [HAC/L]

**WEBB John,** Flt. Sgt.(Air Bomber) 1034331 R.A.F. (V.R.) 51 Sqdn. 17 February 1945. His Halifax III bomber took-off from Snaith but caught fire and crashed near Horsham; Sussex. The pilot and Sgt. Webb died and three other members of the crew were injured. Aged 22. *s of John & Mary, Bickershaw; h of Kathleen, Wigan.* ABRAM (ST JOHN) CHURCHYARD. [B]

**WEBB William.** His name has been added to the Wigan Cenotaph but, unfortunately, in the wrong section. He was in fact a First World War casualty and was killed at Arras in 1917.

**WEBBER William,** Pte. 4038909 8th Bn. The York & Lancaster Regiment. Died of wounds in Burma 7 May 1944. Aged 28. *s of William & Elizabeth, Aspull.* TAUKKYAN WAR CEMETERY, BURMA. [AS/HDC]

**WEBLEY William Cecil,** Flt. Sgt.(W.Op.[Air] ) 1032389 R.A.F. (V.R.) 186 Sqdn. 3 February 1945. His Lancaster bomber left Stradishall to attack the benzol facility at Dortmund but it crashed and all members of the crew died. They were initially buried at Dortmund. Aged 23. *s of Frederick Cecil & Elizabeth, Atherton; h of Doris.* REICHSWALD FOREST WAR CEMETERY, GERMANY. [X]

**WEBSTER Frank,** Pte. 3856939 2nd Bn. The Loyal Regiment (North Lancashire) Captured at the fall of Singapore and died 11 June 1943 whilst being held as a PoW of the Japanese. Aged 33. *s of Edward & Mary.* KANCHANABURI WAR CEMETERY, THAILAND. [L]

**WEBSTER James,** Fus. 3523539 1st Bn. The Lancashire Fusiliers. Died in India 24 May 1944. Aged 33. TAUKKYAN WAR CEMETERY, BURMA. [A]

**WEBSTER James Richard,** Fus. 3454137 2/5th Bn. The Lancashire Fusiliers. Killed 7 August 1944. Aged 28. *s of Joseph & Margaret; h of Rachel, Standish.* FONTENAY-LE-PESNEL CEMETERY. [STC]

**WEBSTER John,** Pte. 4206240 9th Bn. The York & Lancaster Regiment. Died 22 November 1944. Aged 23. *s of John & Ellen, Leigh;* TAUKKYAN WAR CEMETERY, BURMA [L]

**WELLINGS Thomas,** Fus. 3459493 2nd Bn. The Royal Fusiliers (City of London Regiment) Killed in Italy 29 July 1944. *s of Mr. & Mrs. J.H.Wellings; h of Elsie, Hindley.* FRIANO DELLA CHIANO WAR CEMETERY. [X]

**WELLS Edward,** Pte. 3531059 8th Bn. The Manchester Regiment. Killed 10 January 1944 on Malta. *s of Harry & Polly; h of Mary Alice.* PEMBROKE MILITARY CEMETERY, MALTA. [BHC/W]

**WERRILL Roy,** Sgt. 2205575 R.A.F. (V.R.) 514 Sqdn. 17 January 1945. His Lancaster bomber left Waterbeach to attack a benzol plant at Wanne-Eickel. It was lost without trace and therefore all eight members of the crew are commemorated on the Runnymede Memorial. Aged 21. *s of Allan & Olive, Whelley, Wigan.* RUNNYMEDE MEMORIAL. [ISM/SSC]

**WEST Frederick,** Tpr. 3855885 18<sup>th</sup>(5<sup>th</sup> Bn. The Loyal Regiment [North Lancashire]) Regiment, Reconnaissance Corps. Died 3 August 1943 while a PoW of the Japanese. Aged 32. *s of Caleb & Harriet; h of Margaret.* THANBYUZAYAT WAR CEMETERY, BURMA. [X]

**WEST Stanley,** Cpl. 969161 R.A.F. (V.R.) Accidentally killed in Wales 11 July 1942. CAERNARVON CEMETERY. [W]

**WESTON Cecil Stanley,** Sgt (W.Op./Air Gnr.) 1109648 R.A.F. (V.R.) 115 Sqdn. 26 July 1942. Aged 22. His Wellington III bomber from Marham crashed near Krefeld. All five crew members were killed. *s of Stanley & Annie, Atherton.* REICHSWALD FOREST WAR CEMETERY, GERMANY. [A]

**WESTWELL Albert,** Pte. 3858760 1<sup>st</sup> Bn. The Loyal Regiment (North Lancashire) Died 26 March 1946. *h of Catherine, Hindley.* HINDLEY CEMETERY. [X]

**WESTWELL Hector,** Pte. 3456272 2<sup>nd</sup> Bn. The Wiltshire Regiment. Killed in Italy 5 August 1943. CATANIA WAR CEMETERY, ITALY. [ABC]

**WESTWELL Vincent,** Pte. 6093611 4<sup>th</sup> Bn. The Buffs (Royal East Kent Regiment) Lost on board a ship in the Aegean Sea, 23 October 1943. Aged 25. *s of Richard & Rebecca.* ATHENS MEMORIAL. [A]

**WESTWOOD Henry,** Fus. 3458030 11<sup>th</sup> Bn. The Lancashire Fusiliers. Killed in action in Italy 2 September 1944. Aged 31. *h of Margaret, Atherton.* FLORENCE WAR CEMETERY, ITALY. [A]

**WHARTON Horace,** Sgt. 1073453 R.A.F. (V.R.) 612 Sqdn. Killed 4 August 1943. Aged 23. He has no known grave. *s of Alfred & Mary Ann, Pemberton.* RUNNYMEDE MEMORIAL. [W]

**WHEALE Ronald George,** Sgt. (W.Op./Air Gnr.) 1310119 R.A.F. (V.R.) 221 Sqdn. Died in a Middle East hospital on 15 September 1942. Aged 22. *s of Richard & Harriet Wheale, Tyldesley.* ALEXANDRIA WAR MEMORIAL CEMETERY, EGYPT. [T/TC/TMC]

**WHELAN John,** Flt. Sgt. 1376153 R.A.F. (V.R.) 221 Sqdn. His aircraft failed to return from operations in North Africa 6 December 1942. Aged 27. *s of Frederick & Florence; h of Rina, Liverpool.* ALAMEIN MEMORIAL [AGS]

**WHITE Arthur Cyril,** Pilot Offr. (Obs.) 11523 R.A.F. (V.R.) 26 O.T.U. 31 May 1942. Aged 23. His Wellington I bomber was shot down and crashed near Oss in Holland. The pilot was captured but the rest of the crew perished and rest in Uden War Cemetery. *s of The Venerable Arthur White, M.A. & Elizabeth White, Orrell.* UDEN WAR CEMETERY, HOLLAND. [BC]

**WHITE Harold,** Pte. 1824299 81 Coy., The Pioneer Corps. Killed in North Africa 25 November 1942. Aged 32. *s of Mr. & Mrs. George; h of Sarah Hannah, UpHolland.* BONE CEMETERY, ALGERIA. [UPC/UPH]

**WHITE James Helier,** Capt. 130714 The South Lancashire Regiment attd. 5th Bn. The East Yorkshire Regiment (The Duke of York's Own.) Killed in Normandy on D-Day, 6 June 1944. Aged 35. *s of Dr. Robert Prosser & Clarice. He was born in Wigan.* BAYEAUX WAR CEMETERY, FRANCE. [X]

**WHITE William,** Sgt. (W.Op./Air Gnr.) 995408 R.A.F. (V.R.) 608 Sqdn. Killed in a Coastal Command operation 20 October 1941. Aged 26. *s of Robert & Mary; h of Phyllis, Orrell.* FRDERICKSHAVN CEMETERY, DENMARK. [OC/OUC]

**WHITEHEAD Dennis,** Fus. 3608185 6th Bn. The Royal Inniskilling Fusiliers. Killed in North Africa 11 February 1943. Aged 25. *s of John & Elixabeth Jane; h of Nellie.* ENFIDAVILLE WAR CEMETERY. [HIC/W]

**WHITEHEAD Jack Kenneth,** Tpr. 7939179 2nd Derbyshire Yeomanry, R.A.C. Killed 18 May 1943 in the Middle East. Aged 21. *s of John & Mary.* ALEXANDRIA WAR MEMORIAL CEMETERY, EGYPT. [SMC/W]

**WHITEHEAD Wilfred,** Flt. Sgt. (Air Gnr.) 1511705 R.A.F. (V.R.) 103 Sqdn. Killed 17 March 1945. The Lancaster I bomber took-off from Elsham Woods to bomb Nuremburg, but it was brought down resulting in the deaths of all seven crew members. Aged 21. *s of Wilfred & Maggie.* DURNBACH WAR CEMETERY, GERMANY. [BDC/L]

**WHITTAKER Edward,** Ldg. Smn. D/JX132459. *D.S.M.* R.N. H.M. Submarine *Salmon.* 9 July 1940. Aged 27. This submarine was sunk by a mine off southern Norway. Forty-one members of the crew died. *s of James & Ellen; h of Edith Sophia.* PLYMOUTH NAVAL MEMORIAL. [BCC/BL]

**WHITTAKER Samuel,** Dvr. T/281577 53 Infantry Bde. Group Coy., Royal Army Service Corps. Captured at the fall of Singapore and died 22 November 1943 whilst being held as a PoW of the Japanese. Aged 30. KANCHANABURI WAR CEMETERY, THAILAND. [SCC/W/WSB]

**WHITTER James,** Flying Offr. (Air Gnr.) 178853 *D.F.M.* R.A.F. (V.R.) 578 Sqdn. Killed 15 January 1945. His Halifax III bomber left Burn to attack a Luftwaffe fuel storage depot but it did not return. He had earlier flown for some time with 76 Squadron and his *D.F.M.* was published in February 1944. Aged 23. *s of James & Ann Whitter, Ashton-in-Makerfield.* REICHSWALD FOREST WAR CEMETERY, GERMANY. [AMS]

**WHITTER Joseph,** L.A.C. 1107515 R.A.F. (V.R.) 171 Sqdn. Killed in India 25 June 1943. Aged 31. *s of John & Mary, Standish; h of Elsie May, Haigh.* KIRKEE CEMETERY, INDIA. [AS/HDC]

**WHITTER Walter,** Gnr. 1676088 4 H.A.A. Regiment, Royal Artillery. Died 7 March 1942 in Malta. Aged 31. *h of Elizabeth (Betty), Standish Lower Ground; parents lived in Standish Lower Ground.* PEMBROKE MILITARY CEMETERY, MALTA. [SCC/ST/STC/W]
(Some sources give the spelling of his surname as *Witter*)

**WHITTLE Arthur,** Dvr. T192000 Royal Army Service Corps. Killed in the Middle East 11 February 1943. Aged 29. *s of Richard & Alice, Worsley Mesnes; h of Ellen.* BENGHAZI WAR CEMETERY. [SAC/W]

**WHITTLE Cyril,** Sgt (Flt. Eng.) 1106196 R.A.F. (V.R.) 103 Sqdn. 23 April 1944. Aged 23. This Lancaster I bomber was returning to Elsham Wolds after a raid on Dusseldorf when it flew into the side of a hill near Hemsley, Yorkshire. *s of John William & Elizabeth.* NEWCHURCH CHURCHYARD, GOLBORNE. [X]

**WHITTLE Francis,** L.Sjt. 2622729 Grenadier Guards. Killed in Holland 31 March 1945. Aged 22. *s of Joseph & Annie, Leigh.* EIBERGEN PROTESTANT CEMETERY, HOLLAND. [L/LTA]

**WHITTLE John,** Pte. 14735729 1$^{st}$ Bn. The Herefordshire Regiment. Died of wounds in Germany 1 March 1945. Aged 20. REICHSWALD FOREST WAR CEMETERY. [T]

**WHITTLE Joseph,** A.C.2. 1528829 R.A.F. (V.R.) 21 Sqdn. Killed in a road accident 25 December 1941. WIGAN CEMETERY. [W]

**WHITTLE Leonard,** Sgt. (W.Op/Air Gnr.) 533685 R.A.F. 58 Sqdn. 19 June 1940. A Whitley V bomber from Linton-on-Ouse crashed near Krefeld, Germany. All five members of the crew perished. *He had family connections with Ashton-in-Makerfield and Bamfurlong.* REICHSWALD FOREST WAR CEMETERY, GERMANY. [AIM/AMS/BMC]

**WHITTLE Robert,** Sgt. 1811022 R.A.F. (V.R.) 21 O.T.U. 30 August 1944. Aged 21. This Wellington X bomber took-off from Moreton-in-Marsh on a diversion operation but it was lost without trace. The average age of the crew was 22. *s of Norman Wilfred & Florence.* RUNNYMEDE MEMORIAL. [A/HBC]

**WHITTLE Sydney,** Gnr. 1738494 152 Bty., 51 Lt. A.A. Regiment, Royal Artillery. Killed in Italy 13 July 1944. Aged 37. *s of Edward Walsh & Eliza, Leigh.* AREZZO WAR CEMETERY. [L]

**WHITTON Thomas,** Flt. Sgt. 1451064 R.A.F. (V.R.) 223 Sqdn. Killed 22 July 1944. Aged 22. He has no known grave. *s of James & Mary, Pemberton.* MALTA MEMORIAL. [W]

**WILCOCK Charles,** Pilot Offr. (W.Op/Air Gnr.) 46167 R.A.F. 62 sqdn. Killed 21 May 1942 while flying an air operation in the Far East. Aged 21. He has no known grave. *s of Gilbert & Annie, Atherton.* SINGAPORE MEMORIAL. [A/ABL]

**WILCOCK James,** Pte. 5126017 156$^{th}$ Bn. The Parachute Regiment, A.A.C. Killed 11 September 1943. Aged 26. BARI WAR CEMETERY, ITALY. [L]

**WILCOCK Joseph,** Sjt. 3387915 4$^{th}$ Bn. The East Lancashire Regiment. Died in the U.K. 2 February 1943. Aged 24. *h of Mary Theresa.* CHORLEY (ST GREGORY) R.C. CHURCHYARD. [X]

**WILD Gerald Marsden,** Sgt. (Pilot) 580291 R.A.F. 50 Sqdn. 12 April 1940 Aged 25. His Hampden bomber took-off from Waddington on an operation to Kristiansand but was shot down by German fighter planes. All four crew-members were killed. *s of Edward & Ethel, Orrell.* RUNNYMEDE MEMORIAL. [AGS/UPC/UPH]

**WILDE Alan Raymond,** Flt. Sgt. (Pilot) R/191982 R.C.A.F. Died 13 October 1944. Aged 20. *He was born in Pemberton and emigrated to Canada with his family in the 1930's. s of Stanley & Emily Wilde, London, Ontario, Canada.* GOOSE GREEN (ST PAUL) CHURCHYARD. [GGC]

**WILDE Stanley,** Fus. 3451975 11<sup>th</sup> Bn. The Lancashire Fusiliers. Killed 19 September 1944 in Italy. Aged 26. *s of Thomas & Annie, Pemberton.* FLORENCE WAR CEMETERY, ITALY. [PC/W]
(Some local sources use the spelling *Wild.*)

**WILDGOOSE Harry,** 3<sup>rd</sup> Engineer Officer Merchant Navy. Died 18 June 1945 in Wigan Infirmary. Aged 28. He had been a PoW in Germany for over four years and had only recently returned to Britain. His ship *s.s. Kantara*, which was en route from the U.K. to the West Indies, was sunk by the German battlecruisers *Gneisenau* and *Scharnhorst* west of Newfoundland in February 1941. *s of William David & Edith; h of Evelyn, Wigan.* PRESCOT CEMETERY. [W]

**WILKINSON Alfred,** Pilot Offr. (Obs.) 115993 R.A.F. (V.R.) 150 Sqdn. 28 April 1942. Aged 24. His Wellington III bomber was lost on a raid on Cologne. All six crew-members were killed. *s of Joseph & Beatrice, Leigh.* RHEINBERG WAR CEMETERY, GERMANY. [L/LGS]
(His brother George was also killed on active service with the R.A.F. They were both stationed on the same base with the same squadron, and were killed over Germany within six weeks of each other.)

**WILKINSON Arthur,** Steward, D/LX536667 R.N. *H.M.S. Drake.* 24 March 1946. Aged 42. *h of Amy Edna.* WIGAN CEMETERY. [W]

**WILKINSON George,** Pilot Offr.(Pilot) 103045 R.A.F.(V.R.) 150 Sqdn. 9 March 1942. Aged 30. His Wellington I bomber from Snaith was on a mission to bomb Essen but was brought down with the total loss of the crew. *s of Joseph & Beatrice, Leigh; h of Phyllis.* REICHSWALD FOREST WAR CEMETERY, GERMANY. [L]
(His brother Alfred was also killed on active service with the R.A.F.)

**WILKINSON George Winston,** Pilot Offr. 110571 R.A.F. (V.R.) 7 Sqdn. 27 April 1942. Aged 27. This Stirling I bomber was on a minelaying operation and was presumed lost over the North Sea. Only one body (that of P.O.Wilkinson) was recovered. It was washed ashore on to Romo Island 6 October 1942 - five months after the aircraft was lost. *s of William and stepson of Florence, Kitt Green.* KIRKEBY CEMETERY, DENMARK. [X]

**WILKINSON Joseph,** Pte. 3775677 2/6<sup>th</sup> Bn. The South Staffordshire Regiment. Killed in France 3 August 1944. Aged 27. *s of George & Isabel, Leigh; h of Jesse, Atherton.* FONTENAY-LE-PESNEL CEMETERY. [A/L]

**WILLIAMS Alan Wilfred,** Tpr. 3860026 The Royal Scots Greys (2nd. Dragoons), R.A.C. Killed in Italy 18 October 1943. Aged 29. *s of Thomas & Agnes, Ashton-in-Makerfield; h of Nora.* MINTURNO WAR CEMETERY, ITALY. [X]

**WILLIAMS Clifford,** Pte. 14512930 1st Bn. The Loyal Regiment (North Lancashire) Killed in Italy 19 February 1944. Aged 19. *s of Mr. & Mrs. W.T., Ashton-in-Makerfield.* ANZIO WAR CEMETERY, ITALY. [AIM/AMS]

**WILLIAMS Frank,** Pte. 3778254 The King's Regiment (Liverpool) and No. 1 Commando. Killed 28 March 1943 in North Africa. Aged 29. *s of John Henry & Sarah Ellen; h of Edith, Pemberton.* TABARKA RAS RAJEL WAR CEMETERY, TUNISIA. [NC/W]

**WILLIAMS John Clifford,** A.C.2. (W.Op.) 1117980 R.A.F. (V.R.) Killed in an air accident 14 February 1942. Aged 28. *s of John & Frances; h of Ada, Tyldesley.* UXBRIDGE (HILLINGDON) CEMETERY. [X]

**WILLIAMS Joseph,** Boy 1st Class. P/JX157723 R.N. H.M.S. *Royal Oak.* 14 October 1939. Aged 17. The German submarine *U-47* penetrated the defences at Scapa Flow and torpedoed the battleship which sunk with the loss of 833 crew. *s of Edward & Sarah Ellen, Platt Bridge. He joined the Royal Navy in June 1939 aged 16.* PORTSMOUTH NAVAL MEMORIAL. [PBC]

**WILLIAMS Reginald,** L.Cpl. 4081590 3rd Bn. The Monmouthshire Regiment. Killed in France 30 July 1944. Aged 28. *s of Benjamin & Edith; h of Agnes, Platt Bridge.* ST CHARLES DE PERCY WAR CEMETERY. [PBC]

**WILLIAMS Robert,** Flt. Sgt (Pilot) 1140108 R.A.F. 101 Sqdn. His Wellington bomber took off from Stradishall to bomb Duisburg but was lost without trace 7 September 1942. Aged 22. *s of Mr & Mrs Joseph, Hindley.* RUNNYMEDE MEMORIAL [HGS]

**WILLIAMS Wilfred,** Pte. 3389451 1st Bn. The East Lancashire Regiment. Died as a PoW on 27 February 1945. Aged 28. *His family connections were in Aspull.* BERLIN 1939-45 WAR CEMETERY, GERMANY. [AS/ASC/NSC]

**WILLIAMS William Anthony,** Flt. Sgt. (Pilot) 1235518 R.A.F. (V.R.) 211 Sqdn. Killed in Burma 27 July 1944. Aged 23. *s of Robert & Nellie, Wigan.* TAUKKYAN WAR CEMETERY, BURMA. [W/WGS]

**WILLIAMSON Robert,** Bdr. 826093 3 Regiment, Royal Horse Artillery. Killed in action in the Middle East 14 April 1941. Aged 31. *s of Robert & Ann, Platt Bridge.* KNIGHTSBRIDGE WAR CEMETERY, LIBYA. [PBC]

**WILSON Ernest,** Sgt. (Flt. Eng.) 995196 R.A.F. (V.R.) 90 Sqdn. 26 June 1943. Aged 30. This Stirling III from West Wickham crashed at Anaus. All the crew-members were killed and were originally buried at Legden. *s of Thomas & Elizabeth, Wigan; h of Beatrice Elizabeth.* REICHSWALD FOREST WAR CEMETERY, GERMANY. [W]

**WILSON Henry,** Pte. 2188847 Auxiliary Military Pioneer Corps Lost in the sinking of s.s. *Lancastria,* 17 June 1940 Aged 47. *s of Thomas & Mary, Scholes, Wigan.* LE CLION-SUR-MER CEMETERY. [SCC]
(Twelve other local men perished when this ship was sunk. See the **Herbert Cunliffe** entry for names and details of the sinking.)

**WILSON James,** Pte. 4393416 6th Bn. The Green Howards (Alexandra, Princess of Wales's Own Yorkshire Regiment) Killed in North Africa 6 April 1943. Aged 25. *s of William & Ellen, Billinge.* ENFIDAVILLE WAR CEMETERY, TUNISIA. [BC]

**WILSON Thomas,** Pte. 2620818 1st Bn. The Parachute Regiment, A.A.C. Killed in action 10 March 1943. Aged 26. He has no known grave. *s of Thomas & Margaret Ellen, Standish.* MEDJEZ-EL-BAB MEMORIAL, TUNISIA. [SSM/ST]

**WILSON William Donald,** Capt. 250335 Royal Army Medical Corps. Died in Germany 24 April 1945. Aged 25. *s of William & Kate Mary, Wigan.* BECKLINGEN WAR CEMETERY. [W/WGS]

**WILTON Leonard,** Dvr. 2378934 Royal Corps of Signals, XII Corps. Sigs. Killed in a road accident 5 February 1945 in Holland. Aged 24. *s of Michael & Mary Ann, Ashton-in-Makerfield.* WEERT CHURCHYARD, HOLLAND. [X]

**WINNARD Charles,** Gnr. 1589400 2/1 Maritime Regiment, Royal Artillery. Killed 31 January 1942 at sea. PORTSMOUTH NAVAL MEMORIAL. [PC/W]

**WINNARD John Edward,** Pte. 13075415 243 Coy., The Pioneer Corps. Died 14 October 1943. Aged 33. *s of John Edward & Catherine, Hindley.* CATANIA WAR CEMETERY, ITALY. [X]

**WINROW James Robert,** Pte. 4465247 9th Bn. The Border Regiment. Died 28 May 1943. Aged 30. *s of Thomas & Anna; h of Catherine, Hindley Green.* WESTHOUGHTON CEMETERY. [X]

**WINSTANLEY Alfred,** Pte. 3526568 The Pioneer Corps. Died 6 April 1944. *h of Mary Jane, Beech Hill, Wigan.* WIGAN CEMETERY. [X]

**WINSTANLEY Arthur,** L.Cpl. 936675 The Hallamshire Bn. The York & Lancaster Regiment. Killed in action in France 16 July 1944. Aged 24. *s of Arthur & Gertrude Annie Winstanley.* ST. MANVIEU WAR CEMETERY, NORMANDY, FRANCE. [JC/W]

**WINSTANLEY David,** Gnr. 860380 5 Field Regiment, Royal Artillery. Died 21 October 1943 while a PoW of the Japanese. Aged 26. *s of John & M.A. Winstanley, Platt Bridge.* THANBYUZAYAT WAR CEMETERY, BURMA. [PBC]

**WINSTANLEY Ernest,** L.A.C. 1057700 R.A.F.(V.R.) Died 6 June 1945 whilst being held as a PoW of the Japanese. *h of Mary Winstanley, Top Lock; he also had immediate family connections in the Ince-in-Makerfield area.* DJAKARTA WAR CEMETERY, INDONESIA. [AS/IN/NSC]

**WINSTANLEY James,** Sgt. (Pilot) 1057286 R.A.F. (V.R.) Died 29 June 1945 in the Middle East. Aged 24. *s of Peter James & Ellen; h of Audrey.* FAYID WAR CEMETERY, EGYPT. [W]

**WINSTANLEY John,** Fus. 1619690 2nd Bn. The Lancashire Fusiliers. Killed 16 April 1945 in Italy. Aged 31. *h of E. E. Winstanley Goose Green.* FAENZA WAR CEMETERY, ITALY. [GGC/W]

**WINSTANLEY John,** Ordnance Artificer D/MX62803 R.N. H.M.S. *Bramble.* 31 December 1942. Aged 23. While on convoy escort duty to Russia, this minesweeper was sunk by the German heavy cruiser *Admiral Hipper* north of North Cape. *s of James & Jane, Higher Ince.* PLYMOUTH NAVAL MEMORIAL. [W] (See also Walter Houghton who died in the action.)

**WINSTANLEY Leonard John,** Pte. 3662179 4th Bn. The Northamptonshire Regiment. Died 2 February 1946. Aged 34. *s of William & Ada; h of Eva, Lowton.* LOWTON (ST LUKE) CHURCHYARD. [X]

**WINSTANLEY Walter,** Cpl. 1033372 R.A.F. (V.R.) Killed in a road accident 2 February 1946. Aged 25. He had only recently returned from India. *s of Joseph & Emma, Westleigh.* WESTLEIGH CEMETERY. [L]

**WINTERSGILL Sydney,** Sgt. (Pilot) 1051879 R.A.F. (V.R.) 9 Sqdn. 12 August 1941. Aged 21. His Wellington I bomber was on a raid to Kiel but crashed into the River Weser. Four bodies of crew members were recovered. *s of Rev. John & Ethel, Orrell.* BECKLINGEN WAR CEMETERY, GERMANY. [OC]

**WINWARD John,** S.B.A. D/MX100792 R.N. H.M.S. *Mounsey.* Died 1 November 1944. Aged 21. *s of John & Dora, Leigh.* PLYMOUTH NAVAL MEMORIAL. [L]

**WISEMAN Jack,** Cpl. 949951 R.A.F. (V.R.) Died in a military hospital in South Africa on 9 May 1944. Aged 31. *s of Amos & Louise Wiseman; h of Ada Margaret Wiseman.* JOHANNESBURG (WEST PARK) CEMETERY, SOUTH AFRICA. [W/WGS]

**WOOD Arnold,** Capt. 94832 The West Yorkshire Regiment (The Prince of Wales's Own) Killed in Germany 15 April 1945. Aged 27. *s of Arnold & Mary Jane, Leigh.* BECKLINGEN WAR CEMETERY, GERMANY. [L/LGS/LMC]

**WOOD Charles,** Gnr. 779548 58 Anti-Tank Regiment, Royal Artillery. Died in a military hospital in Milan 21 October 1945. Aged 38. *s of Squire & Alice; h of Mary Josephine, Leigh.* MILAN WAR CEMETERY, ITALY. [L/LMC]

**WOOD John,** Cpl. 519650 R.A.F. Died 10 December 1940 Aged 23. *s of John & Orpah.* HAIGH (ST DAVID) CHURCHYARD. [AS]

**WOOD Stanley,** Gnr. 3608020 65 (The Norfolk Yeomanry) Anti-Tank Regiment, Royal Artillery. Killed in action in Germany 12 December 1944. Aged 20. REICHSWALD FOREST WAR CEMETERY, GERMANY. [L/LTC]

**WOOD Thomas,** Fus. 3452309 2nd Bn. The Lancashire Fusiliers. Killed 22 May 1940 during the withdrawal to Dunkirk.. Aged 21. *s of William & Mary, Ashton-in-Makerfield.* HEVERLEE WAR CEMETERY, BELGIUM. [AIM/AMS]

**WOOD Walter Bertram,** Pte. 3656238 1st Bn. The South Lancashire Regiment (The Prince of Wales's Volunteers) Killed in action on D-Day 6 June 1944. Aged 24. *s of Thomas Bertram & Florence E.* HERMANVILLE WAR CEMETERY, NORMANDY. [AS]

**WOOD William Dominic,** Craftsman 10574836 170 Field Regiment, L.A.D. Royal Electrical & Mechanical Engineers. Died 28 July 1943 in Devizes Hospital following an accident. Aged 21. HAIGH (ST DAVID) CHURCHYARD. [NSC/W]

**WOODALL Alfred,** L.Sjt. 950730 95 Anti-Tank Regiment, Royal Artillery. Killed in action in the Middle East 6 June 1942. *h of Jean, Wigan.* KNIGHTSBRIDGE WAR CEMETERY, LIBYA. [BHC/W]

**WOODCOCK William,** Cpl. 3455486 51st (The Leeds Rifles) Royal Tank Regiment, R.A.C. Killed in Italy 22 May 1944. Aged 28. *s of William & Josephine, Wigan; h of Hilda, Hindley.* CASSINO WAR CEMETERY, ITALY. [SAC/W]

**WOODS Albert,** Sjt. 3855327 18th(5th Bn. The Loyal Regiment [North Lancashire]) Regiment, Reconnaissance Corps. Died 11 November 1943 while a PoW of the Japanese and working on the Burma-Siam railway. Aged 32. *s of Edward & Mary, Higher Ince.* THANBYUZAYAT WAR CEMETERY, BURMA. [IN]

**WOODS Alexandre,** Gnr. 1731842 99 Bty., 18 Lt. A.A. Regiment, Royal Artillery. Killed in the Middle East 7 September 1942. Aged 27. *s of Thomas & Eleanor; h of Emma, Leigh.* BASRA WAR CEMETERY, IRAQ [L]

**WOODS Clifford,** Cpl. T/176722 Royal Army Service Corps. Died 13 September 1941 in the Far East. Aged 31. *s of Mary Ann, Aspull.* BAGHDAD (NORTH GATE) WAR CEMETERY. [AS/ASC]

**WOOLEY Joseph Patrick,** Gnr. 4206984 170th Field Regiment, Royal Artillery. Died 23 February 1942. Aged 21. *s of Joseph & Ellen, Lower Ince.* INCE CEMETERY. [X]

**WOOLEY Stanley,** Gnr. 968197 5 Survey Regiment, Royal Artillery. Died of wounds 27 February 1943 in North Africa. Aged 26. *s of Edward & Clarice, Hindley Green; h of Vera, Hindley.* MEDJEZ-EL-BAB WAR CEMETERY, TUNISIA. [HGC]

**WOOLMAN John,** Sgt. (Nav.) 1049966 R.A.F. (V.R.) 104 Sqdn. Killed 16 October 1943 during air operations in Italy. Aged 30. *s of Arthur & Alice; h of Mary.* BOLSENA WAR CEMETERY, ITALY. [L]

**WOOSNAM John,** Pte. D/15011 5th Bn. The Manchester Regiment. Died 27 January 1945. Aged 60. *h of Isabella, Whelley, Wigan.* WIGAN CEMETERY, [X]

**WORGAN William**, Pte. 14242743 1/7<sup>th</sup> Bn. The Royal Warwickshire Regiment. Killed in France 30 July 1944. *He had family connections with Wigan & Hindley.* SECQUEVILLE-EN-BESSIN WAR CEMETERY, FRANCE. [X]

**WORRALL Herbert**, A.B. D/JX192852 R.N. H.M.S. *Galatea* 15 December 1941 Aged 22. While returning from North Africa, this cruiser was sunk by the German U-boat *U-557* off Alexandria. *s of Frank & Annis Skeat, Tyldesley.* PLYMOUTH NAVAL MEMORIAL. [HAC/T/TC]
(See also Ernest Cashin and Fred Mann who also died in this action.)

**WORTHINGTON Hendry (Harry)**, Sgt. 3135624 11<sup>th</sup> Bn. The Royal Scots Fusiliers. Died in a military hospital 6 June 1944. Aged 31. *s of Christopher & Margaret, Ince; h of Margaret, Bradford.* BRADFORD (UNDERCLIFFE) CEMETERY. [X]

**WORTHINGTON Robert Sherwin**, L.A.C. 965157 R.A.F. (V.R.) Died 18 September 1944 in the Far East. Aged 24. He has no known grave. *s of Robert Stanley & Mary Martha, Downholland.* SINGAPORE MEMORIAL [X]

**WORTHINGTON Stanley**, Pte. 14657920 5<sup>th</sup> Bn. The Queen's Own Cameron Highlanders. He died of wounds in Normandy, France 23 June 1944. Aged 23. *s of Thomas & Mary Alice Worthington.* BAYEAUX WAR CEMETERY, FRANCE. [ST/STC]

**WRIGHT James Issac**, Pte. 3571400 5<sup>th</sup> Bn. The Manchester Regiment. He died 9 January 1940 in Watergate Hospital, Newcastle-on-Tyne. Aged 21. ASHTON-IN-MAKERFIELD (HOLY TRINITY) CHURCHYARD. [AC/AGS/NAV]

**WRIGHT John Edwin**, Spr. 1877032 236 Field Coy., Royal Engineers. Died 6 September 1940 Aged 37. *s of William & E, Hindley; h of Henrietta.* HINDLEY (ALL SAINTS) CHURCHYARD. [X]

**WRIGHT Kenneth Jack**, Cpl. 3453804 2<sup>nd</sup> Bn. The Lancashire Fusiliers. Killed in North Africa 19 May 1943. Aged 26. *s of Jack & Harriet, h of Mary, Pemberton.* OUED ZARGA WAR CEMETERY, TUNISIA. [HIY/W]

**WRIGHT Robert George**, Gnr. B/11040 12 Field Regiment, Royal Canadian Artillery. Killed 14 August 1944 in France. Aged 26. *s of Alice; h of Hilda, Astley.* BENY-SUR-MER CANADIAN WAR CEMETERY, FRANCE. [X]

**WRIGHT Sidney**, Fus. 3453131 1/8<sup>th</sup> Bn. The Lancashire Fusiliers. Died of wounds 30 April 1944. Aged 24. *s of Thites & Mary, Wigan; h of Jane.* IMPHAL WAR CEMETERY, INDIA. [W]

**WRIGHT Terence Patrick**, Sgt. 1006115 R.A.F. (V.R.) 7 Sqdn. Killed 18 December 1941. Aged 21. His Stirling bomber took-off from Oakington on an operation to bomb Brest but was shot down by German ME 109s off the French coast. All the members of the crew died and have no known graves. *s of Capt. James Lewis, RE & Elizabeth Ellen, Bolton.* RUNNYMEDE MEMORIAL [HGS]

**WROTH Ernest,** Gnr. 1145510 12 (Honourable Artillery Coy.) Regiment, Royal Horse Artillery. Died of wounds in North Africa 31 January 1943. Aged 39. *s of David & Elizabeth; h of Frances.* BEJA WAR CEMETERY, TUNISIA. [W]

**WYATT John,** Flt. Sgt. (W.Op.) 1536328 R.A.F. (V.R.) 171 Sqdn. Killed 7 March 1945 when his Halifax bomber from North Creake was lost over Germany whilst on a bombing operation to Munster. The pilot was the only survivor from a crew of eight and was held by the Germans as a PoW for a few weeks. *h of Dorothy, Standish. He also had connections with Hindley Green.* REICHSWALD FOREST WAR CEMETERY, GERMANY. [STC]

**WYKE William,** Gnr. 1823847 658 Bty., 194 H.A.A. Regiment, Royal Artillery. Died 16 March 1947. *h of Emily, Hindley.* HINDLEY CEMETERY. [X]

**YATES Bernard Colin,** Pte. 14323067 1st Bn. The Loyal Regiment (North Lancashire). Killed in Italy 18 February 1944. Aged 19. ANZIO WAR CEMETERY, ITALY. [SAC/W]

**YATES Eldred,** Lieut. 174936 The Buffs (The Royal East Kent Regiment) attd. 4th Bn. 6th Rajputana Rifles. Killed in North Africa 20 April 1943. Aged 29. *s of Richard & Mary Elizabeth, Leigh.* ENFIDAVILLE WAR CEMETERY. [L/LGS/LTC]

**YATES John William,** Pte. 3527815 5th Bn. The Manchester Regiment. Died 4 December 1939. Aged 21. *s of James & Harriet, Leigh.* LEIGH CEMETERY. [LTC]

**YATES William,** Gnr. 886495 5 Medium Regiment, Royal Artillery. Killed in action in France 21 May 1940 during the withdrawal to Dunkirk. Aged 20. LILLE SOUTHERN CEMETERY, FRANCE. [L]

**YOUNG Alfred,** Gnr. 950772 95 Anti-Tank Regiment, Royal Artillery. He was captured in the Middle East and died as a PoW of the Italians 10 December 1942. Aged 25. *h of Margaret, Astley.* CASERTA WAR CEMETERY, ITALY. [X]

**YOUNG George Albert,** Gnr. 3453503 165 Field Regiment, Royal Artillery. Killed 8 September 1943 in Italy. Aged 25. *s of John Edward & Margaret.* SALERNO WAR CEMETERY, ITALY. [G/GOC]

**YOUNG William,** Bdr. 1510612 3 Bty., 1 Lt. A.A. Regiment, Royal Artillery. Killed in the Middle East 17 June 1941. Aged 22. He has no known grave. ALAMEIN MEMORIAL. [AS/ASC]

# APPENDIX ONE

This Appendix contains the names and details (where available) of those who are *commemorated on at least one local memorial* but who do not qualify for inclusion in the main body of this Roll of Honour. It has been considered necessary to confine the main named list to those whose graves/memorials remain the responsibility of the Commonwealth War Graves Commission i.e. those Commonwealth citizens who died in service in the Armed Forces (and in some cases Merchant Navy) in the period September 1939 to December 1947.

The Appendix therefore lists:

- Those who died but who were not members of the Armed Forces
- Civilians
- Foreign nationals
- Those for whom it has not been possible to make positive and definite identification

**BOARDMAN Eric**. *Positive identification has not been possible. On the Atherton memorial he is shown as being a Gnr. in the Royal Artillery. No CWGC listing is given, but an Eric Boardman died in Wrightington Hospital in November 1946. He is buried in Atherton Cemetery. No other information has been obtained* [A]

**BOOTH Leslie**. *Positive identification has not been possible but it is likely that he was a Trooper in The Loyal Regiment who was killed in the Far East and is buried in Sai Wan War Cemetery, Hong Kong. All references to this soldier indicate ties with Bolton but, in spite of some indications, it has been impossible to establish any direct links with Standish.* [ST]

**BRADSHAW Henry**, Merchant Navy. Accidentally drowned in East Africa 29 January 1945. Aged 18. It is understood that he was buried near KILINDONI, EAST AFRICA, but no confirmatory record can be found and CWGC has no listing. [OC/OCY]

**CASSIDY John**. *In spite of every effort, no definite information could be obtained and therefore positive identification has not been possible* . [NSC]

**CLARKSON Francis**. *In spite of every effort, positive identification has not been possible. There is a likelihood that he is the Royal Air Force Sergeant who is buried in Hanover War Cemetery having been killed in action in 1944.* [SSM]

**CLEWES Leslie,** Fireman in the National Fire Service. He died in a motor accident in Tyldesley while returning from duty 29 August 1941. Aged 27. ATHERTON CEMETERY [T]

**CLOSE John**. *He is shown on the Wigan Cenotaph as serving in The Border Regiment. There is no CWGC listing and no soldier of that name served in The Border Regiment during WW2 although George Henry Close of the Border Regiment is commemorated at Wigan. Positive identification has not been possible.* [W]

**CROMPTON Lambert**. *In spite of every effort, no definite information could be obtained and therefore positive identification has not been possible.* [AS/NSC]

**CUNLIFFE Arthur**. *Positive identification has not been possible, but he may be the Arthur Cunliffe who was serving with 1$^{st}$ (Airborne) Bn. Border Regiment when he was killed in Italy in July 1943.* AIM/AMS]

**DAVIDSON Sydney**. *In spite of every effort, no definite information could be obtained and therefore positive identification has not been possible.* [SMC]

**DEAN John**. *He is shown on the Wigan Cenotaph as serving in the Reconnaissance Corps. There is no relevant CWGC listing and no information has been obtained. Positive identification has not been possible.* [W]

**DEMPSEY Peter Patrick**. A former regular soldier, he served with the Manchester Regiment and Commandos from 1939 but was discharged on medical grounds in 1941. He died 15 February 1948, aged 44. LEIGH CEMETERY [L]

**DUNN Joseph.** *In spite of every effort, no definite information could be obtained and therefore positive identification has not been possible.* [L]

**DUTTON Harry,** He served for several years in the Royal Air Force but was discharged because of illness. He died 10 May 1947. Aged 35. *h of Irene, Hindley.* HINDLEY CEMETERY [HC]

**EDGE Oswald Rogerson.** *He was born in Leigh in 1896 and entered Leigh Grammar School aged 12 years 5 months. He was thus aged 43 when war was declared and therefore is unlikely to have been conscripted into the Armed Forces. No other information could be obtained.* [LGS]

**EDMONDSON Harold Roy,** Sgt. Royal Marines. *BEM* He died 27 November 1949 as a result of war wounds received in Normandy in 1944. *s of Mr & Mrs J.H.* GIDLOW CEMETERY, WIGAN. [SGC/W/WSB]

**FAZACKERLEY W.** *In spite of every effort, no definite information could be obtained and therefore positive identification has not been possible.* [L]

**FISHWICK William.** *In spite of every effort, no definite information could be obtained and therefore positive identification has not been possible.* [WGS]

**FRANCE Arthur.** *In spite of every effort, no definite information could be obtained and therefore positive identification has not been possible.* [PBC]

**GLAISTER Arthur Cecil,** He was a full-time A.R.P. Warden who died of injuries which he received following a road accident 9 January 1941. Aged 56. TYLDESLEY CEMETERY [T]

**HADDOCK Jerry.** *In spite of every effort, no definite information could be obtained and therefore positive identification has not been possible.* [NSC]

**HARDIE J.R.** *In spite of every effort, no definite information could be obtained and therefore positive identification has not been possible.* [L]

**HARRISON K.** *In spite of every effort, no definite information could be obtained. One possibility is the Sergeant in the Royal Air Force who died in 1941 and is buried in nearby Bolton (Tonge) Cemetery. No link with Aspull has been established.* [AS]

**HAYES Thomas.** *In spite of every effort, no definite information could be obtained and therefore positive identification has not been possible.* [WPC]

**HESKETH John Gray.** He served as a Gunner in the Royal Artillery for most of the war but died 12 April 1946 some time after he was demobilised. Aged 35. *s of Joseph & Anne, Appley Bridge; h of Martha, Appley Bridge.* PARBOLD (CHRIST CHURCH) CHURCHYARD. [AP/APC/PCC]

**HITCHEN Ralph.** *In spite of every effort, no definite information could be obtained and therefore positive identification has not been possible.* [AB]

**JOHNSON A.** *In spite of every effort, no definite information could be obtained but he may be the Sergeant Albert Johnson who died in 1944 whilst serving with the RAF and is buried in Jonkerbos War Cemetery.* [G]

**JOHNSON B.** *In spite of every effort, no definite information could be obtained and therefore positive identification has not been possible.* [SSC]

**JOHNSON Harry.** *In spite of every effort, no definite information could be obtained but a Harry Johnson of 53, Green Lane, Leigh died in 1944 aged 43 and is buried in Leigh Cemetery.* [L]

**JOHNSON Richard.** *In spite of every effort, no definite information could be obtained and therefore positive identification has not been possible.* [IN]

**KEARSLEY William.** *Wigan Grammar School Magazine shows L.Cpl. William Kearsley (Royal Corps of Signals) as a PoW from 1942, but no death is recorded or commemoration on the school's Roll of Honour. He is commemorated on the Wigan Cenotaph. It is likely he died soon after demobilisation but no additional information has been obtained.* [W]

**KELSALL Frederick.** A former soldier and miner, he enlisted at the outbreak of war. Due to the country's need for coal, he was released from the army but lost his life in a mining accident 30 September 1942. Aged 36. HINDLEY CEMETERY [HC]

**LAWRENCE Gordon.** *He is shown on the Wigan Cenotaph as serving in the Loyal Regiment. There is no CWGC listing and no other information has been obtained. Positive identification has not been possible.* [W]

**LEE Eric.** *In spite of every effort, no definite information could be obtained and therefore positive identification has not been possible.* [NC]

**LOUGH T.I.** *His rank on the Bickershaw memorial is given as Corporal, but in spite of every effort, no definite information could be obtained and therefore positive identification has not been possible.* [B]

**LYTHGOE Fred.** A Fireman in the National Fire Service, he died from electric shock 1 December 1942 in the N.F.S. workshops, Wigan. Aged 32. *Family connections in Shevington.* ST WILFRID'S CHURCHYARD, STANDISH. [STC]

**McDOWELL Joseph.** A former Leading Telegraphist in the Royal Navy. He died of tubercolosis 23 September 1946. Aged 29. *s of Lilian & Joseph, Leigh.* LEIGH CEMETERY [BDC/L/LGS]

**McNAMARA John.** *In spite of every effort, no definite information could be obtained and therefore positive identification has not been possible.* [S]

**MEADOWS Elizabeth (Betty).** A civilian aged 21, she was killed by a stray shell or jettisoned bomb in Platt Bridge September 1940. Seven other people were injured. INCE CEMETERY [PBC]

**MEADOWS Harold.** *In spite of every effort, no definite information could be obtained and therefore positive identification has not been possible.* [L/LGS]

**O'HAGAN John James.** He died 25 December 1948. Aged 39. No other detail or information regarding his service could be obtained. LEIGH CEMETERY [L]

**ORMESHER Sandylands.** A former soldier in the Royal Army Service Corps for over three years, he served in North Africa and Italy. He died, aged 40, on 22 September 1946 a few months after being demobilised. *He had many family connections in the Scholes area of Wigan.* WIGAN CEMETERY [WPC] (Some sources give his first name as *Sandiman.*)

**RIGBY Harry.** *In spite of every effort, no definite information could be obtained and therefore positive identification has not been possible.* [PBC/IN]

**ROBB David Wills,** Boatswain. Merchant Navy. Died in 1941 while serving on board *s.s. Leeds City* during a voyage to Montreal. He had formerly served in the Royal Navy. *h of Marjorie, Wigan.* SOREL CEMETERY, CANADA. [SAC]

**ROBERTS Harold.** *In spite of every effort, no definite information could be obtained and therefore positive identification has not been possible.* [WSB]

**ROBERTS John T.** *In spite of every effort, no definite information could be obtained and therefore positive identification has not been possible.* [JC]

**ROBERTS Kenneth.** *In spite of every effort, no definite information could be obtained and therefore positive identification has not been possible.* [AMS]

**RYDER William.** *In spite of every effort, no definite information could be obtained and therefore positive identification has not been possible.* [JC]

**SCHOONJANS Rene,** Fireman. Merchant Navy. Died in Beverley Base Hospital, Yorkshire 23 June 1945 during treatment for a foot wound. Aged 26. *A Belgian national, he had made his home in Leigh.* LEIGH CEMETERY [L/LMC]

**SHAKESHAFT Horace James,** An A.R.P. Warden. Died 3 July 1943. Aged 36 *h of Eva, Tyldesley.* LEIGH CEMETERY [T/TC]

**SHAW Peter Arthur,** Deputy Head Warden, A.R.P. Died 16 May 1941 due to enemy action. Aged 49. ATHERTON CEMETERY [A/CUC]

**SMITH Arthur.** *In spite of every effort, no definite information could be obtained and therefore positive identification has not been possible.* [L/LPC]

**SMITH Joseph.** *In spite of every effort, no definite information could be obtained and therefore positive identification has not been possible.* [IN]

**SPEAK John.** *In spite of every effort, no definite information could be obtained and therefore positive identification has not been possible.* [BL/BCC]

**STEWART John.** *On the Atherton memorial he is listed as a Private serving in the Scots Guards. Clearly there is some mistake. Positive identification has not been possible.* [A]

**SUTTON Richard.** *In spite of every effort, no definite information could be obtained and therefore positive identification has not been possible.* [BL/BCC]

**TAYLOR J.** *In spite of every effort, no definite information could be obtained and therefore positive identification has not been possible.* [G]

**THOMAS Norman.** *In spite of every effort, no definite information could be obtained and therefore positive identification has not been possible* [WSB]

**TWISS Harold.** *In spite of every effort, no definite information could be obtained and therefore positive identification has not been possible* [AIM]

**WALKER James.** *In spite of every effort, no definite information could be obtained and therefore positive identification has not been possible* [HC]

**WARD W.J.** *In spite of every effort, no definite information could be obtained and therefore positive identification has not been possible.* [G]

**WATT Joseph,** Ldg. Fireman in the National Fire Service. He died 4 August 1944 in a railway accident at Bootle. Aged 34. TYLDESLEY CEMETERY [T]

**WHITTLE F.A.** *In spite of every effort, no definite information could be obtained and therefore positive identification has not been possible.* [G]

**WILCOCK Frederick.** He served in the R.A.F. from 1939 but had been discharged because of illness and he died at home 4 June 1943. Aged 23. *s of Fred & Elsie, Hindley; h of Hilda.* HINDLEY CEMETERY [HGC]

**WILMAN John.** He served as a Gunner in the Royal Artillery and for some time was in the Far East. He contracted tuberculosis and was in a South African hospital before being demobbed in 1947. He died in Wrightington Hospital 27 October 1948. Aged 26. *s of Thomas & Annie, Leigh.* LEIGH CEMETERY [L]

**WILSON R.** *The Wigan Cenotaph lists him as having served in the Royal Engineers, but there is no listing in CWGC and he most likely died soon after discharge. No positive identification has been possible.* [W]

**ZEGERS Joseph Andre Armand,** Flt. Sgt. 1299837 R.A.F. 609 Sqdn. Killed in action 3 January 1944 over the Cambrai area of France whilst piloting a Typhoon fighter from Manston. Aged 21. He was buried initially in the war cemetery at Grevillers. *A Belgian, he came to England as a civilian refugee in May 1940 and joined the RAF in November 1941. His link with Leigh must have been strong since he is commemmorated on three memorials in the area. It is probable that he joined an already well-established Belgian community which had existed there since the First World War.* BRUSSELS TOWN CEMETERY. [L/LAS/LTC]